JUST LIKE ME

WHEN THE PROS PLAYED ON THE SANDLOT

VOLUME 1

D1551695

KELLY G. PARK

SUNBURY

Mechanicsburg, PA USA

Published by Sunbury Press, Inc.
Mechanicsburg, Pennsylvania

www.sunburypress.com

For information about special discounts for bulk purchases, please contact Sunbury Press
Orders Dept. at (855) 338-8359 or orders@sunburypress.com.

To request one of our authors for speaking engagements or book signings, please contact
Sunbury Press Publicity Dept. at publicity@sunburypress.com.

FIRST SUNBURY PRESS EDITION: August 2020

Set in Adobe Garamond | Interior design by Crystal Devine | Cover by Terry Kennedy | Edited
by Lawrence Knorr.

Publisher's Cataloging-in-Publication Data
Names: Park, Kelly G., author.
Title: Just like me : when the pros played on the sandlot / Kelly G. Park.
Description: First trade paperback edition. | Mechanicsburg, PA : Sunbury Press, 2020.
Summary: Eighteen former major league baseball players are interviewed regarding their early
years in youth baseball from the 1940s to the 1980s.
Identifiers: ISBN 978-1-620064-01-6 (softcover).
Subjects: SPORTS & RECREATION / Baseball / History | SPORTS & RECREATION /
Children's & Youth Sports.

Product of the United States of America
0 1 1 2 3 5 8 13 21 34 55

Continue the Enlightenment!

CONTENTS

"How old would you be if you didn't
know how old you are?"

—Satchell Paige

ACKNOWLEDGMENTS

I MUST BEGIN by thanking every player I interviewed for this book. Each player was gracious with their time. Specifically, I must mention the first four players I interviewed: Jim Hickman, Phil Roof, Hawk Taylor, and Boog Powell. When I first conceived the idea for this book, I knew no one in Major League Baseball. I had no "connections," but these four gentlemen agreed to meet with me, tell me their stories, and encouraged me to see this project through.

At Major League Baseball Players Alumni Association, Ryan Thomas, Chris Torgusen, and Alex Trihias.

The following individuals assisted in scheduling player interviews: Kathy Dampier, Tom Blankenship, Terry Robinson, Bill Hickman, Mike Hostetter, and Steve Alexander.

The following organizations and individuals provided valuable services, advice, and encouragement for me as I worked through the project: Authors Guild, Vanan Transcription, Nick Darnell, Tony Powell Creative, Bill Murphy Photography, Merrie Fidler of the AAGPBL, Mike Henschel, and Carlos Loftus.

To Nolan and Marissa Park and Grant and Alli Park. Because they are my sons and daughters-in-laws, and they make me happy. And to Marissa for a great job transcribing several interviews for me.

At Sunbury Press Lawrence Knorr, Crystal Devine, Joe Walters, and Terry Kennedy.

A big thank you to my youth league coaches and friends I've played with growing up. Coaches like Red and Coy, Mac and Gene, Ron and Leon, Charlie, Joe, and Mike. Buddies Nick, Martin, Billy, Scott, Kerry, Tony, Mick, Kevin, and Mark; really everybody growing up I played with, it was fun. My brothers Phillip and Casey, who kept my interest in baseball going when it could have gotten lost in living life.

A bigger thank you to my wife, Mrs. Kelly, for her encouragement, support, advice, and above all, patience!

The biggest thank you to my parents, Arwood and Sharon Park. Mom religiously bought me (and my brothers) a pack of baseball cards every Friday when she went to Austin's Grocery Store, which I immediately opened, sorted, and prepared for a serious round of trading cards with my friend Scott. Not sure how it happened, but even after some thorough preparation, he usually got the better end of the trade. Because of Mom (and despite my brothers' best efforts), I've still got a fantastic card collection. Mom, thanks for not throwing my cards away when they were left lying all over the house.

"Hey, Dad, you wanna go play pitch?" He heard that a lot during the summer months, and more often than not, he was up for playing pitch, even after being at work all day. He was patient for the first ten wild throws, turning and walking after the ball I had thrown over, under and to the side of him, but with the 11th wild pitch, it was my turn to chase after the wild throws. Slowly the accuracy improved. One such episode occurred at grandma's house. Mama Ola had an old shed in the backyard that Dad stood in front of so he wouldn't have to chase down my wild throws. Well, I unleashed a fastball that flew over Dad's head and hit the front of the shed just below the roof, going through the shed wall and lodging between the interior and exterior walls. Dad didn't get mad; he just got out his pocketknife, cut a hole in the shed wall, and pulled my baseball out so we could keep on playing pitch. As I said, my accuracy was improving, and as I reared back for the very next throw, my hardest fastball ever . . . I hit the exact same spot. The good news was Dad had already cut a second hole in the wall; the bad news was Dad didn't think Mama Ola wanted a swiss cheese looking shed, so our pitching session for the day was over. Dad, thanks for the days of playing pitch.

INTRODUCTION

BOOKS FASCINATE ME, they always have. All the way back to elementary school when the teacher would hand out the Scholastic Book order forms, and I had the tough decision of choosing between the Willie Mays, Tom Seaver, or Hank Aaron book to order.

Reading was always something I enjoyed. When I wasn't outside playing a pickup game of baseball, basketball, or football, I was reading about baseball, basketball, football, or whatever sport I happen to be interested in at that time. It didn't matter the sport; if it involved playing with friends, we were all-in; if the game was in season, we played it.

As I got older, the number of books I was reading decreased to the point I wasn't reading for leisure at all. Around the time our oldest son was born, I happened to walk by a discount book rack, and a book caught my eye. It was titled *Shoeless Joe and Ragtime Baseball*. I bought it, and within a couple of weeks, I had it read and was ready for another one. I began to frequent the local bookstore and found a biography of Babe Ruth by Robert Creamer. This book is a great read, and it just fueled my interest in reading again.

By chance, the focus of my reading became early twentieth-century baseball because the next book I found was *Cobb* by Al Stump. From there, I read biographies on Walter Johnson, Honus Wagner, Christy Mathewson, Lou Gehrig, Rogers Hornsby, Moe Berg, the Gashouse Gang, the crazy 1908 season, and many more sprinkled in. Then I picked up a book called *The Glory of Their Times* by Lawrence Ritter. This book is a collection of interviews with former players from the early twentieth-century; players that were not the stars of the game; they were the steady everyday players that fans who followed their favorite team knew, but others may not.

Well, an interesting thing happened as I read the stories told by these players; many of the stories were a re-telling of stories I had read in the player biographies but from a different perspective. So instead of getting the superstar's version of the play, I got the journeyman's version, which was very intriguing to me. Take the Fred Merkle situation, known as Merkle's Boner. In a 1908 game between the New York Giants and the Chicago Cubs, a 19-year-old Merkle made an alleged, baserunning mistake that ultimately cost the Giants the Pennant. I read versions of this play in Christy Mathewson's bio, in *Crazy '08*, and two-player versions from interviews in *The Glory of Their Times*, all with a slightly different take on the play.

Plays similar to Merkle's Boner occurred throughout the book, so when I finished it, I looked for something similar to read. In my research, I came across a book review of *The Glory of Their Times* that read, "The story is so well written, you feel like you're on the field with the player." My first thought was, "No . . . I didn't feel like I was on the field with the players while reading this book because I never had the skill to be on the field as a professional baseball player." (and my second thought was) . . . "But I sure have some great memories of playing baseball as a kid; I wonder what the pros memories are of playing youth baseball?"

I turned my search to find a book that told these stories . . . and guess what I found? Nothing! I googled every phrase I could think of looking for this book. What I found was an occasional magazine article about youth baseball but nothing covering what I wanted to read.

Well, as the days went by, I couldn't shake the thought of why wasn't there a book about professional baseball players' memories of playing youth baseball? Before I realized what was happening, the thought came to me, "Well, if there are no books on this topic, then why not me? Why can't I interview the players and produce this book I want to read? I'm going to do it!!!" It didn't matter that I've never written a book and that I did not know anyone even remotely associated with Major League Baseball. I was going to give it a try.

My first step was to ask the people whose opinion I respect if this was a good or bad idea, so I asked my wife, knowing the response would be either "you're an idiot, or that sounds like a good idea," and luckily I got the latter. I asked my brothers and some buddies and got a thumbs up from them (but really, did I expect to get an answer other than, "that's a great idea. Not really!").

As I'm trying to figure out how in the world I will get just one player to meet with me, I found myself visiting a client, and out of the blue, my client asked, "Do you know who Jim Hickman is?" I said, "I did," and he pointed to his maintenance man and said, "That's my maintenance supervisor; he's Mr. Hickman's son."

There it was, the opportunity I needed, and before I knew it, I asked if Mr. Hickman still lived in Henning, explained my project, and asked if he would be interested in talking to me? After a long 48 hour wait, I got my answer, YES! And I was off to the races.

As I progressed along interviewing players, I begin to realize the historical aspect of my interviews. These players are telling me stories of their experiences growing up that will never be experienced by kids again. After I had completed fifteen interviews of retired major-league players, I felt a re-evaluation of this project was needed to ensure I was staying true to the book's objective. During the reassessment, I realized that I was ignoring two groups that had a significant impact on baseball and society. To understand this realization, I should briefly explain that my dad had recently died at the age of 87. He was a WWII veteran of the South Pacific, and typical of his generation worked hard and said very little. At Dad's funeral, we lost count of the number of great stories his friends told us that we (his sons) had never heard. I found myself wanting to hear more when one of his few remaining buddies told me, "You'll never know all of the things your dad saw during the war"; I realized then that those stories were gone forever.

So, with this sitting in the back of my mind, it hit me . . . there is more to professional baseball than just the major leagues; I have to interview players from the Negro Leagues and the All American Girls Professional Baseball League.

I researched these two groups of professional baseball players and soon had interviews with All American stars Lois Youngen, and Katie Horstman. From the Negro Leagues, I had the pleasure of interviewing Jim Zapp and Bill Greason, both of whom were teammates of Willie Mays on the Birmingham Black Barons. I learned so much talking with these players and listening to their stories growing up as kids; those interviews are memories I will never forget.

Between my first interview with Jim Hickman to my last interview with Willie Horton, I had a lot of interesting adventures traveling and interviewing players. I've driven through the night to interview players. I've been followed by and then questioned by MLB security. I've been so surprised by an offer from a player to call some of his baseball friends for me to interview that I forgot to pay for lunch and stuck him with the bill (something that still haunts me to this day and I hope I have the opportunity to repay him someday).

When I first started this project, I thought all the stories the players would tell me would be funny and happy stories when they were kids, and then I begin to understand a basic fact, not everything is fun, even in youth baseball. Some players struggled because their families didn't have much money for equipment, while other players simply didn't have the chance to play in youth leagues because of segregation. But then again, there IS a lot of funny and happy stories in youth baseball . . . like how one player really got his famous nickname or why a player wasn't bothered when he peed in his baseball pants. There is even a boys' team that would rather be a winning team with a girl than be a losing team without one. All the stories are relatable, whether you are a boy, a girl, the first chosen, the last chosen, the kid that can blow the biggest bubble gum bubble, or whatever the color of your skin is. Luis Tiant said it perfectly, "How long you gonna be a kid? Not too long, you're going to be old for a long time. Why would you want to take that away from the kid? Let the kid be a kid. Let him enjoy".

So, my goal for this book is:

- The players I have interviewed have been very gracious and accommodating to me, and out of respect for them, I want to allow them to tell their stories.
- For the baseball fan to have an opportunity to read stories of players' memories of playing youth baseball and thinking, "Hey, that's just like me."
- So today's kids can read how kids played and interacted during the 1940s through the 1980s.
- For the baby boomers, their children, and their grandchildren to hear the stories. The baby boomers know what it's like to nail and tape a broken wooden bat to use because it is the only bat they had, but their kids and grandkids only know aluminum and carbon fiber bats that every kid will carry in his bat bag. Kids need to read about how a future pro player had to jump into the Ohio River to retrieve a home run ball hit over the flood wall because it was the only baseball they had.
- That kids understand they do not have to wait for an organized game to play baseball, baseball can be played anywhere, at any time, and with just a couple of friends . . . you just got to get outside and play.

It took ten years from concept to completion, and hopefully, my next project will not take this long, but it's all up to you, the reader. My next project is your stories, so go to my website www.justlikemethebook.com, click on "Your Stories," and tell me your story about youth baseball. There's a good chance you could read your story in my next book, *Just Like Me: Our Stories from The Sandlot.*

As a note to the reader, my interviews with the players are approximately 45 minutes to 1 hour, and instead of interpreting the player's stories, I transcribed our interviews. These stories are taken verbatim from the transcription of our conversations, so the content is from the players. The only changes I've made are to remove word fillers such as "you know," "uh," and the occasional fill-in phrase or slang to clarify the story, but the intent of the story does not change. As you read this book, remember, the stories are recorded conversations, and the transcription of a recorded stream-of-thought interview reads much differently than a prepared written story.

1.

PLAYER BIOS

BOOG POWELL

Boog was born in Lakeland, Florida, on August 17, 1941, and graduated high school from Key West HS in Key West, Florida. Boog played 17 years in MLB. Fourteen with the Baltimore Orioles, 2 with the Cleveland Indians, and 1 with the Los Angeles Dodgers.

Boog is a 4-time All-Star, 2-time World Series Champion, won the MVP award in 1970 and was voted the 1975 Comeback Player of the Year. In 1979 Boog was inducted into the Baltimore Orioles Hall of Fame.

Boog authored the book: *Baltimore, Baseball & Barbecue with Boog Powell: Stories from the Orioles' Smokey Slugger* with Rob Kasper

PHIL ROOF

Phil was born in Paducah, Kentucky, on March 5, 1941, and graduated high school from St. Mary's HS in Paducah, Kentucky. Phil played 15 years in MLB. Six with Minnesota Twins, four with the Oakland A's, two with the Milwaukee Braves, two with the Milwaukee Brewers, and one year each with the Cleveland Indians, California Angels, Toronto Blue Jays, and Chicago White Sox.

Phil managed in the Minnesota Twins minor leagues for 16 years and finished with a record of 1165 wins against 1116 losses and a .511 winning percentage. Phil was the bullpen coach for the San Diego Padres in 1978, Seattle Mariners, for the years of 1983-88 and Chicago Cubs for the 1990-91 seasons.

Phil is an active member of the Knights of Columbus.

HAWK TAYLOR

Hawk was born in Metropolis, Illinois, on April 3, 1939, and passed away on June 9, 2012. Hawk graduated high school from Metropolis Community HS in Metropolis, Illinois. He played 11 years in MLB, five years with the Milwaukee Braves, four years with the New Year Mets, two years with the Kansas City Royals, and one year with the California Angels.

Hawk was a "Bonus Baby," signing a contract with the Milwaukee Braves for a reported $119,000 in 1957. After retiring, Hawk graduated from Murray State University with a master's in health & physical education and coached baseball at the collegiate level at Lambuth College and Paducah Community College.

JIM HICKMAN

Jim was born in Henning, Tennessee, on May 10, 1937, and passed away on June 25, 2016. Jim graduated high school from Ripley HS in Ripley, Tennessee. He played 13 years in MLB, six years with the Chicago Cubs, five years with the New York Mets, and one year each with the St. Louis Cardinals and Los Angeles Dodgers.

Jim was selected in the 1961 expansion draft by the newly created New York Mets. Jim holds many firsts for the Mets franchise. First Met to hit for the cycle, a natural cycle, which was only the sixth natural cycle all-time in 1963 and was the first Met to hit three home runs in one game. Jim also hit the last home run in the final game ever played at the Polo Grounds and then the next year set a pair of firsts at Shea Stadium with the first walk and first hit-by-pitch in the Mets first game at the new stadium.

Jim made the All-Star team in 1970 and had the game-winning hit in the All-Star Game scoring Pete Rose when Pete collided into Ray Fosse. Jim was voted the Comeback Player of the Year in 1970. In 1996 Jim was voted into the Tennessee Hall of Fame.

After retiring, Jim worked as a batting instructor in the Cincinnati Reds minor league system and operated a farm in his hometown of Henning, Tennessee.

BILL GREASON

Bill was born in Atlanta, Georgia, on September 3, 1924, and graduated high school from Booker T. Washington HS in Atlanta, Georgia. Bill played one season in MLB with the St. Louis Cardinals, eight seasons in the minor leagues, and four seasons in the Negro Leagues with the Birmingham Black Barons, Nashville Black Vols, and the Asheville Blues. You could consider that Bill's greatest success was during his 11 seasons playing in the various Latin American Baseball Leagues.

After retiring from baseball, Bill enrolled at Birmingham Easonian Baptist Bible College, completing his Undergraduate studies in Religion and his graduate studies at Samford University. Bill has been the senior pastor of the Bethel Baptist Church of Berney Points for almost five decades.

LOIS YOUNGEN

Lois was born in Westfield Center, Ohio, on October 23, 1933, and graduated high school from Westfield HS in 1951. Lois played four years in the All-American Girls Professional Baseball League for the Kenosha Comets, Fort Wayne Daisies, and the South Bend Blue Sox. Lois then played one year for a national touring team called The All Americans.

Lois graduated from Kent State Teachers College with a bachelor's degree in physical education. In 1971, Lois earned her Doctorate from Ohio State University. Lois taught at the University of Oregon, becoming an Emeritus Professor of Physical Education. Lois has served on the board of the All-American Girls Professional Baseball League for many years. Information regarding the AAGPBL is at www.aagpbl.org.

KATIE HORSTMAN

Katie was born in Minster, Ohio, on April 14, 1935, and graduated high school in 1951. Katie played four years in the All-American Girls Professional Baseball League for the Fort Wayne Daisies and the Kenosha Comets. After the AAGPBL shut down in 1954, Katie played on a national touring team called the All-American All-Stars for three years.

In 1960, she joined a convent and became a Franciscan Nun, becoming the first Nun in the United States to earn a bachelor's degree

...ation from DePaul University. Katie left the convent in ...is a track and cross-country coach, Katie's squads won eight-track state championships and two cross-country state championships. Katie is a member of five Hall of Fames in baseball and track.

The children's book titled: *Horsey the Nun (A Book by ME)* is written and illustrated by Caitlyn Harris and relates the story of how Katie Horstman went from playing in the AAGPBL to becoming a Nun.

JIM KAAT

Jim was born in Zeeland, Michigan, on November 7, 1938, and graduated from Zeeland HS. Jim played 25 years in MLB. Fifteen with the Minnesota Twins, four years with the Philadelphia Phillies, four years with the St. Louis Cardinals, three years with the Chicago White Sox, and two years with the New York Yankees.

Jim is a three-time All-Star, 16-time Gold Glove award winner, the 1966 Sporting News AL Pitcher of the Year, and a World Series winner. Since 1986, Jim has been a baseball analyst and team radio and TV announcer for the Twins and Yankees. Jim has won seven Emmy Awards for sports broadcasting.

Jim has two books available: *Still Pitching: Musings from the Mound and the Microphone* with Phil Pepe and *If These Walls Could Talk: New York Yankees: Stories from the Dugout, Locker Room, and Press Box* with Greg Jennings.

Jim is involved with the Mary Ann Kaat Memorial Fund under the umbrella of the Community Foundation of the Holland/Zeeland Area. He directs the proceeds from the sale of his memorabilia to fund the youth baseball leagues by building ball fields, installing lights, and purchasing equipment for the youth leagues.

LOU PINIELLA

Lou was born in Tampa, Florida, on August 28, 1943, and graduated from Jesuit HS in Tampa, Florida. Lou played 18 years in MLB. Eleven years with the New York Yankees, five years with the Kansas City Royals and one year each with the Cleveland Indians and Baltimore Orioles.

Lou was the Rookie of the Year in 1969, an All-Star in 1972, and a two-time World Series Champ. Lou managed in the MLB for 23 years, winning the Manager of the Year award in 1995 and 2001 for the Seattle Mariners and in 2008 for the Chicago Cubs. As the manager for the Cincinnati Reds, Lou won the 1990 World Series and retired from managing in 2010 with 1835 wins.

Lou authored the book: *Lou: Fifty Years of Kicking Dirt, Playing Hard and Winning Big in the Sweet Spot of Baseball* with Bill Madden.

JIM ZAPP

Jim was born in Nashville, Tennessee, on April 18, 1924, and passed away on September 30, 2016, in Harker Heights, Texas. Jim graduated from the Immaculate Mother Academy in Nashville, Tennessee. After serving in the U.S. Navy during WWII, Jim played ten years in Negro League baseball.

Jim began playing integrated baseball in 1952 in the Mississippi/Ohio Valley League, which is now called the Midwest League. Jim had a batting average of .330 and led the league in home runs and set the league record of 136 RBIs, which still stands. After retirement, Jim worked at the U.S. Air Force's Civil Service Division as their Sports Director.

LOU WHITAKER

Lou was born in Brooklyn, New York, on May 12, 1957, and graduated from Martinsville HS in Martinsville, Virginia. Lou played 19 years in MLB, all with the Detroit Tigers.

Lou started his professional baseball career in 1975, and the following year was named the MVP of the Florida State League. Lou was promoted to the major league team late in 1977 and was the Rookie of the Year in 1978. Lou is a five-time All-Star, winning three Gold Gloves and four Silver Slugger awards. Lou is a World Series winner with the Tigers in 1984 and one of only three MLB second basemen to score 1,000 runs, have 1,000 RBI, collect 2,000 hits, and hit 200 home runs.

STEVE BLASS

Steve was born in Canaan, Connecticut, on April 18, 1942, and graduated from Housatonic HS in Housatonic, Connecticut. Steve played ten years in MLB, all with the Pittsburgh Pirates.

Steve pitched two complete games in the 1971 World Series, allowing only two earned runs in the Pittsburgh Pirates World Series win. In 1972, he was selected for the National League All-Star team and, in 1983, began his broadcast career with the Pirates until his retirement at the end of the 2019 season. Steve's career pitching record stands at 103 wins and 76 losses for a .575 winning percentage.

Steve authored the book *A Pirate for Life* with Erik Sherman.

WHITEY HERZOG

Whitey was born in New Athens, Illinois, on April 17, 1931, and graduated from New Athens HS. Whitey played eight years in MLB, three with Washington Senators, three with the Kansas City Athletics, two with the Baltimore Orioles, and one season with the Detroit Tigers.

After retiring as an active player, Whitey began his managerial career in 1973. Whitey managed 12 years for the St. Louis Cardinals, five years with the Kansas City Royals, and one year each with the California Angels and Texas Rangers. Whitey's postseason record includes three National League Pennants and one World Series win in 1982.

Whitey was voted the 1985 National League Manager of the Year and managed three National League All-Star teams. He is a member of the Baseball Hall of Fame as a manager, elected in 2010.

Whitey's foundation, Whitey Herzog Youth Foundation, was organized and is committed to promoting and improving youth baseball programs throughout Missouri and Illinois.

DOUG FLYNN

Doug was born in Lexington, Kentucky, on April 18, 1951, and graduated from Bryan Station HS in Lexington, Kentucky. Doug played 11 years in MLB, four with the New York Mets, three with the Montreal

Expos, two seasons with the Cincinnati Reds, and one each with the Texas Rangers and Detroit Tigers.

Doug was a member of the 1976 World Series-winning Cincinnati Reds and won a Gold Glove for his play at second base in 1980 with the New York Mets. Along with his 1980 Gold Glove, Doug led the National League in Putouts, and Double Plays turned at second base.

After retiring, Doug has enjoyed a variety of opportunities, including coaching in the Mets minor league organization, leading the state of Kentucky's anti-drug program, announcing games for the Cincinnati Reds, and the University of Kentucky baseball along with participating in fantasy camps.

Doug is a member of the Fellowship of Christian Athletes and supports the Hope for the Warriors and USA Cares organizations for military personnel and their families. Doug also co-hosts, along with Johnny Bench and UK coach Matthew Mitchell the Children's Charity Golf Classic.

FERGIE JENKINS

Fergie was born in Chatham, Ontario, Canada, on December 13, 1942, and graduated from Vocational HS in Chatham, ON. Fergie played 19 years in MLB, 10 with the Chicago Cubs, six with the Texas Rangers, and two with the Boston Red Sox and one with the Philadelphia Phillies.

Fergie is a Baseball Hall of Fame member, elected in 1991. In 1987, he was elected into the Canadian Baseball Hall of Fame and was named by SABR as one of the top 100 players of the Twentieth century. Fergie made three All-Star teams and in 1971 won the National League Cy Young Award and the Sporting News Pitcher of the Year Award. Fergie ended his career with 3,192 strikeouts.

Fergie authored the book *The 1969 Cubs: Long Remembered— Not Forgotten* with George Castle and *Fergie: My Life from the Cubs to Cooperstown* with Lew Freedman. Visit Fergie's foundation web site at www.fergiejenkinsfoundation.org.

WILLIE BLAIR

Willie was born in Paintsville, Kentucky, on December 18, 1965, and graduated from Johnson Central HS in Paintsville. Willie played 12 years in MLB, four with the Detroit Tigers, two years each with the Colorado Rockies and San Diego Padres and one year each with the Toronto Blue Jays, Cleveland Indians, Houston Astros, and split season with the Arizona Diamondbacks and New York Mets.

Willie had the unique experience of pitching for two expansion teams, Colorado Rockies and Arizona Diamondbacks, in their inaugural season. After retiring, Willie has been the bullpen coach for the San Diego Padres and is currently the pitching coach in the Detroit Tigers minor league system.

WILLIE HORTON

Willie was born on October 18, 1942, in Arno, Virginia, and graduated from Northwestern HS in Detroit, Michigan. Willie played 18 years in MLB, 14 years with the Detroit Tigers, two years with the Seattle Mariners, one season with the Texas Rangers, and a split season with the Detroit Tigers, Cleveland Indians, Oakland A's and Toronto Blue Jays.

Willie is a four-time All-Star and a 1968 World Series Champion with the Detroit Tigers. After retiring, Willie created the 360 Willie Horton Community Foundation http://wh360.org focusing on community partnership programs for young and old and the Willie Horton Foundation http://thewilliehortonfoundation.org, focusing on providing scholarships for high school and college students and providing school supplies for Detroit Public schools.

CHARLIE LOYD

Charlie was born in Paducah, Kentucky, on January 28, 1938. Charlie played in the New York Yankees organization for five years, from 1961 to 1965.

During Charlie's tenure in the Yankee organization, the major league team made it to the World Series his first four years, and the 1961 team is considered by many to be one of the best MLB teams of all-time, with the pitching staff led by Whitey Ford.

Charlie played on the Paducah Junior College team that went to the National Junior College Championship and made the All-tournament team in 1959. Charlie held the record for most innings pitched. Charlie pitched for the University of Kentucky in 1960 and 1961 and was selected First Team All-SEC in 61 before being signed by the Yankees.

After retiring from baseball, Charlie had a successful career in sales.

2.

FAMILY & HOMETOWN

BOOG POWELL

There was always somebody to play catch with and Carl Taylor; he took to catching, and he wasn't a very likely candidate to be a catcher. After my mother died when we were 10, and my dad remarried, he married a lady, and henceforth Carl came, and Carl was a non-athlete period and my brother Charlie and I were like rough and tumble out in the woods kinda kids all the time, and when it was football season you played football and basketball (season) you played basketball, and you know we did everything, and Carl was, he played the piano and stuff you know (laughing), so all of a sudden he took to it like I've never seen anything like it, and all of a sudden he was a really good catcher and I was a pitcher, and I was pretty good, and I had pretty good stuff, and he could handle me, he handled me with no problem.

PHIL ROOF

(How many in the extended Roof family played professional baseball?) There's eight that have played professional baseball, and three are still in the game as an active player in the minor leagues, Gene is a member of the Detroit organization as a roving instructor so some people say it must be in the water; well, it could be in the water, but it's more or less in the genes, in the DNA.

My dad was not a big person, 5'10", 145lbs. He said he played against a guy named Johnny Sikes that played right field, and he could throw the ball over the third baseman's head from right field, and he said, "I could barely get it into second base," and he played center. Dad said he could run a little bit, but he wasn't much of a player. But my granddad on my mother's side, my granddad, was a sandlot player in a league in Brownsville, Kentucky, which is just a little community outside of Hickman in the county close to the Tennessee line. He never talked much about it, but there were pictures of him being a first baseman on that Brownsville team.

I was in the big leagues for four or five years before I knew that my Grandfather ever played baseball. He never talked about it! His dad died when he was 12-years-old, and he was the oldest of six children, so he had to take on the dad's role in farming, and once his dad died, he had to stay home and take care of his mom and young children, but on Sundays, he was able to get away and play some baseball. But they had size; my dad didn't have size. From the Roof side of the family, they weren't very big, but on the Lattus side of the family, we're all close to 6 foot and 200 lbs. We're German, part Polish and something else, maybe Lithuanian. We got some size, and I laugh . . . my first wife and I went to France and Germany and Rome in 2001. France is normal people, short you know, Rome was short people, and they argued all the time, and then we get to Germany; shoulders were broad, the height was taller. So, I said, "Now I can see where some of my family might have come from, and that's where we got our size from." All my brothers, nine of us, nine boys and a girl, we're all over 6 foot, and most of them are 6-foot, three, four or five.

(How many Roof brothers played professionally?) Five of us did. Two in the major league level, Gene and I. Adrian could have, Adrian was a Vinegar Bend Mizell with no coaching. He had no coaching back then. Threw the ball hard, he didn't know where it was going, but he could throw the ball hard left-handed, same size as Vinegar Bend Mizell. He was our high school coach as a senior.

We didn't have enough baseballs, didn't have a field; we just threw against each other, or to each other. Catch and pitch, and Gerald was a good pitcher and had a great curveball. He just didn't throw hard. Paul threw the hardest of all of us, Brother Paul. He signed with the Braves a year after I did. Adrian threw hard but didn't know where it was going. Paul got as high as Double A. Adrian just played two years in professional baseball before he came home and went to work.

Louis had the most talent. Broke his leg and was never the same after that. He could run. He was not big at that time. When he was a junior or senior in high school, he was 5' 10", 155 lbs., but he was strong. Grew up on a farm and did everything we did. They called him "Little Man," that was his nickname because he could lift as much as anybody could; he could throw as hard as anybody could; he could run faster than anybody could. And the Cardinals came in; Buddy Lewis, the scout had a three-day Cardinal workout, and they would have signed him that day. Then about the 6th inning that third day this guy jumped into him. He's taking a throw from the catcher and waiting for him to slide, and that guy jumps into his knee and breaks it right above the knee in a V shape, and he was in the hospital for 55 days. It never really healed right. He never had full extension of the leg after that.

David played at Oral Roberts. Set a lot of records there at Oral Roberts and then played two years in professional ball, and then Mike Moore, who was a great pitcher for Seattle and Oakland, broke all those records. David had great control with a good slider. He just couldn't get the fastball into the '90s. He was probably at 85, 86 mph. He needed another five miles per hour.

(And Gene?) He had a great career in basketball at St. Mary's high school. Those two *(Russ Cochran PGA Golfer & Gene)*, I believe they averaged in the mid-80s during their junior and senior year in basketball, they would run and gun, they could outrun you and wear you out, wear you down.

Well, his mother *(Louis & Eddie Haas)* and my dad were brother and sister, so that's the connection (between the Roof's & Haas's). Louis signed the same year I did and played three years of pro ball, and then he got out and got his degree and very, very, very successful in the wholesale drug business.

(Did your parents realize the baseball talents their kids had?) I think they realized that we had some skills. Daddy never pushed much; he

never said much; he was just in the crowd and pleased that his sons were able to complete, but as far as knowing anything about the game, he didn't. He just tried to tell us to keep our cool and not lose your cool at a bad call or a strikeout, and we were all pretty good about that. And he got a lot of compliments from fans, "enjoyed watching your son play," he liked those comments.

HAWK TAYLOR

Ok, well, I'll need to preference that a little bit. In fact, baseball kinda ran in the family. I understand that my mother played baseball when she went to a little high school out in the country, and of course, baseball was in the Taylor family there in Metropolis, Illinois. I had two uncles that played professional baseball, one of them in the major leagues, had a cousin who played professional baseball; dad tried it a little bit, so baseball was always around.

Bennie Taylor and my other uncle that played in the Yankee organization was Jack Taylor, and my cousin was Don Comber. He played a little while in professional ball. My dad, he tried it, but he made more money driving a truck than he did playing baseball (laughing), so there went baseball. So, baseball was always around. I was going to baseball games when I was about yay tall.

I remember my dad saying, "If you're going to have a chance to make it up in the big leagues, you need to do it as a catcher." And I guess the idea that making it to the big leagues in a hurry and having a possible career as a catcher was probably primary; however, I played all the other positions. But I kind of specialized in catching. *(Mrs. Taylor commented: I need to tell you that he really liked running the game, and that's what the catcher gets to do.)* Oh yeah, I liked running the show (laughing). Yeah, you could move the outfielders; you could move the infielders. Tell them to come in; a good bit of that (cockiness) occurred, yes.

The American Legion, yeah, played American Legion. Phil *(Roof)* lived in what was called the St. John's community and it was players from St. John's community played with me and some of my buddies on Legion teams so if we weren't playing against one another we were playing with one another, so it really worked out pretty well. Phil was two years younger than I was, so I played with Phil's older brothers more than I did with Phil.

JIM HICKMAN
Yeah, that's all you can do is be yourself, and my mom always said that, and every time I'd go out to play baseball, "You just gotta be yourself because you can't be somebody else, just gotta do what you do."

And it was pretty good advice. I know you try to copy different players and do different things physically, and it just don't work that way, just like playing golf. You gotta play golf the best way you can play. It's not always the same, the way it ought to be, sometimes at least not with me.

BILL GREASON
I was born in Atlanta and attended school there, elementary and high school: David T. Howard Jr. High and then Booker T. Washington High School. And after that, not long after that, I went into the service in the Marines in 1943, and I came out in 1946. I had a chance to see Nagasaki, where they dropped the second atomic bomb; in fact, we stayed there for occupation duty for about 14 to 16 months. We were headed into Sasebo, Japan, to invade, but they signed the peace treaty and thank God for that, but where I was born and raised up, we were poor; we were a poor family. My father was a laborer, and my mom did washing and ironing for some of the white people around there, but we were able to make it. There was five of us, three boys and two girls. The girls are gone; my other two brothers are alive, one in Atlanta, the other in Detroit. But we didn't have any baseball diamonds when we were growing up.

No, No, No, No. My parents didn't have any opportunity to do that (play sports). In fact, we used to live right across the street from Dr. Martin Luther King's home on Auburn Ave. I don't know if those little shacks are still there. On this side was some little shacks for us poor folks, and on the other side was for people a little above us. You have teachers and professors on Auburn all the way up, and that's where we started because every time the rent man came, we had to move (laughing), but we used to live right across the street from Dr. King's home on Auburn Ave. And then we moved over to some alleys over by David T. Howard school. They had two or three alleys over there; we moved over there, but we learned our lesson, and I try to tell people today that when you all have the same disease, you can get along with each other. So, all of us living in that alley, we know'd one was no better than the other so we can get along, and we lived in the alleys and moved from one to the other. Of course, I'd read it in the Bible about Sodom and Gomorrah when God told Moses and them to get out and told them not to look back. Well, I learned to get out, not only to get out of the alley but to get the alley out of me (laughing). So that was part of our upbringing, but it was a great lesson for us.

My youngest sister played a little softball, but the other ones were trying to find little jobs to help take care of the family. I was the middle child. I had an older brother and sister; in fact, they were twins, and then I had a younger brother and sister. My youngest and oldest sister died, and it's just the three boys left—one in Detroit, one in Atlanta, and myself.

LOIS YOUNGEN

My dad had been a baseball pitcher his whole life, and he was the pitcher and captain of his baseball team in college. And he was just a little too small to make it to the next level. But he had a lot of stuff on his ball, and that's why he was as good as he was. He graduated from Kent State University there in Ohio. And I started a scholarship in his name, a baseball scholarship, which is to be awarded to somebody from our county there in Ohio, it's Tuscarawas County. It's New Philadelphia and Dover.

I'd get dad to throw to me, and he'd stand me up against the garage door, and I could hang on to everything he could throw, so I figured, I'd be OK with the boys.

My dad was a middle-aged guy by then, and the only thing I remember my father doing in sports while I was his child was bowling. There weren't that many—we're talking about the 1930s, and 1940s, and 1950s, you know, there just weren't that many things for people to do.

We worked out that we were going to play against some of the other little town teams, and in Ohio, about every five miles was a little town. So, we walked. We didn't have any soccer moms to take us, or softball or baseball moms. We walked. We played against Lodi, and Seville, and Sterling; I think were the three places. I don't know how we made contact with them, and I have no idea how that happened. But anyway, we walked there, and their kids would walk over to play with us. We must have been on the phone a lot. I don't know how this all got arranged. We didn't have any coaches, we didn't have a manager, and I don't even know how we got an umpire—we must have asked somebody that we were confident in to be our umpires. This was not Little League—this was not any kind of a pre-organized group that helped us do this. We did this on our own.

And so that was pretty much my baseball, and then I got old enough to be involved in softball, and because I played baseball, my name kind of got spread around a little bit. So anyway, I was asked to play on a woman's softball team. I think I was maybe a freshman in high school, could've even been in eighth grade in Wooster, Ohio, for Wooster Lumber.

KATIE HORSTMAN

My mom or dad probably never had a bat in their hand (laughing). My grandfather came from Germany. All we know how to do is auto work, how to milk cows, how to plant corn, how to bale hay, things like that. But my brothers; I had five brothers, and one of my brothers was very good and played for Ohio State University; he was a catcher.

Play with my brothers? Yeah, well, it was just a small town, Minster, Ohio. It was a lot of farmers, and it's a very Catholic town, and we were taught by the nuns in the public school; that's how religion was really one big strong point. We had about five farmers around close, within a mile or two, and they all had big families, at least eight, some had 10, and we would always get together at one house every Sunday if it was nice. We always had like a barnyard where you put the sick cows or any kind of sick animal; anyways, we made a baseball diamond out of it. Everybody had their own baseball diamond, so that made it nice, and the other guys let us play as long as we knew how to play, and they were pretty nice about it, and we caught on real fast. I had a younger brother, I was the second to last, and he was very good at sports too. He was just a little guy, and he really loved baseball, football, and everything. We would play every night after we got through with our chores; we could go play. And we always either played baseball, football, or basketball in the barn.

They were similar, and at that time, it was just after the war had ended, and they had like minor league teams here, and that's what my brother was on. Minster and all these little towns had minor league teams, and we had big crowds, I mean there's 2000 in the town, and there would be easily 900 people there on Sunday afternoon because it was the only thing to do, you know, entertainment.

JIM KAAT

I grew up in a little town, Zeeland, Michigan, in the southwestern part of Michigan, about 20 miles from Grand Rapids. It's kind of a farming community. A lot of our kids in school came from farms, but I grew up in the city of Zeeland. At the time, I think it was about 3,000 people.

My dad, his nickname in Zeeland, they refer to him as Mr. Baseball. That's where I got my inspiration really.

The big sport in those days, growing up in little country towns in southwestern Michigan and I'm sure it was the same in a lot of other towns in America, but the big sport was fast-pitch softball, so I played a lot of fast-pitch softball.

I don't know if you're old enough to remember the TV program the $64,000 Question that was on TV back in the 1950s. A lady in our town actually wanted to send my dad to it because there was a lot of baseball questions, and he had all the record books going back to 1900, so I learned my baseball history at home from my dad from the time I was probably six or seven. So, I was really raised on baseball trivia, which has been so helpful to me to know in the broadcasting business.

Lefty Grove ended up being a Hall of Fame pitcher; that was the first big league baseball hero that I ever heard of: Lefty Grove. And that was my dad's favorite player. He actually drove to Cooperstown in 1947 to see Lefty's induction.

(How did your dad become such an avid fan of baseball?) You know, I talked to my sisters about that often. I have two older sisters. They are 92, and one's about to be 91. I'm 78. And I've always said that I wish that I had asked my dad more questions about life in general and maybe in baseball, of course. As an aside, financially, I wish he had been a baseball card collector back then. I'd have the Honus Wagner card or something (laughing), but I didn't ask him exactly how he got his start, but he was, for some reason, a Connie Mack fan.

Yeah, I think sentimentally, he just liked the fact that here was a guy (Connie Mack) that had to sell a lot of his players off because they didn't make a lot of money. You know Connie Mack and then Lefty Grove. The Philadelphia Athletics became my dad's team.

LOU PINIELLA

My father and my uncles both played in the amateur league here in the Tampa Bay Area. In fact, my mother's brother Joe and my father could've played pro ball, but it was during the war in the 1940s, and it wasn't possible, but I would go watch them play all the time. They played in the old Inter-social League. Probably about eight teams or so; teams like the Loyal Knights and Elks Club.

Centro Espanol Baseball Club, which is a Spanish club. The Italian Club had a team, the Cuban Club had a team, and they'd play on Wednesdays, and then they'd play doubleheaders on Sunday at Old Cuscaden Park. So, I used to go and be the bat boy and watch them play, and I got interested in the sport, and I liked it, and I played it a lot as a kid.

People kept playing into their late 30s, early 40s . . . They kept playing baseball. And I remember going to the skating park, Sundays were special, and they had the doubleheader, four teams played, and I still remember those days. I remember loving to buy snow cones down underneath the stands (laughing), and like I said, being the bat boy for my father's team and for my uncle's team, they played on different teams. I knew a lot of the men that played; a lot of them were right from the neighborhood.

We grew up with baseball. We grew up with baseball, and you know, as I got a little older, we started playing; they did have a PONY League. So, we went into PONY League Baseball. They had a really good American Legion program. We went into American Legion, and from there on, I went on to college for a year. I played one year at the University at Tampa baseball, and then I signed a professional contract.

Tony (LaRussa) was on that team also, but you look at Tampa. Tampa for a long time was as prolific or more prolific an area for Major League Baseball as any city; take a look at the people that come from here, it's long, and it's impressive; you can start with, Wade Boggs a Hall of Famer, we got Tino Martinez, we got Freddy McGriff, we got Garry Sheffield, we got Luis Gonzales, you got Dwight Gooden, my cousin Dave Magadan.

JIM ZAPP

Born and raised in Nashville at the end of Fourth Avenue North, below Clay Street. One brother, one sister, they didn't play baseball. Good childhood, yeah, thanks to my mother, my father couldn't have cared less (laughing). My Mom really saved me when I stopped going to school; when I laid out of school, and when I went back, they had the high school basketball team. When I left school, I went to work at the brickyard. Isn't that something . . . went to work in the brickyard, then I went back to school. My brother, he never did play, he was chasing girls, I guess . . . but I loved baseball when I was a kid.

There was the black sandlot baseball teams. They'd go out of town on Sunday and play like in Franklin, Columbia, places like that. My mother would let me go with them, but I wasn't playing, she was very strict; I'd go with the teams sometimes, but I wasn't playing. Yeah, my dad, he cared less, it's what my momma said, and my momma said, "No." I didn't start playing until I went into the Navy.

We had to register with the Priest, big Church, the convent for Nuns and the Elementary School next to that, four brick buildings, and we had to go to school way out there to go to Catholic school. We were going to a private school. We had to walk most of the time, and we'd end up at Fourth Avenue North. Oh, we had to walk to Nashville, about three miles up and three miles back every day.

LOU WHITAKER

I grew up in Martinsville, Virginia; that's where they race the cars. They do the NASCAR there, and I lived maybe 12 miles or so away from the raceway, Martinsville Speedway.

(Did you want to be a race car driver growing up?) Never even thought about it. I thought it was just a lot of noise as a kid because being that far away, twice a year, you hear those cars going around in circles, and it was just something that I never thought about as a kid. You knew they were there, and really thinking about it now, I could have used that in some of my baseball interviews when they ask questions. Nobody knows where Martinsville is, as far as being a small town. But if I had mentioned race cars, then they would say, "Oh, yeah, I've watched that before (laughing)."

My mom never would say anything, do this, or do that, go here or go there. She left that up to me. And she was just proud that I had just done as well as I did growing up as a kid. I mean, she would always see us as kids out there playing ball in the streets and in the ballpark. But nobody ever went anywhere other than staying local. And now here I am, I've got scouts coming to my house, and they're talking about signing a professional contract to play ball. I mean, that was really my decision.

STEVE BLASS

A small town of about 800 people: the thing is, I was so obsessed, every morning of school vacation, of summer, the first thing I would do when I got out of bed, I would run over to the window to see if the weather was gonna be good enough for me to play ball. That was the first thing that I did and found out if I could play ball. Down in this small town, I was the oldest kid in our family, so I had complete freedom because the town was so small; it wasn't big enough to get in trouble. I was like Huckleberry Finn. My parents, when I woke up in the summer, I would have something to eat, and then they wouldn't see me until dinner; I was either playing ball or chasing after every girl in our town. We had five churches and about 15 girls, and at one time I belonged to all five churches just so I could find a date (laughing). But I've been married 54 years plus four years of bad behavior in high school. I married my high school sweetheart.

Yeah, interestingly enough, my Dad did. He played in what they call an Interstate League. The guys at work had a little town team, and they played Sundays, and I was the batboy, and I would hitchhike about seven miles up from where I lived up to where they played. Back in those days, you could hitchhike; everybody knew everybody. The world was so different. I was their batboy.

Those guys who had worked all week and then played ball on Sunday, after the game, would stop at a bar and drink beer the rest of the afternoon and evening, and I couldn't go in so they would leave me in the car. They would bring me Coca-Cola out on a regular basis. I drank more Coca-Cola than any kid in Connecticut (laughing). I did that, and actually, my dad did pitch before I could remember much about him pitching. Interesting enough, they said one of the big stories about my dad pitching in that Interstate League that one day he threw, in the middle of an inning; he threw a pitch that went over the backstop. And that was ironic because I laughed and laughed, and at the end of my career with the Pirates, I was close to throwing a ball over the backstop (laughing). So, things come in a circle.

Hell, I mowed every lawn in Falls Village, Connecticut, and I sold vegetable seeds and flower seeds to get a BB gun. It was just like a kind of a Tom Sawyer type of existence. Maybe more like Huckleberry Finn (laughing).

WHITEY HERZOG

New Athens, Illinois, is about 35 miles south of St. Louis, and it was a small town of 1,400 people and maybe 100 kids in grade school and 100 kids in high school. We had a group of guys that—we started playing when we were in the sixth grade every day. We'd go up to the school-yard in the summertime and choose-up sides, and some days we'd play uptown against downtown because there was a big hill, but most of the time, we chose up sides every morning, and we start playing about 8:00, and we'd play all day.

I had one brother that was older—a year older than me, and I had a young brother, two years younger than me. We had three boys in the family. And my older brother did sign a contract, a professional contract, and he played in the Cotton States League one year. The Yankees bought his contract, and they were going to move him to the Class A Binghamton, but the postman's job became available in New Athens, and he quit playing ball and became a mail carrier in New Athens so he never really knew whether he had a future in professional baseball. He died about a year and a half ago; I think that was a claw in his spine because he never really answered that question because he didn't give himself the chance.

The other thing that helped me being from a small town; they had a town team. They played every Sunday, and they had a lot of good players, they were all so good, they all could've signed contracts, but they went down with the Cardinals, or they went with somebody else, and they got homesick. I heard that story a lot, "What happened? They didn't make it (laughing)". But the big thing is I ended up playing with them as a sophomore in high school. I was playing center field for that team, and we used to play the Schoendienst brothers from Germantown, Illinois in the fall, and Red would come over; that's when I first met Red in the mid or late 1940s when he came up to the Cardinals.

DOUG FLYNN

Going to watch my dad play when I was probably four or five-years-old. He played amateur ball; he had played with the Brooklyn Dodgers, but I don't remember that . . . that was before I was born, so obviously I don't remember. Then he played in the Blue Grass League here in Kentucky, a league that I played in, Governor Chandler played in, and a lot of players played in, Woodie Fryman was one. I remember going and watching him playing and thinking, "What is my dad doing out there with those young college kids (laughing)," he was only 30 years old. I thought he was so old, but I remember him being really good; that and in the backyard throwing with him and my uncle, my mom's brother, who was a good player. They played semi-pro together and then later playing with mom, but my first recollection is being that young kid and going to the ballpark with him every Sunday after church.

I think the teams around here at the time were Harrodsburg, Frankfort, Greensborough, Flemingsburg, they are all local teams, but they were all good from what I understand.

Dad played basketball at the University of Dayton. He came out of the service and played there under a guy named Tom Blackburn. I loved basketball too, and my favorite player was a guy named Larry Conley that played at Kentucky. He was from Ashland. My dad was a referee with Larry's dad. Dad would tell me about Larry and then on my 15th birthday, Larry was my birthday present to come home for dinner. They just got beat by Texas Western in the 1966 NCAA National Championship game; he was home, and he and dad were friends, so he brought him over to the house for dinner.

Lord, Dad, was good at everything he did. He could shoot pool; he can dive, he can high jump, he used to jump the fence at home and chase rabbits. He played college basketball; he played pro baseball. I saw him do a one and a half off the high dive one day. He was just a natural. I never had those skills, and because he never had fear, I think I always had a little bit of fear as a young kid because I was so little. I mean, I'm up there as a freshman playing baseball against seniors. I was 5'2" as a sophomore and 5'6" as a junior, 5'8" as a senior.

I was always taught a great lesson about humility from my mom and dad, both of them. I mean, dad was a little cockier than mom, but he used to tell me, he said, "If you're any good people will know about it, you don't have to say anything about it.

FERGIE JENKINS

I grew up in Chatham, Ontario, Canada. It's about 65 miles north on the Canadian side of Detroit. The population at the time was probably around twenty-two thousand people. All blue-collar workers, a lot of them were farmers; it's a farming community. We had two industries. We had

Ontario Steel, and we had a Libby's, which was a produce shop that harvested a lot of corn, soybeans, that type thing, and Dekalb and Pioneer.

Growing up in Canada, I think the fact that I didn't wear myself out as a kid, as a 12 or 13-year-old pitching, that probably did help. I see these kids who played Little League baseball in the Little League World Series . . . Rick Wise, he was one guy that signed and got to the big leagues as a player and also pitched in the Little League World Series. I think you wear kids out at 12-13-years-old, and to me, it's not good. Maybe they end up signing as a shortstop or something else but not as a pitcher. I think it was Art Mahaffey with the Phillies; he said, "Jenkins, you only got so many bullets, man." I look back at that, and he was pretty right. I can throw a little bit, but I can't throw as well as I used to. You only got so many bullets!

WILLIE BLAIR

I had four half-brothers and three half-sisters. The closest one in age to me was about 10-years-older than me, and he was the only one that really played sports. He played basketball, and the rest of them played for fun; didn't play on any teams; they just played for fun. We all liked basketball but really just playing in our neighborhood, playing Wiffle ball with the kids, and then my uncle, who was a big Yankees fan when he was younger, kind of pushed me to play baseball. That's where it all started. I was just playing in the backyard playing Wiffle ball.

WILLIE HORTON

My first memory of baseball is with my oldest brother-in-law, George Clayton. He was from Black Mountain, Kentucky, and he cooked all around in them places, and the big town at the time was Harlan, Kentucky. He's the one who first put a ball—I was about four years old, in my hand. He'd be cooking, and then he'd play catch with me and stuff like that, and that's the first time I got introduced to baseball. Then my folks came north to Detroit. They wanted me to play, at that age, they wanted me to play tee-ball, but down there in Kentucky, I'd been used to somebody throwin' to me. So, my mom and dad let me go back and stay with my brother over in Tennessee, and I used my brother's birth certificate to play in an older league at the time, he was a couple of years older than I was, and then after that, I came back, and we started playing baseball in the city of Detroit.

On the way down to the ballpark with my family, we were talking about my brother in law, the person who put the ball in my hand, and I still use his Bar B Que sauce. It's a certain way he makes his Bar B Que sauce. I remember doing a cookbook when I was with the Seattle baseball team years ago; they did a cookbook with all the players and the celebrities; I called him back; at that time, he was living in Atlanta and told him I used his recipe. He said—he'd always say "Young'un, child, young'un you don't have to call me for that." And I said, "That's your recipe," and I do my ribs just like that, and it all started with that little baseball he gave me.

I was introduced to Judge Damon Keith when I was 13 years old. He became my legal advisor, and then that's when I really started enjoying the game. The game taught me how to enjoy and be involved with people. Judge Keith, he's still living, he's got to be about to be 95 now, and he's still like my Father. He's still getting around and still works down at the YMCA. He was a lawyer at the time when I met him, and I remember asking my dad and mom, I said: "Y'all aren't giving me away, are you?" They said, "No, no, no. Putting you with a young man that can help guide you and show you that God gave you some special ability and bring it in and make you recognize you can do things different." And from Judge Keith, through Mr. Ron Thompson to Coach Sam Bishop, I think that's when I really started enjoying baseball and integrating in with people. I never put the game before fans and the people, and I learned that at a young age. You never put the game before fans because its people who make the game, to be able to smile, cheer, or boo you, whatever. That's what makes the game, and I learned that at a young age, but I just am very thankful that it helped me when I got off and when I left.

I got through it because I had a support system. I had people surround me, but that little baseball gave me the people. Like I mentioned about Judge Keith, and Mr. Bishop and my school teachers, your school teacher, and school become like your parents at school, but that game, that little round circle, what Mr. Thompson told us as kids; eight, nine, ten-years-old that was the circle of enjoyment of playing this game, and you can expand and grow, and do many things in life.

I'm close to my older brother. I was born later in my mother's life, and there is about five years between me and Billy. He was a great athlete, but he didn't like it. Billy liked to read and play chess, and I thought he was going to be a great engineer one day. But he was an all-around athlete in all sports, and people used to try to get him to play and do different things, but he didn't want to do it. He went to the service to help my parents, but I look at him, and I think he went to the service to make sure I got out of school and have the opportunity to do things. My brother Billy, to hear people talk about him, could've been a great athlete in football and baseball.

CHARLIE LOYD

Grew up in Paducah, Kentucky, lived here all my life. My older brother was a catcher; he played high school ball, but then he went into the service, he never played organized ball in the summer and never played college, but he always played. I was a pitcher, and he was always my catcher. I was out there throwing to him, and we'd be out in the backyard, and he'd get tired, and my dad would come out there and catch me, but he didn't last long because I was wild and I'd throw 'um . . . I'd throw 'um over the garage or out in the alley, and he'd have to go get 'um (laughing), so he didn't last long.

My brother could've played at Paducah Junior College. He couldn't have played in major college; I don't think. He wasn't eatin' up with it like I was. He had other things that he did.

My dad would take me up to St. Louis two or three times a year and a lot of time he'd have some business up there, and this is hard to believe, but if you didn't have a ticket you could go and sit in the bleachers for a dollar, and he'd go to a meeting, and he'd drop me off at the ballpark, and I'd sit out there in the bleachers all afternoon for a dollar.

We used to stay in the Chase Hotel. The visiting team was always staying at the Chase Hotel, and I'd meet all those guys hanging around the lobby down there. I'd go up there sometimes to see the St. Louis Browns because that was an American League team. Around here, you never got to know anything about American League teams because St. Louis (Cardinals) didn't play them. But I'd meet guys down there. It was interesting.

I wouldn't trade my childhood for anybody. We had the biggest time. I've talked to some guys I've played with, and they said, "You know we grew up in the best of times. We could leave home in the morning, and our parents didn't have to worry about you; there wasn't any drugs or anything. If your parents were gone, your neighbors watched after you. It was really a good time to grow up.

3.

GETTING STARTED

PHIL ROOF

Well, my dad was interested in baseball. He loved Cardinal baseball, and he would listen to that radio every night back in the late 1940s. In fact my brother Paul and I; he's a year and half younger, we would listen to Harry Caray, we could name every Cardinal on that ball club, and daddy would let us listen some nights until 8:00 before we went to bed so we'd get one round of line up before we went to bed and that was the motivation to play. Once Adrian got big enough, he is the oldest, and he didn't start playing until he was in the eighth or ninth grade; I know once he started playing organized baseball, all the rest of us followed suit. We lived out in the country, and we farmed, and with one car, we didn't have a lot of transportation, so we just played among ourselves. On Sunday, back when we were kids, on Sunday, Johnny Wurth and somebody else would take a group of kids out and just work them out, take a little batting practice, stuff like that, so by the time, I started playing it was more or less organized.

I can't remember the name of the league that we first started playing in. On Sunday, it was a sandlot league, and it seems like when I got in high school, we became a Twin States team. That was organized, it was well organized, and it was well written up in the paper by James Elkins, and whoever else was sportswriters for the Paducah Sun. The one team that I played for was the Poodle Hounds in the seventh grade in Lone

Oak, and then the next year, I made the high school team. I also played in the Khoury League that summer.

If you went out for the baseball team, you got a uniform, whether you were good enough or not, 12 guys . . . wasn't but 40 in the whole high school.

HAWK TAYLOR

My first recollection of organized ball, in fact, I was probably even too young for it, but I pestered so many people (laughing) they probably decided it would be best to let me be on the team. They had what they called a city league in Metropolis, Illinois. It seemed like the earliest age group then was about six, and that's my early recollection. The city league, taken as a whole, did a pretty decent job, but it was about that time a program from the St. Louis area was starting to grow big time called Khoury League. The Khoury League took the place of the city league there in Metropolis, so we had many, many different ball fields located all over the city. The city was pretty much set up for the development of baseball.

I started young from that standpoint, from the organized baseball standpoint, but most of my baseball was learned whenever my uncles would come home from playing their summertime baseball, and I'd pester them to let me play in Sunday afternoon games, they'd stick me out in right field or whatever, they'd show me how to hit; do this and do that, so it was just natural for me, and when I learned how to play baseball I learned how to do it the right way, I didn't have to unlearn anything.

Most places that had country stores or had a high school out in the country usually had a baseball team associated that used the high school field. When my uncles came home, the local teams all had already played their schedules and if the weather was still nice . . . what I remember is in the Fall each year we'd go to those different high schools and we'd have some pretty good crowds out there, they'd want to see the country boys knock off the big city players who played the pro ball, didn't happen very often, but I'd get a chance to play. That's how my baseball got started.

BILL GREASON

I guess I started playing fastpitch softball in Atlanta, only had one park that we played at, that was Washington Park, and I would just be on the playground and playing and picked up a ball and started playing with it and some of the older fellas saw me, and from that day they said, "You can play baseball."

I didn't know anything about baseball; didn't know where to play. So, I think it was with the Scripto Black Cats, they called them in Atlanta. Yeah, I believe it was the Scripto Black Cats. They had this pencil factory, Scripto, made pencils. They had a plant there, and they sponsored a team in Atlanta. We played on a field in Atlanta; I believe it was on Jackson Street. I've forgotten the name (laughing), it's been a long time, but he let me throw a few balls and so forth. I don't know; all of my life as I look back over it, I see God gifting me with everything that I've been able to do.

LOIS YOUNGEN

Well, my first memories of playing, I was six years old, and my father was a basketball coach along with other things in this very small town in Ohio. I would beg to go to practice with him, and then after basketball practice, my mom told me that I always wanted to go out there and shoot the ball a little bit. I don't know if I got the ball anywhere close to the basket, but I'm sure with my dad's help, I did. But I enjoyed going and sitting through his basketball practice. So that's my first recollection of being involved with balls, and then in elementary school, I played any kind of ball with the local kids. We played football in the fall because it was easier, we didn't need as big a space to throw the ball.

Then, in elementary school, we moved, and in the town I lived in, on my street, there were only boys, and they all play ball. We had houses on one side of the street, and it was pretty much pasture field and farmland on the other side of the street so my first real recollection of playing baseball was when the boys said, "Well, you can play with us, but you've got to either play right field or be a catcher." And not being too stupid (laughing), I said, "Well, I'm not going to play right field. Everybody knows in elementary school, the only person that plays in right field is somebody who can't play (laughing)." As opposed to the major leagues, where you better have a great right fielder with a rocket arm. So anyway, I said, "I'm gonna catch"; that way, I knew I'd be in on every pitch, and that's how I learned to catch with the boys in the neighborhood because there weren't any girls to play with.

But anyway, one summer . . . later my mother told me this; I think I probably repressed it. But anyway, the boys came down and they told me they didn't want me to be on the team anymore. My mother said it absolutely—it absolutely crushed me. I was just floored,—that's the worst thing that had ever happened to me, and then I was obviously off the team. I mean, they didn't want me to play, I wasn't going to play. Mom said it wasn't longer than about a week and a half later; they were back asking if I would come back and play because they hadn't won a game since (laughing).

(Did they give you a reason?) None of the other teams had a girl on the team, and the other boys made fun of them, and they got bullied into asking me to quit but eventually, somebody must have explained to them that it was more important to win with a girl than to lose without one (laughing) and take the ridicule of having a girl on the team (laughing). Nowadays, it seems ludicrous, but I said, "Well, I guess I wasn't very proud; I just went right back on the team (laughing)." I never gave it a second thought. I just said, "Okay, let's go," I just wanted to play.

KATIE HORSTMAN

We had organized softball. A young priest came here, Father Schuwey, and he said: "Well, don't the girls play around here?" He was from Kentucky; I think Louisville or Lexington, one of the two, and this was his first parish; he says, "Well, I think the girls should have something too" because he saw us playing on the playground. He said, "Do you think we could get a team together?" I was only in the sixth grade when he came, and we said, "Oh yeah!" and so, it was mostly the farm girls that came out. We were the best because we all did the same thing; played with our brothers and sisters and neighbors, and so he says "Well, we could start a CYO team, and I says, "Oh geez." You know, Catholic Youth Organization, that's what it stood for, and so he says, "Okay." Well, he was so handsome that 40 girls came out. Some didn't even know how to hold a bat. He was really handsome and very, very nice. He dwindled it down to about 15, and most of them, I'd say 10 out of 15 were farm girls. So, all the other schools did the same thing, all the other little towns like Maria Stein, St. Henry, Coldwater, Fort Laramie, St. Mary's, New Greenland; so we had about 12 small towns, and we played against each other.

Oh, we were number one. We really were. The others either didn't have big families or they didn't come out, or they didn't have a good coach or something. We just happened to have everything line up.

That was always my dream. Every night I would go to bed, I'd pray that there was someplace where they either had a girl's baseball or basket-ball or football. I didn't care; any of the three, I loved them all. I figured they wouldn't have football. I never knew soccer existed until I came to Fort Wayne, and I would have loved to have been a soccer star too.

(What did you think when you heard about the AAGPBL?) Oh my gosh, I was on top of the world (laughing). You know, I was still grieving for my dad, dying overnight, and a year later, here I am playing baseball. And he knew I loved baseball and I swear it was a miracle. It was simply a miracle because I thought, "Who would know where Minster, Ohio, is?" We were famous for Wooden Shoe beer. Now we're famous for Danyon yogurt. The biggest plant is right here; it went from beer to yogurt; ev-erybody laughs about it (laughing)!

Oh, my gosh . . . yes! We would hurry up, get off the school bus and boy, I'd get the cows in because our games started at 5:00 and we had to milk them either after or before (the game), and we would always try to do it before because normally after the game our coaches would have us over for snacks with iced tea or milk to drink afterward. So I wasn't going to miss that; I mean, that's where you did all of your gossiping and talked about the game and what was going to be next and who was going to be next and everything.

JIM KAAT

I was the youngest of four, so my brother was nine-years-older than me, and he had no interest in sports whatsoever, but my dad had bought him a catcher's glove—a Ray "Cracker" Schalk catcher's glove. I know there is a picture that I have- a little black and white probably 2x4 picture of me squatting down with a mask and a catcher's glove and I was probably four or five-years-old then, and my sisters tell me when I started to play catch that I wanted to throw the ball left-handed. Of course, it was not socially acceptable in those days to be left-handed, so they would always put the ball in my right hand, but invariably I would put it back in my left hand (laughing). So, I stayed a lefty, but I probably started playing catch just in the yard with my dad. In those days families tended to congregate in one area, and I had a big family; aunts and uncles in Grand Rapids, Michigan, so we would have a big family reunion every 4th of July, and I always looked forward to that because I would be playing catch and playing baseball with my uncles and cousins.

The first organized ball that I actually played was fastpitch softball. Probably from the time I was 11 or 12, we had an organized league in town, and I would pitch the windmill fastpitch softball. I didn't really play organized baseball until American Legion baseball when I was like 14.

LOU PINIELLA

When I grew up here, Little League wasn't formed. I played in all the Youth Leagues here in the Tampa Area. Growing up, they had a really good park recreational league, which basically took the place of today's Little League.

And I played in the Boys Club leagues; different Boys Clubs here in the Tampa Bay and (the) central part of the state, but mostly playgrounds. That was a really good recreational playground league. I was born in West Tampa, which is the Latin section of, at that time, Tampa; that and Ybor City, and I played for West Tampa Heights. I played at MacFarlane Park. Tony LaRussa and I both played at MacFarlane Park. We grew up probably about a mile apart, so we played a lot of baseball together, youth wise. He played shortstop, and I pitched, and I played the outfield.

Me and Tony went to different schools. I went to Catholic school; I went to the St. Josephs Elementary, and then I went to Jesuit High School, and he went to MacFarlane Elementary, West Tampa Junior High, and . . . and then on to Jefferson High School. We played baseball together, but we didn't hang out all that much.

JIM ZAPP

I loved baseball always as a kid. In those days, all the black sandlot baseball teams was on the Southside of Nashville, and I lived in the Northside. My mother wouldn't let me go to the South Side to play baseball, so that's why I didn't start playing until I went into the Navy.

LOU WHITAKER

We just played as kids all day long, from sunup to sundown, and I didn't start playing organized baseball until I was ten years of age, and that was the beginning of playing organized baseball.

I know quite a few of my friends that were great to me, just watching them, even my uncle, who was 10-years-older, so I'm an eight-year-old and all of us little kids out there watching them as we grew up. They just played the game right, and that's something that I always admired is watching my uncles and my cousins play baseball.

STEVE BLASS

I was hooked early on baseball, just throwing the ball all of the time. I think I broke every knick-knack that my mother had throwing the ball against the door inside the house during the winter (laughing). So, I was hooked really early on.

I played Little League baseball, my dad was our coach, and I tried to trick him one time and force him into letting me pitch. He came home from work, and I said, "I'm not gonna give you the car keys to go to the game until you tell me that I'm gonna pitch tonight." Well, that didn't work too well. I didn't pitch for the next two weeks (laughing). I got a little life lesson right there: you don't try to trick the coach, even if he's your dad.

Here is the interesting thing about my Little League. When I was eight years old, it was the first year of organized Little League in our town, and I was playing for the Yankees. The night before the opening game, we got the uniforms out, and they didn't have a Yankee uniform small enough to fit me, so I got traded to the Giants! I'm the only kid that ever got traded in the Falls Village, Canaan, Connecticut Little League the night before the game. So, I played my entire Little League career as a member of the Giants team (laughing). I played 3rd base, I pitched, and I lead the Little League in home runs one year by hitting two. They came in the same game, and that lead the league that year.

WHITEY HERZOG

Well, basically, there wasn't much else to do. You're talking about a town where you had a theatre with a movie on Tuesday and Friday. There's German, all German people there in the town, most of the men were, what you would call consumers of beer (laughing), and they'd get off of work and stop at the tavern, get a couple of beers, come home take a shower, eat dinner, and then go back down to the tavern and play Rummy. So, all the kids had to have something to do. We played a lot of cart ball, a lot of the Indian ball. We were always doing some kind of games; mumbly peg, marbles; every day, we were doing something, but come summertime, it was baseball every day. We played baseball every day from 8:00 in the morning till our mothers came up to the schoolyard and said it's time to go home and eat. In those days, they didn't call it dinner, they'd say it's time for supper and they'd come get you.

In those days, there was not any Little league. There was nothing organized; not too many small schools had grade school baseball teams. We really didn't play any organized baseball or put on a uniform until you got into high school. So, it was just for fun. We had the same group of kids who seemed to play against each other and with each other for six years through high school. And we ended up, as Juniors in high school going to the state finals in the state of Illinois, and that's when there was no classification. We'd beat two teams on the way to the state champion-ship, teams that had more teachers than we had students. So, it's a little bit different today, you know, with the 4-A, 5-A, 3-A, and so forth. And a school like New Athens today, I think, is in 1-A and that's for small schools.

DOUG FLYNN

Playing in the backyard with dad throwing to me and then we'd always play out in the street. What I can remember having is, the front door is first base and a piece of cardboard is second base and back door's third base and playing out in the street when I was younger and being the last one to get picked because nobody wanted me on the team (laugh-ing). Yeah, I was a little younger than everybody else. Smallest guy in the neighborhood and smallest guy on the Little League team.

As a matter of fact, I remember one of the best players on our street was a girl by the name of Ruth Ann White. She was the best player on our team, so she'd always get me on her team because she knew I was the worst player on the team (laughing). She felt sorry for me, and her father was a preacher, so I feel like this was part of her mission (laughing).

(Did Ruth Ann go on to play anywhere?) She didn't play any. Nobody really did from that street. They were all just good. Back then, you really didn't have any model to look at in Kentucky as to who were the pro ballplayers in the area; there weren't that many. If it was like everybody was doing it, or getting a chance to go, then we would have paid more attention, but that was always something that was "waaaay" out there, out of our reach.

At first, I went five years in Little League, two years of PONY League, one year of Thoroughbred League, a year of Colt League, then Connie Mack, so I never quit playing. Then I get to high school, and as a fresh-man, I tried out, and they kept me. I didn't play, but they kept me on the team, and then I started as a sophomore, junior, and senior. But I didn't start as a freshman, and I shouldn't. These guys look so big. I'm glad I was on the bench because I watched them, and I learned from them, and they took care of me too.

FERGIE JENKINS

I started Little League baseball at nine-years-old, and because I was a tall skinny kid, I thought the best position for me was as a first baseman. I played first base until I was 16.

And then I started to pitch. Gene Dziadura, who was the area scout that had played some baseball in the Cubs organization, graduated from the University of Windsor, moved to Chatham, got married, and started a scouting career with the Phillies. He came to see me when I was 15. I turned 16 that winter, my birthday is in December. I was playing hockey in one of the local arenas at Chatham Municipal Center, and I was the defenseman, and I got in a couple of scraps and a fight during the game he was at (laughing). He came in the dressing room after the game and wanted to know why I was so violent? I said, "Well, I was taught to play defense, and those guys are coming in on my goalie, and I gotta stop them the best I can." I was a pretty good skater, but you know, hockey was my first love, basketball second, and baseball third.

During the summer months, I started warming up, throwing, and playing first base, and he saw me, and it caught his eye. He asked me, "With that arm, have you ever tried to pitch"? And I said, "No, because we have pitchers on our ball club, I want to be a regular player, I want to play first base, every day I want to play." He changed my mind to that thinking during that winter; we started to throw a couple of times a week, Tuesdays and Thursdays around 7:00 pm after school was out, and pitching came pretty easy. I was long and lanky at 16-years-old, and throwing the ball, I had pretty good movement. I think at the time I weighed probably 175 pounds (laughing), so that next summer I threw a no-hitter, a couple of 1-hitters. I had a little change-up, a little bit of a breaking ball, but a good fastball. We won a couple of Old Bay Championships. When I played first base, we won one and then we won another one as a pitcher.

There was decent talent, and my talent didn't get good until I became an older teenager. I didn't throw a good curveball until I was 21 (laughing).

WILLIE BLAIR

I was eight years old and I played in what I think was called the minor league. And it actually was coach pitch for part of the game, and then they'd let a kid pitch for maybe a couple innings, and that was probably my first one. It seemed like we had, I don't know how many teams there was, but it seems like we had 20 or 30 kids on a team (laughing). We had kids playing all over the place, so that was probably my first memory of baseball.

Everybody runs to the ball; that's what I remember. There were just people all over the field. Again, I was eight-years-old and don't really remember all of it; I don't know if they just let all the kids come in and play on two teams, but I remember there was a ton of kids out there, so even with all those kids out there you hit a ground ball, and you could score (laughing).

I really only remember throwing one game, and I think I walked the first four and hit the next one, and then they brought the coach back in, so it wasn't the way I wanted my career to start.

WILLIE HORTON

I learned from Buck O'Neal (Negro League ballplayer), my dad played a couple of years in the Negro League, and my dad didn't never tell me that. He never played too much ball with me. He'd always tell me to work, go to the wall and throw the ball off the wall, and hit the ball off the ground, and stuff like that.

As I look back, my dad never drove a car, but Papa was at about every game that I can recall when I was a kid, and I just wondered how he got there. He didn't miss too many games, and he never drove a car (laughing). He would motivate me; he'd sit me down when I did wrong, and he always disciplined to that. The Detroit Tigers had given me a brand-new car, and I had a little skin-up (accident). He got it fixed and sold it, and he said: "Well, next car you own, you'll be 21-years-old." He said, "They didn't sign you to run the streets, they signed you to play baseball," and I just did what Dad told me to do, and actually, I was in the big league then. Then I got a car from Al Kaline, and I left it at my buddy's house, because I was scared to take it home (laughing). I look back at my mom and dad, and I think of them two people, especially mother . . . Papa used to complain about all the kids he got, Mama always bringing other people home, help feeding them, but I respect my dad. He accepted responsibility and worked two or three jobs. He raised all of us, and he did make ends meet, and I had a chance to have an opportunity as a 17-year-old to do some things for my parents, and I signed a hardship case to help them. So, I had a chance to do that, and I did, and that's when I signed with the Tigers.

CHARLIE LOYD

We always played a lot of sandlot baseball, but I guess it was before they even started Little League; we had a league here called the Knot Hole League. The Paducah Chiefs had the pro team here, and down the right-field fence behind first base, there was a great big knothole they had painted in the fence, and you had to stoop down to get in it, and they let all the Knot Hole players get in free and sit in the bleachers down the right-field line. So that's my first memories of organized baseball (laughing).

Probably had 10 or 12 teams, you kinda got your own team together, and I went to St. Mary's and most of those guys would get the guys out of their own school and form a team, so we had a bunch of guys from St. Mary's and we played a little, and we ended up winning the league, and for winning the league we got to go to St. Louis and see the Cardinals and Giants play.

4.

BASEBALL IS BEST
(WHY I PICKED BASEBALL)

BOOG POWELL

I guess I was best at it. I played football, and I was . . . I had 50 football scholarship offers, and I could have gone just about anywhere I wanted, including all three academies. Everybody wanted me. Matter of fact, Bear Bryant drove up in my yard in Key West and got out in a big black limousine and walked over with that Houndstooth hat on and said, "Son we want you to come to Alabama" and I said, "Well thank you, Mr. Bryant, I will certainly consider it." He said, "That's all we can ask; you'll be very happy," he turned around, got in the limousine, and drove off. That was it. Drove all the way to Key West (laughing) and drove in my yard and said we want you to come to Alabama, son. But I mean even back then Bear Bryant was still Bear Bryant.

So anyway, everybody offered me scholarships. I even had one basketball scholarship, Mississippi offered me a basketball scholarship, University of Mississippi. They wanted to get me there to play football, though. They figured if they got me there, "We get this big boy here we'll talk him into playing football," and I said, "Noooo." And Florida State. I ended up signing with Florida. I was always a Gator. I've been a Gator forever, and they all knew that I was probably going to sign with Florida, but of course, I gave it up when I turned professional. I signed with

Florida mainly just so I would have some kind of an insurance policy if something happened to me where I couldn't play, where I couldn't play baseball. And so, you know as things worked out, I think that I did the right thing. I was ready to go.

HAWK TAYLOR

I came from a very athletic family like I told you. My mom played baseball; all the Taylor guys were good athletes in all sports, and baseball just happened to be the primary thing that we took too, but I was pretty good in basketball and other sports too.

In fact, I just happen to look down here in my 1955/56 basketball scorebook. This is from when I played high school. Just look through here real quick, I had a 26 point per game scoring average, and I think my high game in here was 43.

(Were you offered basketball or football scholarships?) No, because it became obvious through the course of time, I could have played football or basketball, at a lot of different colleges but the fact that I excelled in baseball they just knew that when the time came that I would be signing a bonus pro contract.

JIM HICKMAN

Well, I was a little better in baseball than I was in other sports and I enjoyed it more. I wasn't a big fan of football or anything like that or basketball either for that matter, but I just wasn't a very good player in either one of those sports. Of course, you listen to a lot of people tell you different things *(Like what?)*. Well, you know like he'd have a little ability to play baseball, and so I did.

JIM KAAT

I played basketball, but I really followed baseball as a fan. Followed on the radio and with the trading cards and with the newspaper. I always had a desire from the time I was seven years old. You know my aunts and uncles would say, you know the typical "What do you want to be when you grow up?" and I said, "I'm going to be a baseball player" and everyone would say "That's too bad because he is so small." So that was my desire from early on.

LOU PINIELLA

I played some basketball; I played some football, but basically, the sport that I enjoyed the most, all of the time, was baseball and we played; I wouldn't say 12 months out of the year but certainly eight or nine. We played a lot. I mean, we'd get up in the morning, go to the playground and played until it got nightfall.

We looked at it this way, if Al Lopez can do it, why can't a few of us? All my friends; they all played baseball. We'd hitchhike across town just to go play. At that time, it was safe to hitchhike, and we would go from West Tampa to Ybor City. We'd go to Seminole Heights, we'd go to different parts of town and have pickup games and believe it or not, at times we put up a buck or so against the other team, you know what I mean (laughing).

JIM ZAPP

I was playing third base then; I was a pretty good third baseman, good arm, and everything. You had to stay wide-awake over there at third base. Play against guys like Josh Gibson; they'd kill you playing on the infield.

That's when I started playing the outfield. They moved me to the outfield. Let's see, I think; they didn't move me to the outfield until after the war. A guy, manager of the Nashville Elite Giants named Felton Snow. He put me in the outfield . . . said: "You'll get more rest out there than playin' third base (laughing)." So that's when I started playin' the outfield . . . left field.

We played our games just about every day. During the war, all your better major league ballplayers came straight to Hawaii . . . was stationed in Hawaii around Honolulu. Pew Wee Reese, Johnny Mize, all those guys was stationed over there at different bases.

LOU WHITAKER

Well, I just loved to be outdoors playing and guys at the ballpark; they kept the fields in very good condition, and when they cut that grass, it just smelled SO good (laughing).

None of us was really troublemakers as kids, so we didn't just run all over the place. We would get together, we'd go to the ballpark, so parents knew where we were, and we would just be outside playing all day long.

FERGIE JENKINS

Well, Gene Dziadura was kind of a mentor of mine. As I said, I met him when I was 15, going to be 16 that winter. He was kind of telling me that if I wanted to be a professional athlete, then my best opportunity might be to decide to be a pitcher and work hard at it and see what happened. And that is what I tried to do.

He saw something in me that I didn't see. As I started to work, those last two years, 17 and 18, during the winter months, it was remarkable how well I was throwing. As I said, I was playing senior ball at 17 years old against fellows who are 24-25 years old, and I was having some success.

WILLIE BLAIR

I think the biggest thing is competition. I mean, I love to compete in anything I do, and I got that at a young age when I was playing. I played for keeps. It's one of those things where even playing Wiffle ball in the yard I wanted to win, and I wanted to beat the guy, so I think that's the biggest thing and then as I started playing and making friends and all that kind of stuff it became not only a thrill to compete but the camaraderie that you build with being part of a team and that was pretty special.

CHARLIE LOYD

Well, back then, it was like hunting season. The night before a game, you couldn't sleep because you was antsy regardless of what league you were playing in. I was always ready to get out there and compete; I loved to play and the difference in baseball and basketball; it's not near as confining. Seems like basketball you're always running, running laps, running sprints, and if you're not on the starting five, you're always playing defense, and I didn't like that either (laughing). In baseball, you can go out and hit, shag flies, play the infield, just not as confining; you do a lot more things.

I played basketball, and of course, I went to St. Mary's high school, and we had basketball and baseball, no football, nobody ever heard of soccer or anything like that back then.

I grew up down on South Fourth street. During the summer at 8:00 in the morning, there would be 20 guys out there ready to play, and we'd play from daylight to dark every day during the summer; these days, you couldn't find 20 guys to get up 2 two teams. Even now, if you're in high school, if you don't make the Legion team, there's no place for you to play anymore.

I played basketball all during high school, and I was a forward, and I went to Paducah Junior College and played basketball, and I found out in a hurry there wasn't much call for a 6 foot forward in college basketball (laughing). Now I tell everybody I was a great dribbler and real fast; I just couldn't do both of them at the same time (laughing).

5.

COACHES

BOOG POWELL

They just let us go play. There wasn't anything unusual about the team. My dad was with us the whole time, he was there for support, and we took the train from Lakeland all the up; we took the train to Williamsport, and that in itself was quite a thing.

PHIL ROOF

Guy named Mr. Poodle; he drove the bus for Lone Oak. I don't even know what his first name was; I'd have to ask some old guys what his name was. Offhand, maybe Roscoe Keyla, who used to run the barbershop, he would know, oh . . . Don Hicks would know.

Yeah, the school couldn't afford a coach out there, so my brother Adrian took over. He played a little Legion ball the year before and Eddie Haas; when he was a senior, he was our coach out there at that time. He played 2 or 3 years of Legion ball. We just kinda had to teach ourselves, but we sucked up as much knowledge as we could on TV back in the 1950s, and that was our teaching tool, didn't have any professional coaches to come in. When I played Legion ball my freshman, sophomore, and junior year a guy by the name of Walt DeFraites, he had played professional ball for four or five years, and he was a coach for the American Legion team.

HAWK TAYLOR

Primarily the one fella that was very influential in my learning the skills of baseball who happened to be one of my dad's best friends, his name was Del Kreuter, and he and his brothers owned Dr. Pepper. They had a Dr. Pepper bottling plant and a bunch of other things, and they were always sponsors of local baseball teams. He took an interest in me, and he knew quite a bit about baseball, so it helped me out a bunch. He had a son who also played some professional baseball. He didn't quite get the breaks that I got. *(Meaning?)* Having people who were influential in my life who were knowledgeable and able to past on these things that would help me out at times that I needed to learn them.

JIM HICKMAN

I think that's right, you know it's hard to remember back 50 something years or longer than that, 60 something years but, yeah, my dad was the coach of the team.

(Did your dad play professionally?) No, just around here, just country baseball.

That's kinda like my old high school coach. He's gone now, but we played golf together; we'd play every day if we could, and he would say, "I have a hard time hitting that ball; I've just got too many things to think about before I hit it." I said, "Yeah, that's about the truth." He was always concerned about my arm. My arm was my strong point. And that's why I pitched in high school. He just always wanted me to take care of my arm.

BILL GREASON

I remember one guy that gave me a shot at baseball, (his) name was Sammie Haynes. He was the manager of the Atlanta Black; let me see, he was the catcher for the Atlanta Black Crackers. He saw me, and he was the one who gave me a chance to pitch.

That's what it was all about, the abilities I had. No one taught me. Even once I entered professional baseball, nobody, even the manager, they didn't stand on the side and say, "Throw this and try to use this and this and this." When TV first came out, and I saw the Yankees, and they had a pitcher named Vic Raschi, he was a burly big guy, and I said "I'm gonna be like that," and I developed my style after Vic Raschi: used to come right overhand and I said "I'm gonna be like him," and I'd watch him and then when we played I'd sit on the edge of the dugout and watch certain players, see what I could learn from them because during that time they couldn't afford to teach you too much especially another pitcher; because you might take his place (laughing). They didn't help you too much because the talent was limited, and somebody was always ready to move in so . . . "If I show you, I may lose my job," so you had to learn for yourself. I was a pretty good hitter too.

LOIS YOUNGEN

My coaches, while with the AAGPBL, one was Max Carey, and he was a good manager, and he was a teacher. Now, I don't remember anything specific; I can't remember a specific thing that he said to me, but I know I was a better player at the end of that first season than I was at the beginning. I don't know; I'm sure he told me some little things that I forgot about. The next year the manager was Jimmie Foxx, "Double X."

And so those are my two Hall of Fame managers, and I love them both. I was—I thought Jimmie Foxx was, well, first of all, he wasn't like they made him out in the film, A League of Their Own. That was not the Jimmie Foxx that we knew. All the players adored him. He never came drunk; he never berated anybody, he always coached at first base, and he never drank on the bus. All those nasty things that they have in the movie was just Hollywood hyperbole to make money. But Jimmie Foxx was not like that, and every time I get a chance, I tell people that was not the Jimmie Foxx that the women on the team knew. So, we like to rebut the portrayal that Jimmie Dugan in the film was, in fact, a.k.a. Jimmie Foxx because it's not at all true. So, I've had my say, and I say this every opportunity that I get. That's a disservice to him as a person, and that just wasn't the kind of man he was. Now he did . . . it was true; he was an alcoholic. I'm not going to take that away from him. But, if you know anything from any of your mental health or health education classes that you had someplace along the line, you know alcoholics look and act just like everybody else, except they go home and drink at night.

And then they get up the next day and go to work. So, he didn't do a lot of teaching, but he did work with some players more than other players. The only thing he ever said to me that I really remember was; I was at his home . . . Jimmie and his wife lived at a lake north of Fort Wayne during the summer, and I was invited up there a couple of different times, different groups were invited, players were invited up, and he turned to his wife, and he said, "Wouldn't Red Barber love this gal (laughing)." I wasn't even sure who Red Barber was. Then I found that he was a big announcer, so then when we won the pennant that year, we didn't win the World Series, we had the little playoff, but we won the pennant. We had the best record, and he signed my program, "To a fine young lady. Jimmie."

So that's one of my most prized possessions as well. He knew I was going to go on to college, that I had plans other than playing ball although I was really surprised when at the end of my four years, 1954, they terminated the league. And somebody needs to do some good research as to what happened because it wasn't the quality of the players. Somebody asked Jean Faut why they shut-down the league, and she said, "No, it wasn't the quality of the play. In fact, the players were getting better, but for some reason, we weren't getting the fans, and no fans, no money." Obviously, you can't operate ball clubs without fans. But I don't know what was happening in the early 1950s. I think there was a bit of a recession. But that's just something I'd have to research, and I haven't had time to really look into this, but I think that's part of it.

KATIE HORSTMAN

The two coaches also had daughters that was very good. That is why they coached.

I still think they should pay them (MLB players), right after the game because I see mistakes, mental errors galore, and our last coach was Bill Allington. He was super, he went to the rulebook and everything on road trips, not only did we play baseball but we had exams, he would make us get up around 8:00 in the morning on road trips, he'd get the rulebook; everybody had a rule book, and he would go through it from top to bottom and actually give us quizzes. I still have some of his exams.

I was so happy because I would have probably been the same way. I knew all the physical things; of where to throw the ball and stuff because of Coach Bill. If you didn't make that double play right mentally, "Physical errors, anybody can make," he said, "But mental errors, there's no way." Then we would have to be out there at 7:00 in the morning, and he would get that play that you missed mentally and do it at least 25 times. We would be out there at least an hour and a half before we could play again, which was great!

JIM KAAT

Well, I think the skills, and that's what I always appreciated about my dad because I always said that he was the perfect dad for an athlete. He never showed me how to throw a pitch or hold a ball or never said: "I wish the coach would play him more" or anything like that, he was always appreciative of me playing, but he kinda stayed in the background. The first real coach I had was in Holland, Michigan, which was four miles away from Zeeland. They had the tryouts for the American Legion teams. I believe there were four teams, and I went down, and there was a coach named Ned Stuits. He showed me where to stand on the rubber. I was a lefty, so he said "You stand on the first base side of the pitching rubber;" that's the only coaching I ever got, and then as I made one of the teams, Padmos Scrap Iron was the team that I played for the first time, the coach was Clare Van Liere, who was the local insurance man so again he wasn't a coach that instructed us he was just a coach that showed up and organized us and said go out and play (laughing)!

(So, you learned by playing?) Yeah, I did. I think that is what you'll see in the golfers on the Champions Tour and those of us that grew up in that era. We didn't have the refined techniques that a lot of today's athletes have. We sort of found it on our own, and we each had our own style, and quite frankly, I think that was very helpful to us.

LOU PINIELLA

We had people that drove us around, and they didn't really teach us how to play baseball. When you play in the playgrounds before we got to PONY League and so forth, we started to get really good instruction in American Legion ball, and we had this one gentleman that played a little pro-ball, shortstop position, his name was Lingo Rodriguez. He knew the game of baseball and he really started to teach us how to play the game, how to do things that help you get better, and to start instilling in you that winning was important. So, he probably had as much influence on me as a youngster growing up in this area than anybody else from a baseball standpoint.

I never got any instructions at all on hitting. I got instructions on fielding; I got instructions on running the bases. I got some instructions when I pitched, but as far as hitting, just go out there and hit.

JIM ZAPP

I laid out of school for a year, and when I went back, they had a basketball team. So, I played forward and center for the basketball team, and the coach's name was Mr. Goodman. He got at me about going out for the basketball team; I said, "Mr. Goodman, I don't play no sissy game," I said a basketball game was a sissy game during them days, baseball and football was all of it. Pearl High School was the only city high school for blacks, and they wanted me and two other boys from high school to go over there and play football, and my mother said: "No, you ain't going to play no football, you staying right there and playing basketball." Man, I've been thankful many a day for that; football will tear your legs up.

I still didn't get it . . . an education, like I should have. I came out of the Navy, my old basketball Coach Mr. Marquez, he tried to get me to go to Tennessee State. I said, "I'm going to play baseball," he said, "You can play baseball anytime but get your education first," but I didn't listen to him and I started playing baseball and I wound up in Texas.

One of the best guys I ever met, when I went to Texas to play ball at Big Springs, was Bob "Pepper" Martin; he invented the Columbia Bowling Ball.

LOU WHITAKER

Oh, heck all of them, all of them really. I give credit to all my coaches from Little League all the way through. But I guess when I got about 13 years old, there was this one coach, he was the Sheriff of the county and his son was like a year older than me. So, you know, back then, and even today, you may have a father and a son, they're going to be together, and then they pick all the rest of the players. Well, I was picked by this one particular man and another guy; we played from I guess 12 years of age all the way through 18, which was the end of organized ball for me. And the other guy, his name is Roy Clark. He used to be a scout with the Atlanta Braves. He played a little minor league baseball, but he was the scout for the Atlanta Braves, and he's the one that scouted all these players when they became good in the 1990s. And now he works for the Washington Nationals. I think he's the Vice-G.M. right now or some-where in that organization with the Nationals.

This coach, I mean, he wanted me every year. He would start his own baseball team every year. As I got older, he even tried to get me in Connie Mack. They were trying to make a trade that I would play with his team, and they would send some players from their team, but I decided to stay with the Martinsville Henry County Oilers. That's what they were called back then, and they were just well known, and all the players played for this team in my area. I just decided to stay with my own city team. I just can't think of every one of them right now, but each and every coach had a huge impact in my development and even my friends growing up that were years older than me, but they loved to play, and we would always just get together and start a game. Like I said, we played all day long; we just loved to be out there in the ballpark playing.

STEVE BLASS

Yeah, my dad coached my last two years. The first two years I played my coach was a guy named Jerry Fallon, and I always remembered him because we had our first meeting and he said, "I don't know how many games we're going to win, but we're going to have fun, and we're going to learn some fundamentals." Looking back, one of the great introductions I had to the organized aspect of the game.

And I was inducted into our high school Hall of Fame, and I made a talk, and I mentioned Jerry Fallon very specifically. Our high school was a little unique in that it was a little rural high school . . . it was a regional high school that served six towns, and it still only had a graduating class of about 120. But we had three guys out of that high school that made it to the big leagues as pitchers; actually, we had seven boys signed as pitchers professionally, but three of us got to the big leagues, and I'm related to two of them. My brother-in-law was John Lamb, who was a relief pitcher for the Pirates in 1970 & 1971; I married his sister. Also, her cousin is Tom Parsons, who pitched briefly for the Mets and the Pirates. Actually, John Lamb saved a game for me in 1970 or 1971. We had the whole family involved. She was in the stands, I started the game, and he finished. At that time, he was part of our pitching staff that was a mixed grill. We had a Moose, a Veale, and a Lamb (laughing).

I think there was a combination. He was a tremendous coach, and I'll get to him in a moment. I think the planets just aligned. We all had strong arms. I worked on a farm all during high school. I still believe that throwing those hay bales up on the wagons were something that couldn't have been bad but probably helped strengthen my arms and upper body. He was a unique kind of a coach. I just think the world of him. He is still living in Sharon, Connecticut.

Ed Kirby, a great coach. He was particularly tough on me. I hated him. I hated him for a while because he just worked me like a dog, but then I realized that he was aware of the fact that if I signed, and he thought I would, that I would have a lot of challenges along the way. He toughened me up, and I just love him to death for doing that.

WHITEY HERZOG

Well, because we didn't have a grade school team, in the summertime, we would get into some youth leagues. There was a catcher that caught on the town team by the name Harold Wilderman, but everyone called him Handsome Harry, he took a group of us, and we played other towns on Saturday and Sunday every once in a while.

And then in high school, we had a coach by the name of Alonzo J. Woods that also coached the basketball team, and he played on the New Athens town team, and he was a catcher also. He was our high school baseball coach and those guys, I know they didn't get much money in those days, they just took a guy that was a teacher at the school and gave him one or two bucks to be the baseball and basketball coach in a small school, but he was good. He made us all good young men, and we never had any problems. He coached a basketball team, and he used to come in at halftime and say, "Okay, remember now, play good substantial percentage basketball, and you're going the other way this half (laughing)," and we finished 37 and 2.

DOUG FLYNN

Every one of them. I was so lucky. My dad was probably the biggest impact and my mom . . . my mom was a really good player too, fastpitch softball, Mom played here locally. I'd go out and throw with her, and I'd say "Mom, I'm gonna throw some pretty hard, get ready," and I'd let one go as hard I could, and she'd go "Okay, now throw this next one hard" she'd catch it like it was nothing and throw it back to me (laughing). Dad was probably that influential coach and then basketball, Cotton Nash; it's 1963, I'm 12-years-old, remember Cotton Nash, boy what a good player. I never envisioned even playing in college when I was a younger kid. I never envisioned playing professionally as a younger kid in any sport. I just knew I loved it, and I loved to play, and I loved to compete even at my size. I was always playing against somebody who is bigger and older, and I think that was good for me.

I had great Little League coaches Jack Durkin and Garner, great coaches, Luther Wren, they were Little League coaches, and I had them for five years.

I had them for five years in Little League. They were my coaches, and they taught fundamentals. My mom taught me a lot too. I remember one game . . . that game we got beat and I'm sitting on a bench; well, we'd never been beat, I didn't know what gettin' beat in baseball was, so the game is over and I'm sitting there and here comes the opposing team to shake hands, well I don't want to go across the field when all of a sudden I feel and hear a smack and a boom, back of my head and my mom said: "Get your rear-end over there." She said, "for those 50 somethin' games that your team was winning, you weren't afraid to walk across that field; now get over there." She taught me a good lesson.

I was lucky because I kept playing and I played with good people and for good people. I had some wonderful coaches like Wayne Wiley, who was my 13 and 14-year-old coach and a dear friend. They helped us learn how to love the game, and that was so important because it wasn't just "to go out there and it's all work," we had fun, we loved each other, we played for each other, and that's what I tell people now . . . if you get a team that's out there busting their butt for their teammates, they are going to be pretty good. But if they're out there playing for themselves, or for a city, or anything, no, you need to be playing for your buddy.

FERGIE JENKINS

Yeah! I played with some great managers (in the Pros): Leo Durocher, Billy Martin, Don Zimmer, Frank Lucchesi, Billy Hunter; some of these guys were smart managers, and that's why I was fortunate enough to win so many games; they left me in the games. They could see the talent, so I had the chance to stay in ball games. People say, "How come you had so many complete ball games"? In the National League, you could hit, and I wasn't a bad hitter, I could bunt too, but the thing was, a lot of the managers just left me in the ball game because if I come up in the eight-inning or seventh-inning, and I could move the runner up; bunt the runner one base up or hitting behind the runner. I tried to do that. That gave me the opportunity to have some complete ball games.

Leo was the kind of guy and then Billy Martin too; they would say "Hey big fella" and they'd walk by me and say "We're giving the bullpen a rest today" and I went "Okay, thanks Skip" (laughing). I was able to stay out there and complete a ball game a lot of times and just pitch a little longer in the game.

WILLIE BLAIR

There's plenty of them. My first one in that eight-year-old league, his name was Dip Stafford, and I don't remember a ton about him, but I do remember meeting him again after I'd been in pro ball and I was back home visiting my parents, and I met him again, and he said: "You don't remember me do you?" "No, not really," and then he tells me his name, and I remembered him. He made it a lot of fun for us.

In Little League, I had a couple of different coaches; Don Patton and Jim Queen were my first coaches, and then, later on, it ended up being Paul Burchell. I can't remember the other guy's name, but he had four kids on the team. He had one that was 12, he had two that was 11 and one that was nine, so that was fun and then my Babe Ruth coach, his name was James LeMaster, we called him Lemon. I don't know where that name come from, but he was a character. He always went out to the third-base box coaching and had a clipboard, that yellow legal pad. Well, his steal sign was if the yellow was showing, you steal, and you didn't go if it wasn't showing, so that was his steal sign. Then my high school coaches, Mike Collins, who was a really good player, drafted and played pro ball as a catcher. Taught me a lot about the game all the way up to American Legion, where I had Don Hardin and Doc Magrane. Steve Hamilton was my head coach at Morehead (State University). All those guys left an impression on me one way or another. I have good memories about all of them. I was fortunate to have a lot of guys that seem like they really cared for me and that I cared for.

WILLIE HORTON

Mr. Ron Thompson, he really was, truly, the one that sit down with me as a young man and the rest of the young kids at Post Middle School in Detroit, right across the street from the Jeffries Project. He was an ex-football player with the Rams, and he was going to Wayne State, and one day he stopped at the playground, asked us, "You guys want to play organized ball," and first we said "No," and then we said "Yes we do," and he said, "Well you guys meet me; I want you guys to have your bats and your little gloves, then meet me the following Monday." When we met him we thought we would go out there and start playing baseball, and he told us to put our balls and bats in the corner of the playground and made us get in a round circle, and we said: "What's he talking about and making us do this for?" And he said "I want you guys; before you start, you got to love the game, and you have to love each other and know each other before you can play this game because this is about a team sport," and as a little boy, at that age, you don't want to hug no boy (laughing), but we did it, and now I live my life from that, and I lived from that day all the way through my life, through baseball, and from that day, that round circle, he said, "You got to enjoy the game and keep that little boy in you all the time, and as you grow, the higher you go in this game you got to keep having fun and enjoy it." He taught us that it was more than just putting a ball and bat in our hand. He was concerned with us becoming a productive citizen, doing things to help ourselves and try to help your teammates. I learned then at a young age if you couldn't say something good about your teammates, you shouldn't speak at all. And I grew from that area, and he kept us all together till we signed, and our little group still gets together, about 14 still living.

And we went to high school, and some of them became lawyers and doctors. He gave us a way in life that we want to be in something positive in life—we know we want to do something, and I've been fortunate, (I learned) from that when I met Mr. Thompson.

CHARLIE LOYD

My first coaches were Ed Kellow that was the basketball coach at St Mary's and Marshall Jeffords, who was a policeman here for years and years. He always coached; in fact, he also coached the American Legion team. So those guys put in a lot of time, unpaid time, free time.

We had a coach at St. Mary's that would get a lot of films, and I'd watch those films, pick-off plays that other pitchers in the big leagues used, and things like that. It was always something you could learn, always.

6.

NICKNAMES

BOOG POWELL

You know I never was 100% sure; I'd always heard that my dad used to say, "Just look at that little booger run," you know, and somehow it just got shortened. But I was talking to my Aunt Eunice not too long ago, and she said, "Do you really know where that name came from?" and I said, "No." She said, "Well, there was a radio show back in the late 1930s called Dr. Boogit." I'd never heard of it, nobody has ever heard of Dr. Boogit, and Aunt Eunice just started calling me Dr. Boog, and then the Dr. got dropped, and that's what it was, then everybody just started calling me Boog.

And then, of course, when I got here, it's not Boog its "Boooooog!!!" So, it just got . . . so people were booing me and all that stuff, and that was the coolest part of it all. You know, coming up to bat and listening to that, and even like today when we have an event or something out on the field, it's still there, you know the people still boo me, that's pretty cool after all these years, that's pretty cool.

PHIL ROOF

(Did you have a nickname?) No, when I was in the third grade, my name was Phillip. Most everyone around here called me Phillip, and when I came to Sister Mary Jerome RSM in the third grade she said "We're gonna shorten that name, we're gonna call you Phil" and she just started calling me Phil and then about half of the people at St. Johns called me

Phil and the other half kept calling me Phillip but once I got used to the name I just signed my name Phil Roof in high school and of course in pro ball that's all it was . . . Phil Roof.

HAWK TAYLOR

That's a first edition, that book by William Chester, and I think it was written in 1939. They made a movie serial out of that, and that movie serial was called "Hawk of the Wilderness," and there is my namesake here; there's Hawk of the Wilderness. His name is Herman Brix, 1928, 1932 Olympic shot putter. Also played a few roles of Tarzan but he was Hawk of the Wilderness, so that's how I got my nickname because he was playing the role of Hawk of the Wilderness down at the local theatre, and "There's my man, I'm gonna be like him, he is it, Hawk of the Wilderness." I'm five-years-old; I'm nicknamed Hawk of the Wilderness. Based after that book right there, Yep, I was gonna be Hawk of the Wilderness. And I was. I became . . . 'cuz most of my teachers in high school, grade school all called me Hawk, so I was Hawk, Hawk Taylor, I still answer to Hawk.

JIM HICKMAN

Yeah . . . they'd call me Hick.

BILL GREASON

Booster. Yeah, they call me that. My dad pinned that name on me, I don't know where it came from, but like my oldest brother, his name is James Greason Jr. We call him Bro and my youngest brother; his name is Willie; we used to call him "Fat." Yeah, nicknames, just throw 'um out there and so it didn't bother them.

I learned how to catch, and in Atlanta, they called me "Double Duty" because I would catch one game and pitch the next (laughing), but I decided that those foul balls come off there . . . those balls didn't play . . . boy, they'd cut ya!, so I said: "My best out is 60 feet 6 inches from these hitters."

KATIE HORSTMAN

Horsey was my nickname; from Horstman. All of my brothers were called Horsey too when they played ball.

JIM ZAPP

Not among the ballplayers, but anytime I played in Nashville, I could always tell when my neighborhood boys and family was there from the neighborhood because they called me by my nickname . . . "Toots!" They'd yell, "Toots, come on!" (laughing)

They turned out to see me play, and they yelled my nickname so I could tell when they were all there.

My mother said my brother nicknamed me when I was a baby. I could always tell when old-time people were there, "Come on, Toots!" they'd yell. *(How'd that make you feel to hear people yell your nickname?)* That made me feel good when they turned out to see me play.

LOU WHITAKER

Well, I didn't really have any nicknames back then. I guess the coach that I was talking about earlier, C.P. Whit; he used to call me Big Lou.

My friends, some of my friends growing up, they called me Little Whit, like "Little Whitaker," but you know speaking about Whit that was his name, C.P. Whit. They would call me Little Whit. I didn't get the nickname until my first full season in the minor leagues, and that would have been the Florida State League. Players just started calling me Sweet Lou. I don't know why they did it; I know when I got in the big league— Amos Otis and the guys from the Kansas City Royals they referred to me as Sweet Lou, talking about swinging the bat or something like that.

WHITEY HERZOG

Well, my mother misspelled Darrel, and it came out—I was born in my home by a midwife, and on the birth certificate, the (spelling) D-a-r-r-e-l came to look like D-o-r-r-e-l — Dorrel and my nickname was Relly. They took the r-e-l and put l-y behind it. So when I signed a baseball contract, and I was a toe-head, there was a broadcaster at McAlester Oklahoma that nicknamed me Whitey, and I became Whitey, because it's tougher to say, "Here comes Dorrel Herzog to the plate and it wasn't a very good baseball name (laughing).

And it was funny, in the German community everybody had a say, every German baby that was born in New Athens had two middle names. I was called Dorrel Norman Elvert, (spelling) E-l-v-e-r-t, because I had an aunt that was named Elvera, and then my other aunt was Norma, so they called me Norman Elvert. They were my two namesakes.

FERGIE JENKINS
Well, in school, they called me "Plywood" because I was so skinny (laughing). Later on, they just called me "Fly." I wore a lot of different clothes when I got to the big leagues. But my nickname is just Fergie. Everybody called me Fergie.

WILLIE BLAIR
Not in baseball that I remember. I remember in basketball I had a name because I was a pretty good shooter and they used to call me Silk because my shot was smooth as silk (laughing). But I don't really remember a baseball nickname.

WILLIE HORTON
Well, my family nickname is Boozy. I didn't never understand; all of them still living now is Boozy. See, I'm the youngest of 21 kids.

And I'm the only boy left out of 11 boys, and I got one sister left out of 10, but all through my life, I looked up to them, and all they know is Boozy. So, stuff like that, and all people close to the family call me that, but in baseball, you get names thrown at you from different angles as you go into the Big League. And like today a lot of old people still call me that. Most of my older nieces and nephews call me Boozy. Uncle Boozy.

7.

CONFIDENT OR JUST COCKY

BOOG POWELL

No, never. . . . I was, let me put it this way, I wasn't scared, I might have been a little intimidated, but I wasn't scared; I was never scared.

PHIL ROOF

(Laughing) Well, he *(Hawk Taylor)* was. He was a bit more cocky than a normal kid at that age, but Hawk was good at football, he was good at basketball, good in baseball where we just had the baseball out here, and I've known Hawk to come out of the peach orchard at 2:30 p.m., go take a shower and come to the ballpark and put his uniform on, we're playing against him, "What have you been doing all day"? "I've been picking peaches all day." He was just a country boy like me; even though he grew up in the city, he had to work in the summer months just like everybody else did back then and pick up a buck here or there. Hawk was cocky; he was more cocky than a normal kid.

Well, I was probably middle of the road. I knew I could do things; I just didn't try to show off a lot of it. I knew I could catch and out throw any other catcher around here. I hit good to for myself; for the team that I was on, I think before the freshman year ended, I was the cleanup hitter. I was the cleanup hitter all through high school and then cleanup hitter in American Legion too.

HAWK TAYLOR

Yeah, I was probably pretty cocky (laughing), well I tried not to be, but when time came to hit, I knew I was gonna be able to hit.

Well, the only thing that came close to that was before I had a chance to develop that confidence; this was in the developmental stage. I had a chance to pinch-hit; I guess I was 11 years old; if that old. A guy who was a pro pitcher, and I'd never seen anybody that could throw the ball that hard, I'm up there at home plate . . . whoa, three up three down, and it was a humbling thing, but I understand it. Here he was, this guy was a man, and I'm still just a kid and all that, so I learned a little from that (laughing).

JIM HICKMAN

Yeah, I was; I knew I had some ability, but I wasn't a confident player; I was just the opposite of that. I probably did just like everybody; the older you get, the more confidence you got.

BILL GREASON

Oh, yeah. I just believed that if we got a chance, I could make it. I was talking to my friend Martin the other day; Mr. Beavers taught us in high school, he taught Civics. He used to challenge us in a harsh way. He used to say to us, "A negro ain't nothing." That's what he would tell us sometime in the class, "A negro ain't nothing." We'd say, "What about Marian Anderson, W.E.B. Du Bois or Joe Louis?" "That's just a few," and we realized, it was a strange way of doing it, but he was trying to motivate us to try to be the best that we could be, and I remember after I finished playing baseball and we went over to Atlanta to the stadium. They invited former ballplayers over there, and he happened to be, he was an older man, he happened to be on the gate, and he looked up, and he saw me, and he said, "Greason" and I said, "Mr. Beavers," he said, "How you doing boy? You made it, didn't ya". I said, "Yes, I did," and I said, "I thank ya for that motivation." This was motivation because we didn't feel sorry or anything. A few of us got together and said: "We gonna prove to him that we gonna be something." So, we thank God that he enabled us to succeed.

I don't know; I was pretty good (laughing); I was pretty good. I played mostly outfield when I was playing softball, and of course, when Sammie Haynes saw me and gave me a chance to pitch and that changed a lot.

When I pitched, I didn't believe you could hit me until you hit me. Coaches used to . . . sometimes somebody hit a home run off me; they'd tell me to move him back, knock him down or something. If he could hit, he can just hit, and I give him that credit, but I didn't want to endanger anybody when I was playing baseball by throwing at their heads.

LOIS YOUNGEN

I don't think I ever felt inadequate playing softball when I was high school age. I think when you're in high school, you think you can do anything. It doesn't hit you until you're a little bit older because you haven't lived long enough (laughing). You can be kind of smart aleck at 16 or 17, not that I was, but you can have complete confidence in your ability. And it's not until you get a little older and can look back that you think . . . how in the world could I have thought that or done that?

I think maybe that's why we have so many good Olympians that are outstanding sports people at young ages because they're fearless and they have nothing to lose or they have nothing to look back at. Everything is in the moment, they go forward, and they're successful. Then as they get older, the more you learn, the more you're in the world, the more you might start the self-doubting kind of thing. I may be wrong, but I always thought that I probably played as well as I ever did when I was 16 and 17; played with reckless abandon because I didn't know any better.

KATIE HORSTMAN

Well, I was confident at playing ball because when you can play with your brothers . . . my brothers were big, and they knew baseball, and if you did something wrong, you had to do it over and over!

JIM KAAT

Not really, I always took to it; I was pretty natural. I mean just playing a pick-up game, you don't really say "Johnny's real good" or "Billy's not all that good." You just played. I don't think we were really cognizant of who had more ability than another. And then, when I got into Legion Baseball, I was winning most of my games and hitting pretty well for a pitcher, so I knew that I was doing well, and I had some ability to play. I didn't know how much at that time. You know I was always the guy that if we played once a week, I was the pitcher that pitched all of the time.

LOU PINIELLA

I could tell that I had a few more skills than the other players. I mean, I could hit the ball fairly well, and I had a good arm, and I had good hand/eye coordination, so yeah, I could tell that.

I had a lot of success growing up. I was always the best hitter on the team; I would say all the time, probably the best player on the team. So, I did have confidence; I could really hit the baseball. I had a pretty good arm, so when I pitched, we had success . . .

I've always been very confident; I was very successful . . . You know looking back, like when Tony got $100,000 to sign, I thought I was going to be rich because I always considered myself a better ballplayer than Tony, and I probably was. Now, I didn't play a demanding position like he did, and basically, I was an outfielder, and when you look at the skills that I had, I wasn't really a homerun type hitter, although I did hit some home runs. I wasn't a stolen base guy, so basically, I had some athleticism, but I wasn't the speediest guy in the world, and then my throwing arm was average to slightly above average. So, when you look at all the skills growing up, Yeah, you're better than your peers, but when you get into pro-baseball, and you get with the best kids in the country, you start realizing that there's some work to be done.

LOU WHITAKER

Well, I admired quite a few young men or teenagers back then growing up; they were four, five, six-years-older than me. But, as a kid, we would go and watch the older guys play, and they were good. They played well, and I don't ever say that I was better because the ones that I learned from, they taught me and worked with me pitching and throwing. Just the whole game, I learned from them, but I'm the one that made it as far as being a professional ballplayer, but some of these guys that I played with; oh, they were awesome.

One friend, probably would have been drafted by the Yankees but he got in trouble in his teenage years, I think he was about 16, got in a little trouble and it sort of held him back from going further, and eventually, he just grew out of loving to play as much as he did as a kid.

I was a little kid back then when I started out in the minor leagues, and they would sort of tease me being as small as I was. And after getting to the majors, hearing guys talking about how they're going to dominate us; George Brett, Hal McRae . . . Willie Wilson, being about his second year, he didn't say a whole bunch, but he was right there in that little batting group . . . so I would go over there because I loved to go around the other players. I didn't get in to mess with their batting practice or anything like that, but you know when they wasn't doing anything, we'd sit there, and we'd talk, and joke and they pretty much was trying to intimidate me. But playing baseball, I was always confident, and I was never really intimidated by just conversation.

STEVE BLASS

No, I was obnoxious. I was full of confidence. I was a yacker, a talker. I was good at it, and I was dominant in high school, so I thought I was invincible until I get to the rookie league and won 4 games, and I get promoted up to class D where I got my face ripped off (laughing). Then I realized that I wasn't going to run the table.

WHITEY HERZOG

I'll tell you what; I had a classmate by the name of Buddy Wirth, and he was the center on the basketball team, and in high school, him and I pitched on the baseball team. And when he got outta high school, he got a big bonus contract from Detroit, and I got $500 more than

Mickey Mantle got to sign. I got $1500; Mickey only got a thousand. We were the same age, and they should have fired the scout that signed me for crying out loud (laughing), but Buddy was a great athlete. Probably could have played Big Ten basketball; he was 6'4" or five. Probably could have played shooting guard or even handled the ball well enough that he might have been the off guard or something. In those days we didn't have point guards, we had two guards, two forwards and a center that was it and we played like that. But he signed that big contract, and he hurt his back, and he never got higher than Class B. In those days, we had D, C, B, and A, Double A Triple A; there wasn't any of those three-month leagues or rookie leagues.

I was a pretty good player. I had days when I pitched; I'd be a little wild, but we were a pretty good team, and we could hit. I think my last year in high school I hit .585 or something like that, you don't go into slumps when you're hitting .585. You get a hit or two every day.

DOUG FLYNN

No, I just really wasn't very good. I was smart, I knew how to play the game, but I really wasn't that good. I never thought I was good. I never realized I was good.

Even as I got older when I got to high school, I never made All-City. There was another guy that was in town that was better than me, and he made All-City, so I never made All-City; I never hit .300; I was just a so-so player. I wasn't very strong. I had pretty good quickness but not speed. I was good for a team, but I wasn't a guy who was a game-changer on any team, so I could fill in and be a good player. I was smart. I knew how to be heady like on a basketball team. I knew how to set up the offense, played good defense. Baseball, I could turn a double play. I could sacrifice hit and that kind of stuff, but I wasn't a dominating good player. I can understand, people said, "How did you not get drafted?" It was simple; you should have seen me.! It was really easy. Then, after my freshman year in college, I grew three inches, so I started getting a little quicker. Everything started developing as an athlete; my arm got a little stronger. I was just a late bloomer, but that didn't keep me from wanting to compete or trying to compete at an early age. I always thought that attitude of "wanting to compete" was good playing on a high school basketball team that was an underdog. One point kept us from going to the state tournament, so we had a pretty good team, and we had a bunch of guys that just played hard. Football, we had a really good team. Baseball, we were okay.

(Were you the best player on your team?) Absolutely not. Best player on our baseball team . . . we had a kid named Mike Belcher that was the shortstop; he should have gone on and played. He went to Transy and played basketball. He could have gone on and been a really good one. Pat Byrne was a better baseball player than me, both great kids, great guys, still dear friends, and they were much better. In basketball, Belcher was the best basketball player on the team. He's a point guard. Eddie Clark was a good player; he could shoot. Frank LeMaster, who went on and played in the NFL, was on our basketball team and football team. We was just a bunch of guys that really liked each other, and we love playing with each other, and we had a special bond. We stayed at each other's houses. We'd all hang out in the summertime. We just did stuff together all the time.

(Nervous or nervous excitement?) It eventually became that the nervousness at first was of my inability to think I was good enough to compete with the other guys. I love to compete, and I would compete against you, but I never thought I was as good as them, which may have helped me along.

FERGIE JENKINS

Well, you know, I could see once I started playing senior ball, I could see the talent was there, and just a matter of luck, of pitching a no-hitter, one seven-inning no-hitter, a couple of one-hitters, and winning some championships, and the team depended on me to pitch on the weekends, and that's what happened. We played at the most, 30-35 games in the summer. We didn't play like these kids in Georgia, Alabama, Florida, who play 100 games. I might pitch in like eight games in the summer, that was it, and the rest the time I played first base.

(How did you feel your first day as a Pro in Class D ball?) Nervous, I didn't pitch; I didn't pitch for like two weeks. I went down there, and I learned how to run . . . running program, throwing batting practice to your fellow teammates. Andy Seminick was my manager. Thoughtful guy and always told you that "This is a game, you gotta be patient, you gotta work at it, be patient, good things will happen if you do the right things," and he was right. I always thought I should be pitching when I first got down there. Twenty-five guys made the team, but only twenty-two dressed. Now think about that, twenty-two players dressed so that when it came my time to pitch or not pitch, I had to sit in the stands. Until those two weeks were up, then I got a uniform. The uniform was number 25. The Miami Marlins (was the name) they called the team.

WILLIE BLAIR

I'm not sure I had that when I was eight. When I was eight, it was more about just fun; it was fun to go out and play. Probably when I turned 12, it seems like everything started to click. I'd grown, and I got to a point to where I knew that I threw hard, and I knew kids were scared of me. I kind of fed off that; it just made me want to compete that much more, and then I wanted to play against the best. As we moved on into the all-stars, we were able to do that, and I just always felt like I was a kid that nobody really thought that much of as far as; is he the best player or whatever. Even at a young age, I almost felt like people thought other guys were better than me, so I always wanted to prove everybody wrong, and that was; even through my big league career, that's what drove me is I wanted to prove everybody wrong. I wanted to prove to everybody that I could do what other people could do. I think even at a young age, I had that mentality.

Yeah, when I was like nine, I think I only got one hit all year, and I'm playing against 12-year-olds, but I was intimidated at that time, and then when I was 10, I got a little better. I hit better; I played every game, then it was 11 and 12; when I was 11, I was one of the better players, didn't make it to all-star team, but I'd miss like ten games with a broken foot. But as a 12-year-old, I really didn't struggle, I mean, it was almost easy in my league except for a couple of teams, but I can't really remember where I felt like I didn't belong at that point. Now, as I got a little bit older, there were times when I was in high school; my freshman year, I had a really good freshman year, and then my sophomore year, I was like 0 and 5. I was 4-1 as a freshman, and so my sophomore year, I was pitching against all the best teams, so I ended up going 0-5, and I'm like what am I doing? I didn't realize that I'd actually thrown the ball pretty well at times, and maybe my sophomore year, I kind of doubted myself just a little bit at times. Then my freshman year in college may be a little bit; a little bit overmatched there because I was maybe trying to do too much. But that's about it as far as amateur ball.

(Your Sophomore year in high school you pitched as good as your Freshman year?) Right, I would say I was probably pitching just as good if not better, pitching against better teams. That's the biggest thing, and being at that age, you sometimes just don't realize that part of it. All you see is the bottom line; you either win or you lose. You don't see that you're getting better. In Little League, I feel like I was one of the best on my regular-season team. I was probably the best overall; me and one other guy. Definitely, the best pitcher and I could play anywhere in the infield or outfield, and that was a good thing; they played us everywhere, and I enjoyed that. Babe Ruth, I played on some teams with some good players. A couple of them ended up playing college ball, and like I said, I was always the best pitcher. There may have been other guys that were better hitters and maybe a better infielder or something, but I was always really good in the outfield. I would say I was one of the best players. I wouldn't always say I was the best player, but if you'd talk about overall, I was probably one of them.

WILLIE HORTON

I think all great players are cocky because you knew you could do something. I learned when I was a young man, about eight-years-old, I could hit something a long way. I don't know if you call it cocky or not; it's something that I learned. Sticking to baseball, connecting with coaches, I took their advice, and that added to what I did. When they built the freeway in Detroit, John Lodge back then near the projects. I used to take a broomstick, and go out there, and take a ball, and hit it across the construction. And I learned then I could hit something for some reason, and then when I got in baseball I just could pick up a ball and hit it, and you always had confidence in what you can do, but I think with baseball, and through the people that I mentioned they taught me. I listened and learned from the people and learned to respect people; you learned to take it to another level. And that's what it taught me, where you can be cocky, but this is still a team sport, and I think all great hitters know you got to respect pitchers to be a good hitter. That helped me. When I retired, I had two books on every pitcher I faced out of respect.

If you got to be cocky, (then) be great. You do extra things all the time, and you learn how to do things beyond your training schedule, and you would call it cocky or whatever, but I think its confidence and the confidence goes in how you respect and oppose the team with the pitcher you have to face.

I didn't think about playing in the big league. I just thought I was working out, but I guess that's the reason I never get nervous in a game where you want to do good. I challenged myself, wanting to be involved. I envisioned myself with two outs, a man on second, and me and the pitcher. I did that since I was a little boy. I always wanted to be the one with the pressure. I love pressure, and it made me function better. It made me learn; it made my skill expand, but that comes from respecting the pitchers, and I think that started in how you came up in life and your responsibility.

CHARLIE LOYD

I wasn't cocky; I was confident. You know I always figured I could win. Of course, I pitched to both of those guys (Phil Roof & Hawk Taylor); both those guys were my catchers. Neither one of them were cocky they were; they were confident players. We were, I hate to say this, but we were better than most guys around playing, and we knew that we were probably going to do well. And so, we didn't have any cocky attitude about it we was just glad to be out there. We took pride in what we did.

I remember the first game I pitched at the University of Kentucky. Of course, the SEC is a tough league, and we were playing Tennessee, opening game, and it was snowing. It was cold and hard to get loose, and at times it got snowing so hard I could not see the catcher's signals and not being able to get loose; you'd get stiff between innings, and that's the only time I was really nervous. And I find out I can pitch in that league and after that, it didn't bother me, didn't bother me at all.

8.

GAME MEMORIES

BOOG POWELL

Carl and my other brother Charlie, we all played on the same Little League team that went to Williamsport, and we were eliminated the first game of the Little League World Series. I got beat 16 to nothing. And there was a kid; this kid, Bill Masucci, hit one. And I was looking at that Little League Park, I think it's still pretty much the same now, but he hit one, he hit one on the top of the dike up there off of me, you know where those kids were sliding down with those cardboard things, he hit one over that, on the back up there, on the next dike up there, I mean it was a bomb, I looked at it and said, "Son of a bitch!!!!!!" I said, "My goodness," I just admired it, and I ended up; I finally got a base hit, and I did my famous fadeaway hook slide into second base, I had always wanted to do that in the Little League World Series, and I got a chance to do it. I hit a home run, but it went foul right at the last minute, and that was pretty much it. But it was a great experience for a 12-year-old kid, and today I could have played the next year; I could have played at 13, and I was quite a bit bigger and quite a bit stronger in another year. But I couldn't pitch anymore because after that I could hardly throw the ball, I use to try to catch, I couldn't get the ball to second base. *(So, your favorite memory of the Little League World Series is . . .),* my famous fadeaway hook slide (laughing)

PHIL ROOF

Well, I was just a freshman on that team, and all these St. John people had seen me catching in eighth grade and ninth grade in high school. I made the Twin State team, and Charlie Loyd was pitching, and Charlie Loyd could throw in the mid-'90s from down here *(sidearm)*; I mean hard, and the ball was always running, this and that and Joe Felts Jr. Joe Sr's son had just got back from Korea in the mid-1950s, and he was trying to catch Charlie and Charlie's ball was just running all over, and Joe Sr's two brothers-in-law came by and said: "If you don't take him out and put in that Roof kid we're gonna whip your ass right here." He did. He came by, and he said, "You're in the game," and he said, "Sonny, I'm putting you in at second base to help run the infield," which was a nice way of putting it. And Sonny and I are good friends today. He's a great person. He's about 70, 75-years-old, but I loved playing for his dad. He was a UK fan and a baseball fan. He loved to talk sports.

(Charlie Loyd's take) Yeah, he (Joe Felks Jr.) was spending most of his time back at the backstop picking up the ball (laughing). Sometimes I'd throw him a fastball, at that time I threw sidearm and it broke, I mean, I threw extremely hard, and the ball broke so much and sometimes he'd never get a glove on it (laughing).

(Laughing) That's what he (Joe Sr. brothers-in-law) said, that's what he said, and ole' Phil caught from then on.

HAWK TAYLOR

You know, it has all blended in together. The only fair way to answer is I enjoyed it all. All one big part of me and I can't take out any one part of it; it was all one nice time. Now some of the caliber of baseball was a little more advanced than another, but it all was part of growing up, so I enjoyed it all. Man, I'd go through that again in a minute.

Do you know I don't have any specific memories of doing that, it's just I enjoyed all of it, and that's not to take away any individual part of it, but nothing specific comes out, it's just, "Man I had a great time playing Legion ball, man I had a great time doing this." Now one thing I do remember, now that you mentioned it. I had somebody mention it to me. I think I was playing for the American Legion team in Paducah, and we went and played a game in Bowling Green, Kentucky, and they didn't have a fence at Bowling Green, and I got a hold of one and hit it over the left fielders head, and it just kept rolling and rolling, and I think I crossed home plate by the time the guy was picking up the ball out there. That was one of them that I did remember.

JIM HICKMAN

Well, they had a kid over here at Covington that was, at that time, a pretty good pitcher. He threw hard, and you know how kids talk, well, of course, grownups talk that way too, they get to talking about different players, and I imagine the talk was a whole lot worse than what he was and I was just young enough to be scared you know, so that's the way that came about.

I came up with a stomachache, and I didn't play that day. My stomach felt pretty good that day; I just didn't want to play (laughing).

(Did your dad know you were faking?) He knew what was wrong, yeah, he didn't say much, but he wasn't real happy about it.

I'm pretty sure I did, I know one of the last games I pitched; we played seven-inning games, and I think I struck out 20 out of 21 guys.

BILL GREASON

So, I got a chance to start a game with the Scripto Black Cats in 1947. Somebody saw me and invited me to go up to Nashville. In any town that you're in, in the southern states, there was, except for the Memphis Red Sox; the Nashville Black Vols, Birmingham Black Barons, Atlanta Black Crackers, there was the distinguishing mark between the white and black teams. So, I went up and played with the Nashville Black Vols and had a great year there. I think I won 12 and lost 4; I even pitched against Satchel Paige during that time in Nashville. He was barnstorming; he had a team, and we did pretty good against him, and I played that year and the next year. I don't know whether they sold me, traded me whatever, but I went to Ashville, North Carolina, and those were the Ashville Blues (laughing) no more Black there, the Blues. And in spring training the Birmingham Black Barons come for an exhibition game, and our ace of the staff started; they knocked him out in the second inning, and I was put in, and from the second up through the end of the game I shut them out. They didn't score on me, I don't think they got but one hit, and that was on a Monday night, and Friday night, the Skipper said, "Bill, you're going to Birmingham." I said, "For what?" "They bought you or something; I don't know." But anyway, I ended up that Saturday in Birmingham, and that was in 1947.

LOIS YOUNGEN

So, nobody expected me to hit home runs, but I did hit one home run in four years over the fence in Grand Rapids, which I remember vividly in one of your questions what was your most memorable. Well, in 1953, I caught a perfect game thrown by Jean Faut, spelled F-a-u-t, who was the most valuable player in our league on two separate occasions.

And Jean pitched that perfect game against Kalamazoo on September 3rd, 1953, and I was fortunate enough to catch it. And all I remember about that game, two things, I guess. One is; obviously, we didn't talk about it (the chance to pitch a perfect game), we didn't mention it, the big superstition about talking about it. And the second thing was Betty Wagoner was playing right field for us, for South Bend, and she made a sensational catch. And if she hadn't made that catch, that perfect game would've been out the window. In fact, we might not even had a shutout so my hats off to Betty Wagoner for making that catch because as a catcher, I'd get the chance to have a better view of what was going on in the outfield than some of the other players and it was a sensational catch that she made. So, thanks to her, Jean Faut has her perfect game.

And as I often say to Jean in our reunions, "I want y'all to meet Jean Faut, and this is the lady that made me famous (laughing). If it hadn't been for Jean, no one would have ever known that I was a catcher." So there, that's just about true; I was a journeyman player, but I enjoyed every minute of it, and I got better and better as the years went on. My last year, I hit .284, and if you look at the grand list of the players, I'm up there near the top, and I've looked at this but not recently, but one time, I said, "Lois, quit being so self-effacing because you look at the players that you know that are below you in terms of batting average and you look pretty good (laughing)." I never think of myself as being—I don't know why, of being a very good player and then people tell me things and then I think "Well, maybe I was better than I thought I was."

KATIE HORSTMAN

I loved power. I think I hit the longest ball in Fort Wayne; in fact, I didn't even know that until . . . I have all my scrapbooks here, so I went through it, and it said in there I hit the longest ball.

We had three sisters on our team: the Weaver's from Illinois, Southern Illinois. Jo Weaver, she batted .409, I think. The last year, when we went down to a nine-inch ball, a regular baseball, I think mine was .327, so I was about eight in batting average, but my age to was different. Others, they'd been there for about six or seven years. I was probably the youngest besides Jo; Jo Weaver and Betty (Weaver) Foss, she was married. She played first base, and Jo Weaver played the outfield, and they were outstanding. They could have played on any men's team easily. They were good. Super good.

I was pitching batting practice, and there was a girl that would get the ball from the outfield or wherever it went and hand me the ball. She would be talking to me, but I couldn't understand her, so finally I stopped, went to the catcher, and she said: "What's wrong." I said, "I don't know, but that girl that is picking up the ball, where is she from? I don't understand her. I understand German, but I don't understand what she is talking about?" She said, "Well, she's Alveraz, the Cuban." I said, "A Cuban, how did she know about this when I only live 65 miles from here and never heard of it?" And she says, "Well, in '46 I think they had spring training in Cuba, and they outdrew the Yankees because the Cubans were so excited about girls playing baseball that they followed them all the way to the hotel, they needed a police escort." Can you imagine? I said, "Oh my gosh." I almost fainted; I'm not kidding you. I was never so shocked in my life. I thought Cuba?! I thought, Whoa!

JIM KAAT

My sister that is about to be 91, her and her husband live in a nice retirement home in Holland, Michigan, and it overlooks what used to be River View Park, where Hope College is and where I went for one year. That is where we played our baseball games, the football team played the football games there, and we played our summer Legion games there. I hit a home run one game in the bottom of the eight-inning to put us ahead 4-3. We won the game 4-3, and I remember; I always remember the Holland paper the next day had: Little Jimmy Kaat Pitched Padmos Scrap Iron to a win, and he hit a home run over the right-field fence at River View Park, and it put them ahead 4-3. So that stands out to me. And Legion ball, I don't know the specific teams, but the state tournament was played at Bailey Field at Battle Creek Michigan, and they had a big complex. They must have had like six diamonds there so when we went to the regionals, our team, it was an all-star team out of all the Legion teams in Holland, I pitched the first game at 11:00 in the morning, and we won that one, we had another one in the afternoon and I'd pitch the afternoon game at 4:00.

So, when I say that to people now, they say, "you mean they didn't count pitches (laughing)?" You just pitched and tried to figure out a way to get them out!

LOU PINIELLA

I remember that we had really good American Legion teams here, but we could never, for three years, get out of the state tournament. We'd always get beat in the state tournament, and only because we really didn't have dominating pitching. These other teams had a little better pitching, but our offense could score runs, we had some power, we had some speed, we'd catch a ball well, but we'd get out-pitched when we got all the way up, up to the state level. And at the same time that we played American Legion, we played PONY League also, so we played on two teams, and our PONY League team went to the PONY League World Series in Ontario, California. I hurt myself. We were the only undefeated team in the tournament, we had a day off, and they took us up to Mount

Baldy, we'd never been up on a mountain, Florida's flat (laughing), so on the way down, we saw that beautiful waterfall, and I sort of tripped, and I broke my ankle, yeah, broke my ankle. I was supposed to pitch; in fact, if I would have pitched, I think the chances are pretty well that we would have won the PONY World Series over there . . . but, hey I played the last two games, we lost two games in a row, I played left field with a broken ankle, yeah, it was chipped. It bothered me; it bothered me for a long time.

JIM ZAPP

My first memory was the one I hit in Griffith Stadium when I was in the Navy; that's where the Homestead Grays played all their home games. I hit one over the big screen in right-center. Buck Leonard was playing first base during that time, and as years went on by, Buck would always tell his pitcher, "Keep that fastball away from Zapp (laughing)."

"Keep your fastball far away from him," that's when Buck Leonard first saw me with the Grays in 1945. He's dead now too, doggone it; all the guys are gone . . . but he could play and hit, man.

I was the Power hitter; it just came naturally. I wasn't trying to be; I was just strong. I had a good arm during that time; I'd chest catch a ball and let the guy run and still throw him out. Ole' Barney McCosky would yell, "Zapp throw the ball (laughing)," I had a good arm during that time.

(Were you a base-stealer?) No . . . ain't stealing no bases (laughing).

We were playing at Sulphur Dell Park, and we were playing a team out of Memphis, and one of the teams out of Memphis was called the Memphis Red Sox in the old Negro Leagues, but this team we were playing that day was outta Memphis, but it wasn't the Red Sox; anyway we were playing them in Sulphur Dell Park, and I came to bat, and the third baseman was playing in, we had men on base, and he expected me to bunt you know, so somebody hollered "You better move back before you get killed (laughing)," he thought I'd sacrifice (laughing).

LOU WHITAKER

Well, for one, I wasn't a home run hitter, but about the time I got in the 12th grade I could hit the ball every now and then with a little pop, and I think I hit two home runs in a game in my senior year of high school and of course at that time I had scouts following me around and watching me play.

I pitched against some tough schools from time to time. But I remember this one school, Amherst; I'm getting ready to speak about, Amherst High School out of Amherst, Virginia. They had a team about everybody hit about .350 and above.

And I had to pitch against them that game. I pitched with a sore arm, and I think they got one hit. One of their best hitters, right-handed batter got a; hit the ball off the end of the bat, and it went over first base, and he got a single. First baseman was able to get the ball before he made it to second. He stole second; ball went to center field. He got up and went to third, and I'm backing up to third base, but it was so small there; as soon as the ball got past the third baseman, it was passed me about the same time. So, I just didn't have time to react quick enough to knock it down. And they ended up beating us 1-0 that game.

There was one dude, he hit a ball nine miles off of me, but it went foul; it was a curveball. And he hit it about, well I don't know about a mile (laughing), but it was foul. But I mean that was a tough game there. And we knew we were going up against a tough school and that was for our district championship because if we'd have won that game, we'd have went on to the next stage of the league championship.

(Was that loss hard to get over?) No, it didn't linger because playing the game is the enjoyment of the game. Of course, you want to win, but for me, it was about how do you take your loses. When you get beat, hey, you congratulate the other team, and you move on.

There was another game the night that I got drafted. I didn't sign immediately, so I went on and played summer baseball in the Connie Mack League; played about four games before I signed. We ended up playing a 13-inning ball game, and the guy who started pitching, he went about six innings. So, I come in relief, and instead of the game ending in seven innings, or we might have been playing nine, I forget how many we were playing by then. But anyway, we ended up playing about 13 innings that day. I ended up pitching the last seven, and I got a scout, Mr. Lajoie, who came down to sign me. He was out there watching me; I was supposed to be out there playing a position, and he did see me playing the position, but he ended up watching me pitch for the first time, and he learned quite a bit that day about me as a pitcher. But I ended up getting beat in about the 13th inning. A friend of mine who grew up in our neighborhood, he couldn't make the Connie Mack team because of the players we had, so he ended up playing for the man that I was speaking to you earlier; he comes up with his own Connie Mack team. And my friend ended up getting a two-out base hit in about the 13th inning to beat us there.

I signed the next day, and our Connie Mack team ended up going to the Connie Mack World Series. I think they finished third that year. That's the furthest they ever went. I never went that far when I played on the all-star team.

STEVE BLASS

But the interesting story when people ask me my most embarrassing moment . . . it came my first year of Little League when I was eight years old. To make a long story short, I was in the On-Deck Circle getting ready to hit, and I hadn't had a hit all year, and I had to pee; so I thought "Well, I'm just going to go up and strike out like I always do and then I'll have time to go out in back of the dugout and do my business." Well, I got up there and damn if I didn't chuck the ball over the first baseman's head, and I rounded first and feeling good, adrenaline going, and I stand on second, and I remembered my dilemma. That was the bad news. The good news was, we had, in 1950, fifty-pound grey, heavy, wool uniforms, so nobody knew what would happen when I wet my pants out there on second base (laughing). It was okay for about 30 seconds, felt alright; then, you know what happens; you get chaffed a little bit (laughing). But nobody knew it but me, we had those big heavy, wool uniforms, dark grey. Thank goodness. So that was my most embarrassing moment in baseball ever.

WHITEY HERZOG

My junior year in high school, when we went to the finals of the state. We had never played a night game, we didn't have lights in New Athens, and we got to the finals of the State, and we had to play a night game on a better field in Peoria, Illinois. Carl Linthart, who signed a big contract with Detroit from Granite City, we were playing his team in the final. He hit a ball with the bases loaded and beyond the lights, and in the daytime, I just always turned and went back and then turned around; the ball would be there. Well, that night, I went behind the light poles, turned around the light pole—it was dark, I missed it, and he went for a triple (laughing). Another kid came up and got a base hit that made 4-1, and then a guy on our team came up in the ninth inning with the bases loaded and lined into a double play, and that was the end of the game. We finished second in the state championship game. And that was always something that was on my mind all the time; it seemed like a failure.

Another thing, being from a small town, we went to the sectional in basketball. We didn't go over to East St. Louis to practice on the court we were playing. And then we got there, and we hadn't seen the floor or anything, and we had to shoot at glass backboards, and we played a team that slowed the ball down on us because we averaged 68 points a game and the opposition only got about 37. And the game ended up a one-point game, and I had 12 attempts on the field, made six, but I had six free throws and missed all six. I'd never shot a free throw with people waving behind the backboard. In those days, they used to grab the braces and shake the backboards and everything. And I went 0 for six from the free-throw line. So, I kind of had a monkey on my back.

Well, it just seemed like . . . as good as you play all year and I had my junior season end when I lost the fly ball beyond the lights and then my senior season ended in basketball with a one-point defeat on missed free throws. I wasn't a great shooter, but I could shoot 70% or so at the free-throw line. I'd never shot at a glass backboard; it was a lot of difference when they're waving around back there (laughing). *(Next time you'll know to carry a paintbrush with you for the glass backboards)* Yeah. I should've had a spray can and painted the damn thing; you're right.

Finally, after managing Kansas City and losses three times to the Yankees, two times in the ninth inning of the fifth game, and then coming to St. Louis winning the World Series as a manager in 1982 kind of got that monkey off my back. I really felt good about that.

DOUG FLYNN

I could remember a game when I was nine years old. I played Little League as an eight-year-old. I think it was the last year eight-year-olds could play. To this day, I have a friend who was 12 when I was nine that reminds me of this game. We'd won 56 consecutive Little League games; we only played 18 a year, so we had a streak going of three years without a loss. So, the radio station came out to broadcast the game, and as a nine-year-old, we thought this was pretty big. I am pitching. First pitch of the game, I hit the guy in the head; the first pitch!!! And he goes down. Now, I didn't throw hard, but it evidently hit him, and it stunned him. They stopped the game. They call an ambulance. They come over and get him and take him to the hospital. Some guy in the stands yells, "He killed him!" I'm nine-years-old (laughing). He ends up coming back from the hospital, and we get down four to nothing, and I ended up getting a . . . the only reason I know this is because people remind me . . . I end up hitting a bases-loaded triple. As a nine-year-old, we got beat four to three. To this day . . . that was probably, let's see, I was nine, that was 1960. To this day, this guy reminds me, "You lost the first game," and then we went off and ran off a whole bunch more wins (laughing).

I remember that game; I don't remember a whole lot. I remember Little League, we were really good, and people today remember a lot more than I do because that's when their baseball pretty much ended. Now, they are telling me, "Yeah, y'all were somethin', y'all had the best team in the city, and you used to do this, and I'll say, "Yeah, I heard we were pretty good." (Laughing) I really don't remember all that.

FERGIE JENKINS

Not until we got into the playoffs. We would probably play up around the Toronto area, Peterborough, El River, it's up around Ottawa . . . I'm trying to think of the name of the little town. But they always had good teams. We would make the playoffs and then get invited to these tournaments. I got a chance to pitch or play first base.

Here's a name for you: Derek Sanderson, a hockey player. He played with the Boston Bruins. He played center field for Niagara. He was born in the Niagara region. He's a Canadian, and I played against him. He was a center fielder. Same thing with Whitey Stapleton . . . played against him, and he played for Sarnia, Ontario. So, all of us . . . we played all different sports. We might see each other playing hockey or might see each other playing baseball. The no-hitter I pitched was either against Niagara Falls or it was against St. Thomas. We would play seven-innings, Sunday games; we didn't play nine-innings. I pitched a seven-inning no-hitter; pitched a couple of one-hitters. Back then, the talent wasn't bad, so they might have two good players, maybe three. Fortunate enough, I got the good hitters out, and the other hitters got themselves out (laughing). I didn't have any games where I struck out 18 guys; I might strike out six or seven. That type of thing. These phenomenal guys like Nolan Ryan, "Oh, I would strike out 14 guys in a ball game". I didn't do that (laughing). I struck out seven guys in a game, a seven-inning ball game, or eight in a ball game; that was it and won a ball game, and that was it. I look at these high school kids and "Oh, he struck out 22 kids", "Oh, what the hell, who is hitting" (laughing)??

So, we had the opportunity to play, and then we played in some tournaments at 17 . . . this is a great story; I tell people this all of the time. I got invited to a Free Press tournament in Detroit at Tiger's stadium, and I see Willie Horton hit a ball on the roof, 17-years-old, by the way. "Wow! You know" (laughing). There was Johnny Upham, Ed Patrium, Grant Jackson, Alex Johnson, who passed away, and myself, and we're all scouted by the Phillies, and Willie Horton ended up signing with the Tigers, and I think Bill Freehan might have been there too. I think he was a little older in school; he was in college. He might have been 20-21 years old. I could see that for me to sign professionally, I had to be as good as these other guys (laughing), and it just seemed to work.

WILLIE BLAIR

In my senior year, I think I had two no-hitters, and if I'm not mistaken, they were back to back, and one of them was the first game of the year, and it was only like 32 degrees, and it had been snowing, but we were able to play. Probably, the biggest game that I pitched was a game that I lost, and we were playing Madison Central. Back in 1982 they were perfect 40 and 0, and this was 1983 when I played against them, but they still had a really good team and was ranked like two or three in the state, and I was pitching against a kid named Jeff Cruz who also ended up playing college ball and then went on to play professional baseball in the minor leagues so he and I locked up and he beat me, I think it was either 2 to 1 or 3 to 2, and that was fun. I mean, that was one of those games where everybody knew that he and I were probably the top two or three pitchers in the state; that was pretty fun.

I had a few memories. I remember, obviously, I struck out a lot of guys, but I had one game in particular where I ended up striking out all 18 outs. I gave up one hit and had one walk, but all the outs were by strikeout, and I just remember the coach asked me as I'm coming in off the field; he said: "Do you know how many strikeouts you had?" I said, "Yeah, all of them (laughing)." That, and I remember where I had three straight games with a home run. Then playing in all-stars was good and I remember we lost a game in the all-stars when we got beat that we should've won. We should've won that one, and that was one that I remember all the guys being pretty down about. Babe Ruth, the same thing, I remember throwing two or three no-hitters in a row. All-Stars, that was always great because we got to go to other parts of the state and play teams. I remember one game with Babe Ruth, where I pitched a no-hitter and also hit a grand slam in the same game. That's really it, I had other really good games, but those are kinda the ones that really stand out.

(Were you striking everyone out with a curveball?) It was mainly fastball. I didn't really throw a lot of curves. I may have only thrown two or three a game, but it was mainly fastballs.

Like I said, I could tell when I was 12 years old that kids would be scared when they got in there. My uncle used to tell me, "Throw the first one over their head and hit the screen."

I wasn't real wild. I would have a game every now and then where I'd get a little bit wild, but for the most part, I threw strikes. The game I just told you about, 18 strikeouts and one walk, I was wild through my nine, ten and 11-year-old; my 12-year-old year, that's when I got some control. I threw hard, but I was all over the place, and then when I got to be 12, I got a little bigger and a little bit more mature, and I was able to control the pitch a little bit better.

When I was 12 years old, our Little League team was kind of middle of the pack during the regular season. We were good but not the top two or three teams, but we got into the season-ending tournament, and we end up winning it. It was funny because there was one kid on the team that I was the only guy that could catch him, and he was the only guy who could catch me. So, we went back and forth all the time of who was throwing, but that was pretty neat. We come back, and we beat the top two teams in the league and won the championship in the tournament. So that was pretty neat, you know when you have a couple of really good players, how they can dominate in a short playoff situation.

One time I was 13, and we were playing the state tournament in all-stars, and for whatever reason, at least I thought, and all of our parents thought he was squeezing me, and I'd throw balls I thought would be strikes and I'd just shake my head and turn around and get the ball, and he came over in between innings and told our coach, he said, "Tell your pitcher I don't like his looks." And what he meant by that was my facial expression when he didn't call a strike, and my coach said, "What did you say?" "Just tell your pitcher I don't like his looks." Well, we ended up losing that game 3-2 or 2-1, something like that, and I remember our fans were all over him, and he took off; well, I took off after him. He's going out to his car, and I go in and change my shoes, and I take off, and I'm wanting like to give him a mouthful, and I couldn't get to him because my brother got a hold of me, and one of the other players grabbed hold of me. Well, I broke loose from them, picked up a rock and threw it at his car, and I hit his car, but he took off. So, that was obviously not something I'm really proud of.

I wouldn't want my kids doing it. I mean, the time where I threw the rock at the umpire's car, I mean, he had two or three of our parents that were coming after him, and other parents were holding them off of him. I don't know what he said. He must have said something to one of the parents or something, but I didn't hear all that, just saw it going on.

And then, I had another time when I was 15 that we were playing Babe Ruth, and we're playing in our own league. We only had four teams, and all the kids knew each other, and we all played with each other and played all-stars and played with each other from the time we were eight or nine-years-old. So, we're playing; we were one of the best teams, and we were playing the other best team. They had a pitcher that was really good, too. He grunted on every single pitch, so they're yelling at me a little bit, so when he's out there throwing, all of our guys on our team were going "Agh!" every time he threw a pitch. Well, the umpire was a new guy in town. He didn't know any of us, and he comes over and says, "Hey, you know, that's bad sportsmanship; I'm not gonna have that, you guys grunting like that and all that stuff." Our coach is like, "Look, these kids know each other, and they're just playing. It's not a big deal." So, a little bit later, like an inning or two later, our coach says, "You know, don't even worry about it, it's no big deal, you guys can do that." So, we're doing it again, and he comes over, and he says, "That's it; I'm calling the game; that's the worst sportsmanship I've ever seen." And he pointed at me, and he said, "You're the worst one." It was almost like he was challenging me; he points his finger; well, I took off after him, grabbed him, and threw him up against the fence. I was 15 years old, and I did that to a grown man. But I got in trouble for that obviously; got suspended for like a week, but I learned my lesson. I'd never do that again. But that was part of it; man, I cared, I cared about competing and winning, and both of those times, I felt like I got the raw end of the deal. So, those are the two memorable times in my youth baseball career.

WILLIE HORTON

My freshman year in high school, I hit that tower that Reggie hit in the All-Star Game, and the umpire had to tell me to run; it scared me. We had the all city game at Briggs Stadium at the time (now called Tiger Stadium), and I hit that light tower, and the ump had to tell me to go around the bases to get a home run.

I didn't know what I did. When you're a kid, you just play the game, and you just enjoy what you're doing. But I think there's a feeling that you really can't express yourself to, just, you don't know what to say. It's a great feeling at the time. It's just like now; I am so proud in my uniform. Everywhere I played in baseball, my uniform shirt never went on the floor. Never hit the floor. Every clubhouse in this country knows that Willie Horton's shirt don't ever hit the floor. That's the pride that I learned.

CHARLIE LOYD

Well, I just remember playing in the state tournament in Bowling Green, and that's when Hawk Taylor was the catcher for us, and we played; Louisville beat us up there; I think they beat us 4 to 3 or something. They had a super good ball club, and I can remember back then road trips were really something special, we never got to take road trips but going to Bowling Green and playing Louisville, that was a big deal for us because to us a road trip was going to Mayfield or Murray or something.

No, I never had any (arm) problems. In fact, I never got tired either way. I threw hard; it wasn't anything . . . I'd pitch a lot of doubleheaders, even when I was in college at Paducah Junior College. Yeah, we'd go up and play Southern Illinois, and we went up there one year, and we played them down here, I think they were ranked seventh in the country, and we beat them down here something like 3 to 2. Kinda hacked them off, so they wanted to play us at SIU, so we went up there; we shut them out two games and never played them since (laughing). That's when I was at PJC. They didn't like those junior colleges beating them when they were national powers.

We went to the national tournament at PJC, played out in Grand Junction Colorado, and we won the first game, beat Mesa, Colorado; then, we got beat by Northeast Oklahoma and got beat by somebody before that, got beat in 11-innings. Then they beat us in 16-innings, Northeast Oklahoma, beat us. That was the only time we ever got beat by a junior college, but their enrollment was right at 20,000. It was big-time college, they flew in their own planes, and we went out there in 3 cars, and it was a different venue than we'd been in.

We had Billy Martin (not that Billy Martin) that played center field for us. He belongs to the Middle Tennessee Hall of Fame. He died a couple of years ago. He used to catch me sometimes at PJC. He said he didn't like it, but he did it (laughing). But he said, there's never a catcher that didn't try to pass himself off as one (laughing), but he could play center field. He was a player. We went out there, and we went to the National Tournament with ten players; that's all we had. If we'd had any pitching, we could have won it. We played three games in five days, and I pitched two of 'em. One was 11 innings, and one was 15 innings, and I came out in the 15th Inning; we got beat in the 16th inning. We had two guys, we had 12, and two of 'em were ruled ineligible. They couldn't go with us, so we went out there with ten players.

Yeah, I played on a field without an outfield fence when we were in junior college. Of course, being a pitcher, you always remember a base hit that you get (laughing). We were playing; since we didn't have that many junior colleges to play, they made us go to Iowa and play, and when we won in Iowa, it was called the North Central States Championship, and we were the champions of 24 states before we ever got to go to the Nationals. It was the same way in Iowa, Iowa Falls; I hit a home run over the left fielder's head the same way. Of course, that was one of the few home runs I ever hit. If it had a fence, it probably wouldn't have been a home run either (laughing).

(Obviously, PJC had a lot of baseball talent, was most of the players lo-cal?) Yeah, just about all of them are local. We had a couple of guys that were from Missouri or something. What made us so good; we had two guys from here that had been in the service and was going (to college) on the GI Bill, and they had played a lot of baseball. Chilli Hawkins and Jimmy Shemwell, both of those guys, could play.

9.

STORIES YOU JUST NEED TO READ

BOOG POWELL

Well, at that time, there were no rules or anything about how often you could pitch, and I counted the games up, and I pitched nine games to get out of the state of Florida, and it was still single elimination. And then we went to Greenville, North Carolina and that was where the regional tournament was and the first game we played Tennessee, and I shut them out, and I hit a home run. The second game, which was the next day, I played short, and we had another kid named Jimmy McCall, he pitched, and we beat them, I don't remember what the score was, and the next day I pitched again, I pitched 2 out of 3 games in 3 days, and I shut down North Carolina to get us to Williamsport. Then 2 or 3 days later I'm out there again, and I was tired and about half sick but really excited; I didn't feel well, that's no excuse, but my arm was dead. My arm was just hanging, and I went out there, and there was just nothing there, and I gave up a home run to a kid named Bill Masucci, and he played for Schendenty, and Schendenty went on and won it, they won it all that year.

(So that pretty much ruined your arm?) Later on, it came back, it started coming back, but I was a 12-year-old kid, I was developing, and all those bursa sacks and all that crap in your arm and I had no business being out there that many times, but if you asked me, I'd do it. Don't ask me if you don't want me to pitch; don't start me. Don't make the offer (laughing); that's right.

I was the first one to play in the Little League World Series and a Major League World Series because Jim Barberi didn't play. He was with the Dodgers, but he didn't play.

And a lot of just fabulous memories and as a kid growing up we didn't have TV, I don't' think we had TV until about 1955 so when I was growing up on the way home from junior high and stuff we'd stop in front of an appliance store, they had a big overhang out there, and we'd sit there and watch TV, wasn't a big deal. So, I'd just sit out there and watch the games for a little while, but I wasn't obsessed with it; I wanted to do it. Watching it was okay, and I remember the catch that Willie Mays made in that 1954 World Series, that was the year that we went to the Little League World Series too, and I just said, "Man, what a catch." And you go, I wonder if I could do that? Oh sure, it wasn't no big deal, and I probably did make that catch, not exactly that catch, but I probably made that catch. I had a good knuckleball; I had all the pitches; what else do you need? I could hit; I knew I could hit; I used to switch hit until I was about 13. I wasn't that comfortable hitting right-handed. I was looking back on it; if I had to do it again, I probably would have done it. I probably would have tried to keep on switch-hitting. I even thought about it after I started professionally, but once you start professionally, it's pretty hard if you don't have a really good base to fall back on, of course, it's pretty tough hitting some of the harder left-handers like Whitey Ford, Mickey Lolich and Jim Kaat. God all mighty; it was a hard way to make a living man.

PHIL ROOF

I started catching when I was in the seventh grade. We had a field day at St. Johns, and the mothers would come out and help the nuns and put on a feast, and then we'd play a lot of games out there, and then at 12:30, Father Mills would get the seventh and eighth-grade boys and choose sides. He would choose sides and be so many seventh graders and so many eighth-graders on each team, and when he looked at me, he said, "Your gonna be my catcher." Well, I never caught before in my life, never wanted to up to that time, so we did, and I kinda enjoyed it, and if you remember they had those good chest protectors, we didn't have cups back then, just had a flap down there. They got me drafted and put me back there. We played five or six innings until it was time for the bus to come, then it took us home. Then that summer, I played a little bit of left field, and our catcher got hurt, and my dad come down to the coach and said, "My son can catch." So, I go behind the plate and caught ever since. Caught that summer and then made the high school team as an eighth-grader and caught every game, every inning of every game from that point on.

That's right; they played together (Hawk Taylor & Phil's cousin Louis). We played Legion ball against Hawk; he grew up in Metropolis. And then we had a guy named Chili Hawkins; he was probably the best player that I played against around here. And I keep telling Chili; he shoulda made it, he shoulda played big league baseball. He could run, he could throw, he could play second, he could steal bases, he could hit and hit with power, but he was homesick. He went away for a little while and came back; he was homesick.

Martin Scheer volunteered to coach our high school team when I was an eighth-grader. I'm pretty sure I was an eighth-grader because my brother Louis was still playing, and he was a senior when I was an eighth-grader. And when I came on as an eighth-grader, and they saw that I could catch, then he moved from catching to shortstop because he was a better shortstop, but he could catch too. It just made room for me behind the plate. Well, we had a game in Hopkinsville, and we took off in a pickup truck with cattle sides on the pickup truck. I think four people sit in the front; Martin was still the coach; he'd already graduated the year before, and he didn't have a job, so he said he'd coach us. And there's three other guys in the front seat with him, and all the rest of us were in the back end. We had a tire blow out on the way up, didn't have a spare. So he called his dad and brother, and they came up with two spare tires, and we put the one on, and we went on and got there on time, and we had a blow out on the way back and on the way back my two brothers and a couple of other guys and myself, they didn't want to leave me behind, we hitchhiked a ride into downtown Hopkinsville, and we played pool. The game finished about 4:30, 5:00, and then I watched them play pool for about 2 ½ hours. They got out there and got the truck fixed and brought us on in; that was a nightmare. After that, we never scheduled games that far away because that's probably 75 miles from Paducah.

(And guys in the stands were placing bets?) On me, yeah. They were betting, saying, "Hey Roof, can you throw the ball all the way to second"? And I said, "Yeah." Because you know the backstop was only 15 feet from home plate and we were taking infield practice, we didn't get there in time to take batting practice, we were taking infield practice when I caught the ball from the first baseman, and I let it go. It was right there, and they were making bets back there and saying, "Pay me off, pay me off," I could hear them saying, "Pay me off, come on." And you know that was fun because here I am a kid, made the high school team and had no idea how the score turned out or anything like that, but it was a fun trip you know even though we had all the inconveniences of a flat tire and a blowout.

When that one tire blew out, that first blow out we had, it looked like somebody had dumped two buckets full of dirt out of the tire because there was just all kinda stuff coming out of that tire. And rolling on the road and we was lucky he didn't turn it over or something. Happened to be a back tire so it was less damaged there and so we had to wait until we got another spare tire. Why he left with no spare tire, I don't know. Because you know, you take 18 kids, or however many was in the pickup, probably was 12 or 14, at least, anything could happen.

In September of 1958, Coy Stacey, a local Paducah businessman took me and Louis Haas to a St. Louis Cardinals baseball game, and after the game, we went to eat at Musial's restaurant, and for some reason we ordered pizza, and I thought that was the worst food I ever put in my mouth. I never knew what the word pizza meant, never ate any, and two years later, I'm in Cedar Rapids, Iowa, and I'm renting an upstairs apartment from a lady, and a block away was a pizza joint. By midsummer, I thought that was the best food I ever eat, easy to pick (laughing).

HAWK TAYLOR

Well, I've had similar experiences but not quite to that degree, where the whole team hopped in the back of a pickup truck. Remember I was telling you about Del Kreuter, he owned the Dr. Pepper bottling company?

Well, he had these bottling trucks, and when we'd go to a ball game somewhere, we'd put the catcher's gear and all the bats and everything in that thing, and I usually rode with the gear. I was the batboy, and there'd be some ballplayers ride on the truck as well as me and the equipment. And I don't how big it was, probably a deuce and a half truck, well you've seen Coke Cola bottling trucks, they're similar to what they have now but a little more rustic.

JIM HICKMAN

They started a league here in 1949, and that was a little before my time; I played in the 1950s. I can't remember exactly how many; had six or eight teams from the little towns and communities, and they played there, and then we had, which was probably the best team around here, there was a prison team. They had a man down there that knew a little bit about baseball, and they always had a good team. Now, if I remember correctly, I don't think they were a member of that league. But they played a lot of the teams.

(Players were prison guards?) No, this is prisoners, and they would come out here to play.

Yeah, I'm sure they were non-violent offenders because they wouldn't have let them out if they weren't, but now I remember playing up here at Ripley quite a bit, and we'd go down there and play, and nobody thought anything about it.

My thoughts about pitching back when I first started was the fact that I didn't want to wake up every day worrying about how my arm felt, and I didn't have to do that if I was a position player. I know I did that in high school a lot of times. I'd say, "Boy, I sure hope my arm feels good today," and I just didn't want to go through that.

I tried chewing tobacco one time. We were down in Waycross, Georgia. I never will forget it. I was going to chew tobacco that night, and I got out there playing center field, and they had to stop the game and come and get me. Man, I was so sick I couldn't even get back to the dugout. That was it; I never did chew anymore. We had several guys that chewed a little bit, and I was going to be like everybody else; I couldn't even stand up. They stopped the game, I was down on my knees, and that was it; I didn't want any more of that.

LOIS YOUNGEN

You've got to remember, this is the 1940s, and there was very little physical education going on in small schools. And this is a first grade through grade 12 school that I went to, all the little schools that I went to were that size, and they had sports, but primarily for the boys. I can remember being in high school and playing in two or three girls basketball games where we either had teams come to our school or we went—and I think that was organized pretty much again on our own. It was pretty much sports just for boys.

We never had to fire our bus driver like in the movie; a bus driver never quit. I want you to know our bus driver for two years at Fort Wayne; I don't know his last name, but his name was Wally, and Wally looked exactly like Santa Claus in a bus uniform. He was round around the middle, and he had chubby red cheeks. And he was just about as nice a man as you could know. To me, being 17 or so, he probably looked old; maybe he was in his 40s or 50s, at least, but he certainly wasn't old. But I will always remember Wally as just one of the nicest bus drivers and the nicest man we ever had. I just enjoyed looking at him because he looked like Santa Claus.

The main thing about traveling on the bus was that we always sang. That's one thing you won't find the men in the minor leagues or major leagues doing, but we always sang on the bus. And we sang very well, we harmonized, and we would entertain ourselves all evening by singing. And then on the long trips, the one standard rule, you've probably heard this before, the standard rule was—and it's the thread that ran through the leagues of the whole 12 years, you were not allowed to be seen in public, in the hotel lobby of the visiting city, on the bus, on any occasions, no civic occasion when you were invited downtown or to interact with the public in your city, you're never ever to show up in any kind of pants.

No slacks, no blue jeans, always a dress or a skirt. And that rule was one of the few that was enforced all the way through the 12 years that the league was in existence. And one of the questions people always asked me when I speak to groups is what about charm school because they have that in the film. And originally, the first few years, they did have charm school, and that was Mrs. Wrigley's idea that the girls go to charm school. And according to some of the 1943 and '44 players, some of them really enjoyed it. They said they learned a lot, which is a good thing. However, when people ask me about it, what I usually tell people is, "By the time I joined the league in 1951, they'd given up on us (laughing), so no more charm school."

KATIE HORSTMAN

Well, there were a lot of good teams like Little Chickasaw. They had an excellent pitcher. They were close, I mean, the score was always close, but we just had more power, that's all. They had one good one, which was good as far as softball's concerned. You have a good pitcher and strike everybody out; naturally, they're gonna win and Chickasaw, they only had a 100 in the whole town.

Oh, I played every position. I liked every position. There is nothing better. I caught, I pitched, and my best place was probably third base. I loved third base.

(Why did you like third base?) Oh, my gosh. Well . . . probably trying to speed up for a bunt you know or trying to make a double play and back up people. The best thing I can remember is . . . this was right before an AAGPBL game when we had batting practice. Jimmy Foxx . . . The Jimmy Foxx was my manager in Fort Wayne, the second year that I played, which was 1952. He hit a ball down to me, and it took a bad hop; after all, we didn't have the fields like they do now. So, it took a bad hop and hit me in the forehead, and, oh my gosh, it practically knocked me out; I wasn't about to tell anyone, but I was really dizzy. Well, he was very

apologetic, but I went to the dugout and put ice on it and everything, and for at least three weeks, they called me Ricky Raccoon because I had the biggest black eyes I ever had in my life (laughing). That really stands out. But he was so, so, so nice, unbelievable. He was a great guy, and he could hit the ball. Let me tell you when I first met him when he came in 1952, we were having batting practice and he was watching how we bat and I swung at the ball and really hit it good and he says "Boy, were you a farm girl? Are you a farm girl?" And I said, "Oh my gosh, does it look like it?" and he said, "No, you got wrist action that only a farm girl would have milking cows." And I said, "Yeah, I milk every night (laughing); every night and every morning." After that, I never complained when I came home to milk the cows!

We were supposed to play; this was after the AAGPBL league folded and Bill Ellington, our manager from the Fort Wayne Daisies, and he kept bringing girls together, and I was one of them. We spent three sum-mers, we went all the way around, practically the whole Midwest, from Midwest to the West, and we would play like 80-100 games per summer, and we would play against the men. We would switch the battery, the women would pitch against the women, and the men would pitch against the men. And we got quite a big crowd by doing that, especially in the smaller towns around Iowa, Oklahoma, Ohio, Indiana; those places. We went to Texas, and we were supposed to play this team . . . well nobody knew it was a black team, so we come into town, and we didn't see any of our signs, and normally they gave us a ride on the fire truck through town to announce to all of the people that we were there and the game would start at 7:00 p.m. and people came out. So the sheriff came along, and he asked what the heck we were doing because we were looking around and going slow, and so Bill asked him, he says, "Where is this team located" and he said, "Why?" And he said, "Well, we don't see our posters up; we're supposed to play them." He says, "Play them! Girls playing men?" And we said, "Yeah! We have been doing this for two years." This was the third year we were doing it. So, he says, "They play out in the park, and you're not gonna play them," and we asked, "Why" and he said, "Because they're colored," and I said, "Woah." I said, "Boy, that'll be fun." And "Woah," he said, "If I get another peep out of you, you're going to go across the border," and I go, "What border?" (laughing) I didn't know we were that close to Mexico! I was just a young kid; I was only 20 years old at that time. We didn't get to play them. But it was a beautiful ballpark, we went to the ballpark, and they were good, and we were anxious to play them. We were all Yankees; people called us Yankees all the time. And anyway, we didn't get to play them, and I couldn't believe it, and that was Jasper, Texas.

JIM KAAT

So, Bobby Shantz was known as the best fielding pitcher during that time; that was even before they gave out Gold Gloves. So, people will ask me, coaches, and sometimes pitchers will say, "Where did you get your motivation?" or "What did you do to work on becoming such a good fielding pitcher?" And I said, "Well, I learned by listening to the radio." And they kind of look at me and I'd say "When Bobby Shantz would pitch against the Chicago White Sox, and I could listen to eight teams on a Sunday afternoon: the Cubs, the White Sox, the Tigers, and then when the Braves moved to Milwaukee," I was a little more of an older teenager then but every Sunday they played a doubleheader. So when Philadelphia was playing Chicago the announcer would say "and here is Bobby Shantz, when he deliverers the pitch, he lands on the balls of his feet, he's square to the hitter, he's ready to go left or right if the ball is hit there or at him, he's always in a good position, and he's the best fielding pitcher in the game." So I would go in my back yard with a tennis ball or whatever ball I had and throw against the concrete portion of the back of our garage; I would just throw that ball against the garage and try to land like I thought Bobby Shantz was landing. So I would do that by the hour and my first year of spring training in 1958 we were going through the pitcher's fielding drills, and after about two or three rotations of doing the different drills, my pitching coach said to me, "Hey kid you look just like Bobby Shantz (laughing)." So that is really where I learned, and fortunately, I got to meet Bobby later; I think he is still living. He's maybe in his early 90's now, but I got to meet him and talk to him, so that was kind of cool.

LOU PINIELLA

Here in Tampa, at that time, there were two teams in spring training, one was the Cincinnati Reds, and the other one was the Chicago White Sox. So, we got a chance to go and watch major league players play. I remember we used to go behind left field or behind right field and catch a few home run balls in batting practice and then sell them for a quarter and get into the ballgame to watch (laughing). So, I remember those days; it was fun.

Actually, Tony LaRussa signed for a hundred thousand with the Oakland A's. Yeah, he signed for $100,000, which is a very substantial bonus back then in 1961. He was the shortstop on our American Legion team. He hit second in the lineup, and I hit third and pitched and played the outfield, played left field, and the amazing part about it is that Tony was always a really good fielder, really a heady player and it didn't surprise me at all to see that he had such a great managing career.

And myself, I was probably a little more reckless and little wilder. Probably a little more temperamental (laughing) but it's amazing that two kids that grew up a mile from each other and played against each other in high school, but more important, played in the PONY League Program and then the American Legion Program together and hit second and third in the lineups all the time ended up managing in the big leagues. And Tony is now finished with third all-time or maybe second in managerial wins, and I ended up 14th.

I remember that on the American Legion team that I played on, we had three guys that played in the major leagues, which was pretty darn good; we had myself, we had Tony LaRussa, and we had a catcher named Kenny Suarez. He played for Cleveland briefly and with Oakland, so three players out of our American Legion team played in the big leagues.

JIM ZAPP

When I played ball in the Navy, when I first got there, I was stationed in Aiea, outside of Pearl Harbor, about three or four miles outside of Pearl Harbor, and they got the Naval Hospital there. Naval barracks went down below the Naval hospital, and the Naval hospital is still there, the same hospital. Pee Wee Reece stayed there during the war, and after that, my outfit, which was segregated, one side of the highway was white, white sailors, no black sailors, so we finally moved out of there and went and moved to Pearl City, Hawaii. It's about six or seven miles from Aiea and Pearl Harbor, so then I lost track of the integrated baseball team; I played on the all-black team.

When I got there, they had segregated baseball teams in Aiea. The blacks were on this side of the highway and the whites on the other side of the highway, and it was military, so I end up playing with the black team. So, have you ever heard of Edgar "Special Delivery" Jones? Halfback for the Cleveland Browns after the War. He was coaching the white team, so he integrated the white team, took me and another boy from Michigan, put us on the white team . . . Special Delivery Jones. Have you heard of Barney McCosky? He played with the Detroit Tigers. He came in later on. When he came in, I offered to move to Pearl City, so I left them; I left all them guys, but I was the only black, me, and this boy from Michigan, only two blacks on the team at that time.

No, they just saw us. See, we were on one side of the highway, and they were on the other side of the highway. The Lieutenant, he just transferred us over there on the white team. No problem at all. You see, he had quite a few major league ballplayers on the Navy white team. Hugh Casey, you ever heard of him; he played for the Brooklyn Dodgers.

So, I ended up playing with a civilian team in Honolulu called the Wanderers. The guy who was coaching the Navy team; he was the coach for the white team, so he recommended me to the Wanderers in Honolulu, and I'd go down and play with them; make a little extra money. And I was the only black on that team. It was just about six or seven miles. Had a boy named, can't remember his name now, he played in the Texas League after the war, he was in the Army, and he played, but the rest of them were local boys, the manager of the team was a little guy named Johnny Kerr, I think he's dead now, I was the only black on the team. Got about $200 a game.

When I came out of the Navy, I played with Nashville Cubs; they were kind of a farm team to Baltimore Elite Giants.

Yeah, so we had a Polish boy playing outfield for us one day; I can't remember his name now, he said "Zapp," he was from Baltimore, he said "If I recommend you to the Elite Giants will you go and play with them on weekends?" and I said "Yeah, I sure will," because I heard about all these guys; I had read about them in Pittsburgh, Kansas City, Chicago; Roy Campanella and all those guys. So, I go down and played with the Elite Giants on weekends, and that's where I first met Campanella in 1945.

I was playing with Nashville, kind of a farm team with the Elite Giants, the guy that owned the team was Tom Wilson, but the guy who took care of all his business was in Nashville; his name was Dr. Jackson. So, he tells us every day; he says, "Zapp, they're (Major League Baseball is) going to sign a black boy." We weren't paying him no attention; he was coming over there chasing them gals, and every night he'd say, "They are going to sign a black boy, some of 'em saying Jackie." It was 1947 when they signed Jackie Robinson.

LOU WHITAKER

As a kid, either you want to play a certain sport or you don't, and I never really had a desire or wanted to; I could've have played football because there are wide receivers. I threw the ball as far as anybody; quarterbacking would have been my thing. We had to go out there and see who could throw a football the furthest, and I could probably hang with them. But you know growing up as a little kid we used to have little games where you got little first place, second place, third place prizes, and all that stuff. We had the softball contest; I won first place. I pretty much won all my track and field events, first place. As a kid, I lived on the East side of Martinsville; we had quite a few athletes on that side of town that was my own age. They used to brag that there was a kid on the West side of Martinsville that was fast. So, we got our opportunity to see who was the fastest in this track and field event, and I won that. So, it was no more about who was the fastest anymore because as kids, kids used to brag about and get on other kids about who was the best. So once I won that particular contest, I never heard anything the rest of my . . . and this probably happened when there were about 20 of us, so never, through the rest of my junior high school or high school days did I hear anything about who's the fastest. But I never walked around school with my chest poked out or anything like that; I was pretty much just a laid-back kid who loved to play, wait for baseball season. But when it came to the athletes at Martinsville High School where I went, none ever mentioned who was the best around in my little area.

In my area it wasn't about oh, this person is the best, this person is the best, that person is the best because you could look left or right and say well whatever you guys say, there's a guy over there and it's going to take a lot for you to prove yourself, that you're better than him.

I had an opportunity to attend a Major League Baseball game when I was about 16 or 17-years-old; there was some people much older than me that we played ball together. And they were going to Pittsburgh to watch Pirates and the Dodgers, and they asked me if I wanted to go, and I told them, "No, I don't want to go because we were getting ready to play some ball ourselves." So, I just turned down going to a major league game just to play in the park with my friends (laughing).

But I never went to a major league game before I turned pro. I may have saw a minor league game somewhere being played, but we didn't really watch it or anything. I didn't really know what minor league baseball was. I'm not much on watching; I'd watch Game of the Week as a kid but just going to watch a game—when I was a kid, I'd watch my friends play in the city, but I'm not much on watching baseball. I've always felt more like playing than watching.

STEVE BLASS

The interesting thing was my wife's brother, Art Lamb; the younger brother John made it, but Art signed and blew his arm out. I had to wait for him to graduate; he was a year ahead of me. He was the man, and I said: "I hope your grades are alright Art because I need to get you out of here so I can pitch on a more regular basis (laughing)." I had three no-hitters my junior year and then two more my senior year. Because of the guys that had come before me, including her cousin Tom Parsons who had signed, the scouts were aware of our little high school. I got scouted pretty heavily. It was a unique atmosphere. Our little high school played more high school playoff games in Connecticut than any other team at any level. And never won it completely, but we played more of those games because our pitching was so dominant.

During high school, I was just obsessed. No, not any particular memories. I played right field because I had the strong arm in high school until my brother-in-law graduated.

DOUG FLYNN

After my senior year, I played on a team called South Lexington because a lot of high schools will not take their seniors and put them on their Connie Mack Team. They were trying to rebuild for the next year. So South Lexington got all the guys that were seniors, and we went and played together. Played with Rick Derrickson, who signed professional, Derek Bryant signed professionally. We had a good team. We ended up getting beat in Florida, but we had a really nice ball club.

We won at several different places. We went to Tennessee and played some guy who was supposed to be a first-round draft choice, a big left-hander, we ate him up. And then we went to Florida, and I don't know what happened, something happened. I know we had a couple of really interesting calls playing away from home, but we ended up getting beat, but it was fun. I love that I thought, "I can do this for a while."

I loved youth baseball. I mean, it's some of the best memories of my life. The travel that we had, because the families got to go watch you play, and the cookouts after the games were over. We had a lady with us one year; God love her; her name was Mrs. Fister. Her son and I were good friends; his name was Nick Fister, and Nick and I played Little League and then PONY League All-Stars. Mrs. Fister was kind of a larger lady, and she told us, "If we won this little tournament that she'd go into the pool." And we all went, "You would not," so we win the tournament. We get back to the hotel, and we thought, "Here she comes," and she said, "I promised," and she just waded down in that pool, and it was the most precious thing I could remember. But our little all-star team, it was fun; we loved each other. We were all buddies, and then we put together a team when I was; I guess it was the team we had that was pretty good right before I signed professionally, and we won our area so that we got a chance to go to Wichita, Kansas. I get out to Wichita, and we look, and we're not even seeded at all; I don't know how many teams, but we're not seeded. We're thinking, "Well, who are these guys?" So, we're playing a number two seed from Boulder, Colorado. The first inning, our leadoff guy gets up, and he hits a base hit. I get up, and I hit a home run . . . we're up two to nothing. The next inning, we come in, they score one in the bottom. We come back in the next inning, we score. We're up three to one. They don't score in the bottom of the second. We're thinking, "Come on, we can win this thing." We got beat 18 to four in five-inning (laughing), and I'm talking to the guys on the field, and finally, I'm talking to the first baseman; he looked at me and said, "What school you go to"? I went, "Oh, you wouldn't have heard of it; it's a little junior college. He says, "Yeah, really? You got a good baseball team?" "Well, we don't have a baseball team." He looked at me and said, "Well, where do all those go?" I said "Well, very few of us are in college, we just all live in the same town and play together, what about you?" he said, "Well, I go to Texas, but I come out here to play ball, and he goes to Arizona State, and he goes to Southern Cal, and he goes . . . " I'm thinking, "hot dang." The pitcher was some guy named Burt Hooton (laughing).

And then they had a team from Alaska, and these were all the best players in college, and all had played on these teams. We were ready to "whoop everybody," and then we ended up gettin' beat nine to eight the next game. So, we got beat two straight games, but it was fun.

FERGIE JENKINS

In Chatham, they ended up renaming the ballpark after me. It was called Rotary Park, and now it's called Fergie Jenkins Diamond (laughing), but the thing was, I won a bunch of ball games there, and the crowds used to come out on Saturday afternoon, or Sunday, and watch us play, and the crowds were like 100 people, and when I pitched, it was maybe 600 people (laughing).

So, there was something there that Gene could see. And Gene, he ended up our shortstop, and he coached the team from time to time, but the thing was, at 17, when all these scouts were coming to my house, and my mom, she had glaucoma, she lost her sight after I was born so my mom was blind and she didn't know what all these men wanted, coming to the house and trying to inquire about her son (laughing). And my dad would reiterate, "Your son's got a talent, Mom," he used to always call her Mom, and he might want to be a professional baseball player. I was an only child, so she had some second thoughts about me leaving to go play baseball. Every mom has that.

So, in retrospect, when I signed, it was devastating for her. There was nobody there at the house. My dad worked all of the time, he was a chef and a chauffeur, but before that, he played in the Negro Leagues in Canada; he barnstormed. So, my dad was a good athlete. He was a center fielder . . . he hit left-handed, threw left-handed. And I'm right-handed all the way (laughing). But to make a long story short, it came easy, but I had to work at it. Nothing ever comes easy, but I had the talent; it was all God-given. I had a good arm. Never had a sore arm in the 21 years I played professionally.

Never tried to pitch two games in a day or two days. I played first base. We had two young guys, no we had three: we had Dennis Robuck, who was scouted by Detroit. Larry Meyers, left-hander and Jack Howell . . . those were our pitchers in Chatham, and they had great talent. Scouts looked at them too, but I was the end result. I ended up signing.

I think under supervision, you are going to get better, which really helped me. Gene Dziadura was an ex-pro player, and as I said, he was kind of my mentor. He didn't give me tips; he told me what and how things were gonna happen. He told me, "You're going to play in the South, and people are not going to like you," and it didn't hit home until I went . . . "Alright, the color of my skin." He said, "The number one thing you gotta continue to focus in on, you're a ballplayer. Go out there and play baseball; don't let the crowd rattle you; don't let somebody get under your skin." Which did happen in Chattanooga and Little Rock where I played; I played with Dick Allen. When I went to AAA in 1964, there were four players of color on the team: Dick Allen from the United States, Marcelino Lopez from Cuba, Ricardo Quiroz from Panama, and a kid named Jenkins from Canada (laughing). We get a chance to play. My manager, he would always tell me, "Hey, focus in on what the job is. What you're supposed to do when you are out there." I was a pitcher. I was supposed to pitch.

WILLIE BLAIR

I wasn't a position player every year like my freshman year; I just pitched. My sophomore and junior year, I played outfield and shortstop a couple of times when our shortstop pitched or whatever and then my senior year, I played very little. I was coming off in injury in basketball, where I separated my left shoulder, and my coach knew that there's some colleges interested, and he didn't really want me to take a chance on getting hurt, so he just let me pitch. I'd play every now and then or DH every now and then but not as much.

The first major league game I went to, I think I was 12 or 13-years-old, but a buddy of mine, his dad was a preacher, and he knew some people in the church there across the river from the (Cincinnati Reds) stadium, and they let us stay at the church that night. We went to the game and then spent the night at the church and came back the next day.

This is late 1970s. I remember Bob Horner was with the Braves because I distinctly remember that was the first time I'd ever heard anybody rag a player, and somebody was yelling at him, "You can't hit your weight." That always stuck out in my mind (laughing). I'm trying to remember who all they had. George Foster, I remember watching him take batting practice, and that was just unbelievable.

WILLIE HORTON

Well, I think things stick out in my mind . . . in Kingsport playing in an older league, and Coach Strong took all the kids to Kentucky, I think that's the first time I played against the kids in Kentucky. I played with Eddie Brinkman and Pete Rose when we was kids. The next thing that sticks out in my mind . . . we won the 1959 National Babe Ruth

League down in Altoona, Pennsylvania. That was the older league, the Bill Freehan team picked me up to go with them, and I think I made three outs the whole week, and I met Eddie Brinkman and Pete Rose again, and John Havlicek the Hall of Fame basketball player. He was the pitcher on that team, and we won the national championship that year, and those things will always be a part of you growing up.

Going to that Babe Ruth World Series, Freehan and I went out to the Northwestern field, and I went out there and slept on the field the whole night because I didn't want to miss the bus (laughing).

CHARLIE LOYD

(You had two elite catchers, Phil Roof & Hawk Taylor, in these youth leagues you were pitching to, were you the best pitcher in the league?)

(Reluctantly answering) Probably, yeah. I threw sidearm until I was a senior at the University of Kentucky, then I started throwing overhand because you couldn't get much attention throwing sidearm back then, I was before my time. Now they got all those side arm relievers, and back then you couldn't get anybody interested in you if you threw sidearm because they said you threw a flat curveball, which you did unless you really turn it over on the side, but they didn't take into consideration all side-armers keep the ball low, and it breaks into a left-handed hitter and breaks away from a right-handed hitter, but it took them 30 years to realize that. When I was a senior, I thought, "If I can throw sidearm, surely I can throw overhand," so I threw overhand and did even better than I did sidearm. I never had a good curveball (laughing); I just used my curveball to change speeds. I never had any confidence in anything that was less than 90 mph (laughing). I was a strikeout pitcher; I just threw real hard.

10.

THE GAMES WE PLAYED
(MY FRIENDS AND OUR IMAGINATION)

BOOG POWELL

My brother Charlie and I; we had another game we played all day long called wall ball, and we'd go over there next to Dixieland school. We lived very close to Dixieland school, and there was a wall about the size of that wall right there, maybe 12 feet and you get one guy hitting, and every time you hit a ground ball, and it hit the wall it was a base hit, in the air, it was a double, if it hit the soffit, up there it was a triple, if it went on the roof without going over the roof it was a home run, but if it went on the roof and went over you were out just like at grandma's house, because one of us had to go get the damn ball and most of the time we didn't have more than one (laughing), but that in itself taught me more bat control. It's like pepper used to be, you know it's too bad these young guys don't know about pepper today, we used to have some great pepper games, and it wasn't for kids. This pepper game you better have your shin guards on; it was some good pepper games. But we'd do that same thing, we'd start over there at the Dixieland school in the morning, and I'd get over there 7:00 in the morning so I'd be the first hitter and I'd hit until the bell rung (laughing).

Another game we called workup. You had to get down to second base and get back to home before they got the ball back to the pitcher. There was three guys usually, and then if they got you out, you had to go to center; you had to go be the outfielder, and the pitcher got to hit. Then you worked yourself back up to being the hitter.

PHIL ROOF

We did in grade school. In fact, and I can't remember what year it was, probably third grade when Louis Haas and I played the rest of the grade . . . beat them. We were, for some reason, we were more advanced than the rest of the grade was. Then as they got a little bit older, we didn't have to choose up sides because they always separated us, Louis had to be on one side, and I had to be on another side.

I can remember being in about the fourth grade; my brother Gerald would have been about two grades ahead of me, and I'd catch him, and he'd catch me. And then he'd tell me to put down 1 (finger) for a fastball and 2 (fingers) for a breaking ball, and I'd do that and then when I got ready to pitch, he was catching me. When he put down 1 (finger) well I would try to throw a fastball with just one finger on the ball, and he saw it, and he said, "Phil you can't do it that way, you've got to have both fingers on the ball and the thumb underneath," but at the time I was so young and naïve that I didn't know very much, but he corrected me on that. *(So, you thought the number of fingers he put down was how many fingers you put on the ball?) Yes,* that is what you put on the ball.

HAWK TAYLOR

Oh, I'm sure I played all of them. One old cat, two old cat. Well, that is essentially the same games as you're talking about only with different names. I had to teach a history of baseball course at one time, and I had to go into hitting, so that's where I came up with those names

(Do you feel these made up games improved a player's skills?) Well, the fact that you'd learn and you'd get better by repeating skills, if you catch a ball, catch another ball, catch another ball, well that's how you get good at doing things so at that standpoint . . . yes.

JIM HICKMAN

Played a lot of cork ball and stuff like that. Just have a cork and a broom handle, and that was about it. But as far as pepper, hell, we wasn't good enough to play pepper (laughing). No, I can't think of any little games we played like that, we didn't have anything like a batting tee or anything like that

BILL GREASON

We did that pepper thing when we were playing professional ball; we didn't know anything about pepper when we were kids. We played stick-ball with a tennis ball, have a pitcher pitch it to him with a stick in his hand, but we used to play with that tennis ball, and that's how I learned to twist that baseball, with a tennis ball, *(To throw a curveball?).* Yeah and I had another fellow, he had played a little baseball, he showed us how to throw that fast baseball without the seams, through the middle but I learned that curveball and learned to throw it sidearm, three quarter, overhand. I had a great downer, yeah; I'd get in the low 90's with my fastball. So, I said, "if I got two strikes on ya, I'd wave bye (laughing)."

KATIE HORSTMAN

Oh, we just took turns. If you made three outs, then you went out in the outfield, and then you had to be a fielder and rotated around. We started at first then the outfield and then leftfield and then shortstop and then back into home to bat.

JIM KAAT

Well, one game we played if we didn't have enough players to actually play a game, we played three dollars. We had one of the players; they had a bat and ball. We didn't have fungo bats; then, it was just a regular bat and a ball. And he would hit. We'd be out there, maybe say 200 feet, 150 feet and he would hit, try to hit fly balls and if you caught the ball, it was a dollar. If you got it on one hop, it was 50 cents, and if you fielded the ball, it was a quarter. And you might have three or four kids out there sort of in a scrum trying to either catch the ball or field it. And then whoever got to three dollars first, then you'd switch, and one of the other guys would hit the ball, so that was a game we played that was not a traditional baseball game, but just to pass the time. And we play pickle. Getting in the run down, we played that game as well.

Oh, no question that was helpful. One of the games I played at the professional level is called pepper. Now, if you mentioned that to kids today, they probably wouldn't even know what pepper is.

But you probably heard of the game of pepper. You might have three kids standing 25-30 feet away, and they would throw a ball. It was almost like bunting it to each one of them. When I coached for Pete Rose, we talked a lot about playing pepper. And Pete and I and Tommy Helms, one of his coaches, we would still go out and play pepper with Pete because he really attributed a lot of his bat control to that. And then the games you've mentioned, Boog Powell would probably be the same way because he was a left-hand hitter. I was the only lefty, so our game would actually be pitcher's hands out, so if I'm standing at the plate, I have to hit the ball to the left-field side (when the pitcher was right-handed). If I hit it to the right side, I was out because we didn't have any fielders over there, so it really helped my hitting. In hitting, for years, hitting coaches have said, "Keep that shoulder in, keep that shoulder in," and that, of course, is why they have had so many left-hand batting champions in Fenway Park because they learn to hit the ball to left field off the Green Monster. So, I grew up having to purposely hit the ball to left field. You would run from home to second, right across the pitcher's mound, which wasn't much of a mound. And then if the ball got to the pitcher before you reached second base, then you were out, it's called Pitcher's Mounds Out. And if you hit one far enough where you could go to second and then all the way back to home, that was like a home run. So, if you did that before they got the ball in, then that was a run.

LOU PINIELLA

We played pickup games. We used to play home run derby, played a lot of Indian ball. Indian ball is where you hit the ball; this is when you're young, and you put the bat down after somebody gets the ball, and they'll try to roll it and hit the bat, and you gotta catch it, if not you lose your turn.

We played home run derby, but we played a lot of pickup games, and then we played a couple of games a week. They didn't have it organized like they do now on weekends and all these practices. You had to practice on your own.

The more you play helps develop your skills and the more you play, the more you have a bat in your hand, and the more you have a glove on your hand, the better you're gonna get, and truthfully it's more fun doing it spontaneously as opposed to organized workouts all the time.

The home run derby game we used to play, we'd play with a pitcher an infielder an outfielder and only play half the field. So, all you needed were six players to play.

JIM ZAPP

On the streets, hit balls in the streets before I played on an organized team. Oh, I played out in an open lot with a bunch of kids. There's an all girl's school right there on eighth Avenue; I guess they call it a boarding school. It's still there, but they had a big open lot. They were on eighth Avenue, had a big open lot between seventh & sixth. Big lot and we'd play ball on that field.

Just happened to get together out on Sixth Avenue. I lived at the end of fourth Avenue North, but we'd get in the streets then we had an open field next to St. Cecilia Academy, and we'd play in there some time, it's just a bunch of guys playing.

LOU WHITAKER

We played ball all day long as kids. It was nothing to start with one person—I'd start off just by myself. I'd be at the bottom of the road. I'd find me a stick, and I'd start throwing rocks up and hitting them in the woods, and then one person would come, maybe we'd play a game of strike out with just a stick in the woods, hitting rocks and if you caught it, you got to hit and if you struck out the other person you got to hit. But from there, another two kids would come, and we'd play what we called Catch the Ball and Get the Bat. So, you'd hit until you either caught it in the air or on the first bounce, then you got to hit. A few more kids would come; we'd start a little game in the street. A few more kids would come, we had a bigger game, and then we'd get maybe nine, ten or so, we would go out to the ballpark, which it was only 1/8 of a mile away from where I lived. So, we pretty much lived watching baseball growing up as kids. Chasing foul balls, we would turn them all in, maybe except one because we were gonna find one ball that we're going to play with later the next day or whenever (laughing).

STEVE BLASS

I had that yellow legal tablet, and I would make up a line-up. It was the Indians against the Yankees, and I was always Bob Lennon or Early Wynn, great Indians pitchers. I would throw the ball up against the wall, and however it would bounce, that would be a base hit, or I would catch it, and it would be an out, and I just did nine-inning games, so when we did win the World Series with the Pirates, they asked me about winning the World Series, and I said, "Hell, I've won the World Series 25-30 times against the side of the barn (laughing)."

DOUG FLYNN

I think the key for me, just making it to the big leagues, that I just continued to play. And it wasn't about winning and losing; it was about competing and continually playing. If there's a field open, we were playing. If there was time after school, we were playing.

We played with a tennis ball, and we would build a home run fence, and we kept statistics, all that kind of stuff, and that was a lot of fun. Then we played the games in the backyard, in the field; actually, it wasn't really games, it was just that sometimes you have to say "Okay right fields dead," because you don't have enough players, so right field is dead, or the right side is dead, and that was good, but then, we were lucky we didn't have cell phones, we didn't have computers so you had to entertain yourself and I'm very thankful that we got a chance to do that.

No, we didn't want parents around. The only thing they want to do is make you come home. My dad has that distinctive whistle . . . boy, he could whistle, and you'd go "Dang," . . . You'd be out there, and you'd have to go to the bathroom and "I ain't going, we're playing ball (laughing)." I was lucky; we had friends and people around me everywhere. I lived at two places; I lived on Halls Lane, we'd play in the street, then they had a field behind us we played up until I was 12. Then when I moved away, we had a park at the end of the street, it was like three doors down from me, so you could play football, basketball, baseball; we played it all right there in that park, and I'd always play with the guys older than me, and they beat the living snot out of me, but it was good, and I learned how to compete . . . and I learned how to fail.

FERGIE JENKINS

Yeah, that story is true (laughing). I lived in the east end of town, and the Chesapeake and Ohio Railroad company had a spur, and the railroad cars used to go by; 25-30 mph, and at a young age, kids would have contest throwing rocks in open boxcars if there was a door open. I used to do it; it was just a knack. And then there was a Terry's Coal Yard across the street from where I lived. The company used to have an ice shoot that the ice would slide down into the boxcars, the freezer cars. I could hit that ice shoot eight out of 10 times. Control was kind of uncanny for me. When I started throwing in the local gymnasium, we threw between badminton strings. Put a strike zone up and move the cord one side down and up, and I could hit it eight to nine times out of 10. I think that did help me when I started pitching. I didn't walk a lot of people. I had some strikeouts, a lot of innings pitched. I was durable. It was the right position. I don't think I would have been an NHL Hockey player, though I tried hard. I played three years with the Globetrotters; I knew I could play basketball (laughing); I could shoot. That was a real gift; I could jump, shoot, throw. Pitching was the sport I ended up playing; 21 seasons.

WILLIE BLAIR

Yeah, we had a couple of games. I can't remember exactly what they were. I think we called it Roller Bat or something. I can't remember exactly what it was, but somebody pitched, and you'd hit. When you hit the ball, you'd lay your bat down on the ground, and if they rolled the ball in and it hit the bat, then they got to hit; if they missed, then you got to keep hitting. That was one and then, "Over the Line," we played a game called "Over the Line." I just remember the game; I can't remember exactly how we played it. I think you hit it, and you had one base you had to run like where the second base would be and then run back before they hit you with the ball or before they got a force out at second or whatever. I think that's called "Over the Line." The ball, you have to hit over a certain point; if you hit it on the ground before it got to that line, then it's an out.

Obviously, we played Wiffle ball all the time. We'd tape the Wiffle ball bat. We'd tape the balls to make them go farther, to make them break, curve, or whatever, we did that quite a bit. You have to tape up the bats; we played with them so much within a couple of weeks they're broken.

WILLIE HORTON

Well, "Strikeout," you don't need no catcher, you mark a wall, a block on the wall, and you have a game. You have a game, and you make a tape ball, and back then, we had a rubber ball, tear them up, we tape them up, and use them, but you go out there, we always had a game. There's no such thing that you can't have a game, it'd be raining, and you can still be playing "Strikeout."

CHARLIE LOYD

We had a group of black guys in town that we played, and we played them just about every day. They lived over on South 10th and 11th, and we lived on South fourth. We'd play together every day; never had that first fight, never had that first argument, and one of them was Robert Lee

Patterson, who became Chief of Police here. We always got along fine. A lot of times, those black guys, they'd play a team over in Littleville, which is really a hardcore place. They'd come and get me and my catcher; was a guy named Bob Bundy, to pitch and catch for them so we'd go over, and you can imagine the catcalls that we got (laughing).

11.

BATS, BALLS, GLOVES, FIELDS & LEAGUES

BOOG POWELL

When the Tigers had spring training down there, my brother Charlie and I would go out there and hang around the outside in the perimeters waiting for somebody to hit a home run so we could go chase the ball down, or they had one fence, they had one doorway over there that the ball would roll under, and we knew that and Charlie would stay there, and I would go watch the other place, and we would come home with five or six balls and those balls were going to last us all year and we played with them, and we taped them up, and we had bats that were nailed and taped and everything else, we even made our own field.

We had a vacant lot in back of where we lived, and my dad said, "I'll help you boys put up a backstop if you want to make the field," he said, "We'll start right here, here's home plate." So, we went and got hoes, and we got rakes, and there wasn't nothing out there but sand spurs and, oh, it was awful! We dug it all out, we dug the base paths out and made a mound and everything else and then we had the backstop; wasn't anything special, it was just three or four 2x4's with a bunch of chicken wire tacked on it (laughing), but it worked. So anyway that was our first baseball field and if you hit . . . my grandmother's house was kind of next to our house, and it was a two story house, and if you hit the ball over the house, you were out because somebody had to go get it (laughing). So we use to try to keep it in play, so you learned a little bat control, you used to try to hit the back porch, and if you hit the back porch up there, it was a double, if it stayed on the back porch you got a triple.

PHIL ROOF

Oh yeah . . . well, what equipment? Catcher's mask and shin guards and maybe half a dozen bats that would be it; wouldn't be no more than that. But back then, you didn't have many bats. Everyone used the same bat. I can remember Jerry Girten, I was probably a freshman in high school, and he bought a brand new bat, I don't know what he paid for it, five or six dollars and he hit third in the lineup and I, at that time I hit about sixth or seventh because I was still just a young kid, I was probably a freshman. I asked him if I could use it. I broke his bat!!! He said, "You broke my bat." That killed him! Whatever it cost five or six or seven dollars back then and I hated it, but I hit the ball halfway decent, it was just one of those things, maybe I had the grain in the wrong spot, and I hated that worse than anything.

Did I tell you the story about us going to Brooks Stadium when we were kids? When we'd go in, we'd get in for 50 cents apiece. Sometimes Daddy would get us in over on the press gate, four or five of us, and we would scatter out. One on first base side, one behind the plate, one down the third base, and we would come home every night with two or three baseballs, at least two or three balls.

Ewing Hayden was the general manager, and he would give you a pass if you turned the ball back in. But as soon as we got it, we headed out to the car, and we hid it in the trunk of the car. We always had baseballs; we made it a point that we were going to get baseballs. (**Per Charlie Loyd**, I knew a guy that got so many out there that Poke Brooks, owner of the club, went by his house tryin' to buy them back from him (laughing).)

We used that Jackie Robinson bat, which is that big thick barrel, thick handle, and no knob. We tape bats if they were checking at the big part of the barrel; we tape them up too. I mean, equipment was hard to come by back then. I think Daddy bought gloves for us at different times, but we made those things last a long time. When I signed in 1959 and went to Milwaukee and worked out for a week, I got a 20-year contract from Spalding for a glove contract, 20 years and that winter in the Instructional League down in Florida, Louisville Slugger signed me to a contract for bats, and I got a whole set of golf clubs and a bag. If I would have kept them today and never used them, they would be worth about $4000. It was a collector's item. But I used them and abused them and probably gave them away.

There was something else that happened to me when I was a kid. Back then, in the 1950s, before TV came out, I couldn't have been over the fourth grade, and the nuns would let us listen to the World Series on the radio. So, this was before TV came in, we listened to the game on somebody's radio. So now we're outside of school, and for some reason, I've got my glove there with a ball and somebody else has got a glove, and we're playing catch in front of school out on the main road and Leon Neihoff, I'll never forget, he took his big radio outside, it was about as big as that vase there, and it was sitting on the front porch of the school. The road leaned toward the school. I'd thrown several throws to whoever I was throwing with, and I let this one go, and it hit the pavement and rolled over and hit that radio and busted the front of that radio. We had a reunion back in the summer of 2009, and I told him, I said I was scared because he was like a senior in high school, and I was like a fourth-grader, and he told me, "Put the damn ball up, you don't need to be throwing the baseball anymore the season is over, you don't need to be throwing anymore, put it up." And my comment was, "50 years later, I finally decided to give it up." He laughed about it. He didn't remember who did it, that's what he told me. He said, "I don't remember who did it," I said, "I'm the one." Because I mean he made me feel like a peanut. And I felt bad about it, absolutely felt bad about it because it broke his radio.

It was a sandlot league, and then a couple of years, it was a Twin State League, which was a well-organized league at that time. There were a lot of veteran college players and then two or three professional players that came back and played.

HAWK TAYLOR

Well, my earliest recollection of the equipment was they had some kind of a program at the local Kroger store where they had this catching outfit, and you got, seems like it was General Mills tickets or proof of purchase. And I remember I had shoeboxes full of the tickets and I wanted to win that catchers equipment and I happened to get up there a little bit late, but they held up the drawing, they knew I wanted it pretty bad. So, I won and got a full set of catching outfit, and I must have been seven or eight-years-old so that kinda set me up.

The other thing that helped me out was that having an uncle who played professional ball, he had a player's contract with the glove company called Nokona. And he would get four or five Nokona gloves every year, and I would get a new Nokona glove, and those were gloves that I used so I had high-quality equipment then, and I guess I used to get their leftover gloves and leftover spikes and things like that so growing up I was pretty much into the gear. I have very fawn memories of growing up using the equipment that those guys gave me.

(Did you get any of their used uniforms?) Actually, I did; I did. I wished I still had them, but I can remember them coming back, they were way too big for me, but I thought, "Man, you can never beat a baseball uniform, can never be too big." So, I have no idea what happened to those, but I do remember getting some uniforms growing up. Probably wore them until they wore out.

JIM HICKMAN

We played with old baseballs and everything else, but we always seemed to have what we needed. If I remember correctly, we'd have about two balls a game and tried to keep the game going, and that was it. I know we bought them at a sporting goods store or something like that, wherever we could get them. You know, and I guess that's basically how we did it. Oh yeah, yeah, we nailed them bats up too.

BILL GREASON

We had a softball league; I've forgot what it was. There was several teams. The team that sponsored us was a funeral home. I'll never forget that . . . Handley Funeral Home, it was down off Auburn Ave. They bought us shirts and little pants and gloves and sponsored us and a couple of other funeral homes sponsored teams, and then when we'd go to the ballparks to play, we'd get on a truck, take us across town and then bring us back. That's how that happened.

Yeah, it was unusual having the funeral homes sponsor teams because we didn't have that type of thing (youth leagues) on the side of town we lived, and to go to the west side, we had this park called Washington Park. That's where most of our people used to go for entertainment and recreation because there was a big swimming pool there, the only one. And then they had a field over there where you could play softball, and it had a picnic hut . . . Washington Park, I'll never forget that. What happened was we'd get ready to go across town, we'd go and wait around in the funeral home, and sometime we'd ease into the morgue, and the fellow would see us going into the morgue and then he would cut the lights out, and you could imagine what would happen (laughing), but it was a lot of fun, and we enjoyed it.

They bought new stuff for us. The funeral home had them; they kept them, we were just on the team, and they kept that stuff because they knew if we took it home, it probably wouldn't come back (laughing).

LOIS YOUNGEN

We grew up with the neighborhood kids. I couldn't remember what we had for bases, but I know we had one bat, one ball. And as the next couple of years went on, this is in upper elementary school; we put more and more black electrical tape on our ball (laughing), not sure what it resembled when we were finished. But anyway, somehow, we managed.

The hardest part was—now you got to remember this; nothing was made for women. We had no gloves that were made especially for women. We had no bats that were special for women. We had no catcher's gear that was made for women—you should have seen me taking the catcher's stuff apart and then taping it back together because I looked like I was a tank. I'm five-foot-three, and it wasn't easy. If you look at any of my pictures, I'm one of the runts on the team.

KATIE HORSTMAN

Adequate equipment?! We thought we had the greatest if we had two baseballs, and we had wooden bats. And then when we started the league, I needed spikes, and there weren't any girl spikes, women spikes, so we had to wear men's spikes. Thank God I had a big foot because I didn't have any problems (laughing)." But people that had a size 6 in the ladies' size, they had to wait and order theirs, and I still have my spikes.

JIM KAAT

Well, we had two parks. We had, as you mentioned, the city park in Zeeland, where we had a small dirt diamond and no fences or anything like that, but it was designed to play baseball. So that was our amateur park, so to speak. And then the high school field where I eventually played and played semi-pro, what we call town ball there. Each one of those were like a two-minute bike ride for me.

Yeah, I would say I either rode my bike most of the time, and I could actually have walked. I would say for the most part we, unlike organized Little League Baseball, we had, sometimes eight, sometimes 10 of us that would meet down at the Berghorst Gas Station on the corner where I lived, we would meet and figure out how many players we had and then we would bike off to the city park and play, you know, four on four; five on five, whatever we had.

Well, I got my first glove, and I got a bat with Weatherbird stamps. They were stamps, I guess like S & H Green stamps if your parents bought a certain amount of groceries or merchandise then they got Weatherbird stamps, and you would fill out the little booklet until you had it all full of stamps and then, say for three books you got a bat or a glove, so my first glove, even though I was left-handed, was a Kenny Keltner model. He played third base for the Indians. He was kind of famous for making two good plays when they broke Joe DiMaggio's hitting streak at 56 games, and then in Grand Rapids, there was a pitcher for the Tigers named Stubby Overmire. A little short left-hand pitcher and my uncle John in Grand Rapids knew Stubby's family, so one day, they arranged for me to meet him. I was probably eight or nine-years-old. And Stubby was a lefty, so he gave me one of his gloves. So, I got my first one with Weatherbird stamps, and then I got a Stubby Overmire glove that I used for quite a while (laughing).

LOU PINIELLA

We always had equipment, especially when we got into PONY and American Legion; we had good equipment. In American Legion, we had this gentleman Sam Castellano that supported the team a lot, and he'd buy equipment. We always traveled fairly well, and they always made sure that we got something to eat like McDonald's. It wasn't that bad here. We had almost like a minivan that we traveled in, and like I said, we'd get there to play, and they'd always bring in some sandwiches, like Cuban sandwiches, or they'd bring in McDonald's.

I remember having these old big Riddell shoes. We didn't know at that time that if your shoe size was a 12 that you could fit into a 10-baseball shoe. Your baseball shoes are probably two sizes smaller than your regular shoe, and the reason being is at that time we had the kangaroo leather, and it expanded, and you wanted a shoe that fit real tight where if not, your shoes will get real loose.

And I played about two or three games with these Riddell shoes and Pinky May, the manager, came over and he said: "Son, what size shoes you're wearing?" And I told him I said, "A 12." He says, "You're not supposed to be wearing 12." So, he gave me a pair of 10 Wilson kangaroo shoes. He says, "Here put this on; you'll enjoy this a lot more." You know, I still have those shoes; I kept them. I kept those shoes, and I laughed because, as a youngster, you bought your street size; you're supposed to buy shoes that really are tight. You put them in water, and once you put them in water, you then put them in a shoehorn, and that expands the shoe a little bit, and you're foot grows right into the shoes the right way.

You know these kids today they don't break in baseball gloves the way we did. We'd dip 'em in the water, get a baseball, put in there, and then wrap it around with tape and let it sit for two or three days until it dried.

JIM ZAPP

No, we had these old ratty balls, and a little glove out in the streets was all.

Oh yeah, on Saturday was Boys Day, and a lot of time, we had to sneak away from home because I lived at the far end of North Nashville, so me and my brothers would slip away from home on Saturdays and go to the ballgame when it was Boys Day.

Have you heard of Sulphur Dell Ballpark? From the left-field line all the way round to the right-field line, kind of a mountain like, all the way around. In right field, they'd call it a dump. It was only about 220 down the line. They had a tall fence and screen on top so the Nashville Vols would get the left-hand pull hitters, hit that ball up on the screen. Hard to hit it over because of the tall fence and screen on top of that, and you gotta get it over that screen. *(Would you give the balls back?)* NO! (laughing), we'd get them balls and sell 'em back to the team. Yeah, kids outside the ballpark. It was an everyday thing for us.

We would put a little bat together, and you'll tape a ball together, stuff like that, and we would play in the open field at St. Cecilia. I had to go all the way around to the Southside to play on an organized team and the ballplayers in my neighborhood; they went all the way to South Nashville.

LOU WHITAKER

Well, I would always steal my uncle's glove. The one I was talking about being 10-years-older than me. When he went to work or wherever he went, I knew where he kept his glove so I'd go get his glove and I'd probably head to the ballpark, and now he's coming home looking for his glove because they have a game, so now he's basically saying, "Where is that damn Lou at, he's got my glove again (laughing)."

So, he had to track me down. But I loved that glove that he used to have back then. It was a big glove for me, but I was able to use it. But baseball bats, of course back then—and they do still now—the teams provided, and we used to use wood bats in Little League back then. I never used an aluminum bat until I was in high school; as far as playing, they stopped making the wood bats for the schools, and they started playing with aluminum bats because of the cost of bats. Aluminum bats you can use year after year, a wooden baseball bat if it breaks it's pretty much done with.

Oh, some of the bats I used growing up was Pete Rose bats, Tony Oliva, Rod Carew, and Willie McCovey's back then. But those were the bats I used. When I signed into the minor league, I think I started off with a W215, and I think that was a Ted Williams model.

I was proud to use the bats that I did. Yeah, I mean, you kept up with your equipment. Like for instance, my glove, I didn't just throw my glove around or leave it outside. When I would come home from playing I'd put my stuff where I knew it would be and so when I needed it I'd go right there and get it and it wasn't like I had to go all over the house searching because every minute counted when it's time to play, it's time to get your stuff and let's go (laughing).

STEVE BLASS

The biggest thing in my life was a brand new, white baseball.

I had terrible equipment, but I didn't care because I was playing ball. I actually would get an old pair of baseball cleats that somebody gave up on, or we got them cheap somewhere, and this doesn't sound like one of these "I'm poorer than anybody," but I would get a brand new baseball each Christmas and a new glove each year too. That was huge; I have a glove and a baseball and a pair of cleats. That was big time.

When I think back on it, yeah, because I thought "two home runs in one game!!! hell, I'm going to hit 40 if I hit two in every game." But that was it, the two. But, yeah, that was a big deal. I played in our grammar school, and we had a unique kind of a field because it was on a sidehill, so if you hit the ball, you ran uphill to first base . . . we cut a lot of guys down at first base . . . even from the outfield (laughing). It was level from first to second, and then everybody stole third because it was downhill from second to third . . . kind of a unique kind of a field.

WHITEY HERZOG

You know, I remember when George McQuinn came out with the claw. I remember also when Rawling came out with the Bill Doak models, the hinged fielder's glove for infielders, and I remember when George McQuinn came up with the Trap-eze model, the three-finger, first base glove. I worked carrying papers to save enough money to buy that glove. I didn't come from a family that was very wealthy. In fact, I would tell you we were more poor than wealthy, but my mother and dad never turned down anything that my brother and I needed for baseball . . . spikes, or anything. They always made sure they could get them for us. And the equipment, we used to take the bats that we've broken, put wood screws in them and tape them up and play with them and we had 10 cent string balls we'd play with, and when the covers came off the baseballs, we'd tape them up and play (laughing), until they came flying apart.

DOUG FLYNN

Then we had a field behind our house so we'd go over there and we'd kinda mow what we could to make our own field, and we'd all go and take a wooden bat and if it broke you'd tape it up, or you put little tacks in it then tape it up.

When I was younger, I did. I'd ever have to worry about that. You're always going from one sport to the next, I'd have hand-me-down gloves from dad, and he'd give us whatever he had left. We'd always find a way, and we'd save money if we had to (in order) to find enough equipment to go out and play in the street with. There's no problem there.

We'd lose balls down the gutters in the street, and they'd usually stick my little butt down there to try to pick it out of the gutter so we could find it because I was the smallest one. I mean, we'd lose the ball in high weeds, and you'd spend time trying to find it because that's the only one you had, and everybody would share a bat, and you'd switch off the gloves.

FERGIE JENKINS

You know we had two guys who were good coaches. They were brothers. Bruno Casanova and I'm trying to think of the other one. There were two Casanova brothers. They were from Windsor, Ontario, and they had some professional background; when we didn't play, we did a lot of fundamentals; infield practice, outfield practice, pitching, batting practice, that type thing. Our little town was able to buy a batting cage; we didn't have an L Screen; we didn't know what an L Screen was (laughing). We had a batting cage, and we were lucky enough; we had a sporting goods store called Mulhern's, and they were one of our sponsors; they supplied us with baseballs. We didn't have to play with baseballs that were taped, that type of thing, you see in movies (laughing). Batting practice, we had a couple of new balls, and we used them two to three weeks at a time, and then we got rid of them, and we had more balls because Mulhern was one of our sponsors.

WILLIE BLAIR

I was very, very lucky. The eight-year-old year we played at a city park, and there's just a dirt field, and it "was what it was." It wasn't anything special, and that was my eight and nine-year-old year. After my nine-year-old year, the city built a brand new Little League complex; grass infield, dugouts, it was unbelievable, and since then, they've hosted several state Little League tournaments and stuff like that, but they had three fields there, and I would compare it to any field. They really took care of it, and it was something they took pride in; it's a brand-new park, and the dads went over and took care of it. That was a lot of fun; it was a beautiful park for that time.

Then my high school field was a really nice field too; in fact, we actually had a professional baseball team play on our field during the summer when I was in high school and even a little bit beyond that in the Appalachian League. It started as a co-op team, and then it became the Paintsville Tri-County Yankees. I think the co-op team was called the Paintsville Highlanders and then went to Paintsville Tri-County Yankees, and then it was Paintsville Tri-County Brewers after that, so I got to watch a lot of future big leaguers right there.

(Can you explain what a Co-op Team is?) Back then, a lot of pro teams didn't have a rookie team, so they would get, say, for example, they would have the Twins and Royals just for an example, and they would put together few guys from their organizations on this one team and play as a co-op.

We started using aluminum bats when I was younger, but I do remember having a wooden bat that had been broken and nailed back. The first glove I got was an old raggedy glove, I don't know if he got it at a yard sale or whatever, but my neighbor gave it to me; I didn't have a glove when I was eight-years-old. He gave it to me, and I used that thing for that year, and then after that, I was playing on the team called the Cubs, and our colors was orange and black in Little League, and I had this glove my dad got me somewhere, I don't know if it was from some little cheap store or whatever but it was green and yellow, the glove is green, so I had a green glove with yellow laces and my team was orange and black (laughing). I had that for a couple years, and then I finally got a new Wilson.

At that age, the Wilson glove was my favorite. I think it may have been when I was 12 or 13-years-old, and then as I got on up into pro ball, I got a Rawlings, and I ended up staying with Rawlings for the rest of my career. But as far as bats go, I think the team supplied us with bats in Little League, a few of them and then there's a few kids that had their own, but I remember using a Tennessee Thumper. It was the name of that bat, and I always thought that was pretty cool (laughing). I wouldn't say equipment was plentiful, but we got what we needed.

WILLIE HORTON

Well, I'll tell you, back then, we had a lot of neighborhood stores and community stores, and we had great sponsorships, and our sponsorships helped coaches. And then we learned how to—we would carry people's groceries home to help buy our little balls and bats and stuff. So, we learned to do things, our coach, he taught us how to go out there and do stuff and start getting sponsorships and stuff like that.

CHARLIE LOYD

We had all kinds of different games if we didn't have enough or a lot of guys had to leave and only left five or six of us there, we'd come up with something. We were playing one day over at Third and Norton, that's where we played most of our pickup games, and of course, you'd hit the ball over the flood wall, and it'd go in the river, and we'd have to dive in the river and get it and swim back, and the ball was wet. Well, after a while the cover would come off, so we took the cover off and wrapped it in friction tape and played with it, and then we lost it, and then we found the cover and filled it with rags and wrapped it with friction tape and brought the bases in and played with it (laughing).

It was just a "make do world" back then, and if parents were looking for us, they knew where we were, they'd come find us.

They were pretty good fields, you know, when I was playing in the Knot Hole League, we played at 23rd and Washington, and that's where Tilghman school is now. See, they had a baseball park and a couple of softball parks over there. So, we played over there, and it was a good ballpark, and of course, we played all the Knot Hole games there regardless. All of them were local teams, so all the games were played there, and at that time they had Twin States, and they would play some games there, over on the other corner, I think it was probably Clark Street. It was all in the same block, and it kinda looked like a spring training area where you had three or four ballparks all on the same block.

(Laughing) No, no . . . .. We'd play, and most of the time, when the first baseman came out of the game to hit, he'd give the other guy his first baseman mitt to play while he hit. Sometimes we'd have 18 players and nine gloves (laughing), and when the foul ball went out, the game was stopped until it was found; we didn't have an abundance of anything.

12.

FAVORITE PLAYERS & TEAMS

BOOG POWELL

And Lakeland was the spring training home of the Tigers, and that's where I grew up, and I really always wanted to be a Tiger; I was a big fan of the Detroit Tigers and everything, and I knew a lot about them.

Stan Musial was my favorite player. My dad took me out of school one time in Lakeland to a Cardinal game at Henley field, which is where the Tigers played. Stan Musial was there, and I don't know how but all of a sudden I'm standing there talking to my dad and Stan Musial's right there and my dad says "Why don't you ask him for his autograph, why don't you ask him to sign your glove?" And I handed him my glove, and he signed my glove, and he said, "You gotta be a ballplayer?" and I said, "Yes Sir," and that was it. That's all I needed right there, and he talked to me, and he had a smile, and then he went off and did something else, and he got a couple of hits, and I liked the way he hit, you know all crouched down like that, and I tried to hit like that for years, I did, I tried to emulate everything he ever did, and it didn't work out exactly, I mean some of the things did.

I never followed teams so much; I know I was pulling for the Milwaukee Braves against the Yankees in the 1957 and '58 World Series. I was pulling like hell for Milwaukee; I just hated the Yankees. I didn't have any reason to; I didn't have any reason to hate the Yankees other than they were Yankees (laughing). I didn't have a reason to hate the Yankees, and then all of a sudden, later on in life, I got real close with

Lou Burdett and Warren Spahn from those teams back then and what great guys, great stories too.

PHIL ROOF

Favorite players growing up would have been Musial, Schoendienst, Warren Spann, Eddie Mathews because they were into something in the 1950s, mid-1950s and didn't know it at the time that I would sign with the Braves (Spann and Mathews played for the Braves); we both signed with the Braves in 1959, but the Cardinals were always our favorite team, and I still like the Cardinals because they're close by and whenever I decide to go to St. Louis I call Mike Shannon, and he gets me field passes so I get down on the field and see some of the guys I know that are still hanging on as manager or coaches. I had that privilege of knowing enough people that I can have my guest and take them down by the dugout, so it's a nice perk

HAWK TAYLOR

Well, I'm gonna hand something to you here. Remember, I was telling you about Legion teams, high school teams; look at the uniform that the team was wearing. *(Chicago?)* Yeah, our high school team wore Chicago Cub uniforms.

I was primarily a Chicago Cub fan; I thought I was going to be a Cub and play for the Chicago Cubs. I could probably tell you a few things, but it might get somebody in trouble (laughing).

(Well, I have to ask) I did sneak in to, well they snuck me in, I didn't sneak into Wrigley Field, between my junior and senior year and they put a Cub uniform on me and let me work out, and nobody knew who I was before or after and it was against the rules. I'm sure somebody would have gotten in trouble.

(Was it a team official?) No (laughing). No, but I had a uniform, I put a uniform on, and I was out there taking batting practice with them.

Gosh, you know what, Ted Williams was always my favorite, so all else dwindled down from Ted Williams. He was my favorite; he's my all-time favorite.

JIM HICKMAN

Of course, I was kinda in awe of all those players because being in this area, we'd listen to St. Louis on the radio, and I knew all their names and everything. Well, of course, naturally, Musial was one. I don't know; it was several players there that I followed.

(Did you try and imitate the players?) No, because, heck, I never saw them. I never knew how they batted. Of course, everybody knew how Musial batted and hit, but no, I never saw any of the rest of them.

BILL GREASON

All we had was Joe Louis. People had those battery radios, and whenever Joe was fighting, everybody would gather around where that radio was.

LOIS YOUNGEN

I was a big Cleveland Indians fan, and all I remember is every time I turned around, the Detroit Tigers were whipping us like 15 to 0. I mean, poor Cleveland.

It wasn't until, what was it, 1954 when we had Boudreau at short and Gordon at second, and Keltner at third, Larry Doby, I think, was in the outfield and Hegan was the catcher. I don't know if Bob Feller was still pitching or not, but Bob Lemon was one of the pitchers. Anyway, it wasn't until 1954 that they finally made it to the World Series, and that was when Willie Mays made his sensational over the shoulder catch.

I was discouraged when Ichiro went to the Yankees because you know with the Yankees, you either Luv 'em or hate 'em and I'm on the—I don't care for them very much because they always seem to have the money to buy the players that they want, so that doesn't seem quite fair.

KATIE HORSTMAN

Oh! The Cincinnati Reds, of course, and Wally Post was from St. Henry, Ohio, just down the road 20 miles, and he was good and Ted Kluszewski and then, of course, Pete Rose because my birthday is April 14 also like his, except he is seven years younger. He got in a lot of trouble, though. Ticks me off because he was my hero all this time.

JIM KAAT

Bobby Shantz was really my baseball hero. He was 5'6" tall; won the MVP award in 1951; pitched for the Philadelphia Athletics. He was my hero. Oh yeah, I took to the Athletics when Bobby Shantz came along. He was my hero, and I play a lot of baseball trivia, I am good friends with Bill Parcells, the former football coach and Coach is a real avid baseball fan, and so he will quiz me sometimes on baseball trivia, and he'll say "Remember the Philadelphia Athletics," and I said, "Of course I do." He had me name their starting lineup, and I could go right around Buddy Rosar was the catcher, Ferris Fain, Pete Suder, Eddie Joost. I could go around the whole lineup as well as the pitching staff. I had all of their trading cards, so yeah, that was my team.

LOU PINIELLA

My favorite teams were the Cleveland Indians and the Boston Red Sox; those are my two favorite teams. It's true, American League slant, and it's ironic that I ended up playing 11 years; I was in the Yankee organization about 17 or 18 years, and as a young guy, I rooted against them.

My favorite player growing up was Ted Williams. So, when Boston came to Tampa for spring training games, for sure, I was at the ballpark.

Another hero was Al Rosen, played third base with the Cleveland Indians. In fact, I remember the first TV we ever bought as a family; it was in 1954 to watch the Cleveland Indians and the New York Giants play in the World Series, and the reason being is Al Lopez was the manager. He made it to the big leagues, and he was managing in the big leagues, so basically as young kids growing up, we knew the name, and we knew he was from Tampa. So, it sort of opened up our dreams a little bit . . .

And I remember, you know, I remember watching the game of the week with Dizzy Dean and Buddy Blattner.

JIM ZAPP

I was a Detroit Tiger fan because my aunt lived in Detroit, so therefore, I became a fan of Barney McCosky, Hank Greenberg, and all those guys playing in Detroit.

I think Barney's still living, but he could play center field. He was probably the fourth-best outfielder in the major leagues at that time, behind Dominic DiMaggio. All those guys were stationed over there during the war.

LOU WHITAKER

As I grew up, I started watching Major League Baseball on TV rooting for the Cincinnati Reds and the Baltimore Orioles. I never forget those teams, the Big Red Machine.

Growing up in Virginia, we would get Baltimore channels, and they still get Baltimore in the Martinsville area. But Cincinnati Reds being a dynamic team as they were, they were always on TV, so it's really your area where you watch baseball. I guess if I grew up on the West Coast, I'd have been a Dodger's fan. So, it's a fact of you being in your local area.

Boog Powell, Brooks Robinson, Frank Robinson, Paul Blair, looking at a young Jim Palmer and Cuellar, McNally. And those teams having great managers and as I made the major leagues, I got to play for Sparky Anderson personally, but Sparky was the manager of the Big Red Machine. And then you had Earl Weaver with the Orioles. So, I grew up watching these players and those managers, and you see what those managers turned out to be, Hall of Famers.

STEVE BLASS

Well, it was very rural. I played Little League ball when I was eight years old, but early before that, I was the oldest boy; I had no siblings that I could play with, so I invented my own baseball games. I just, I don't know what prompted it, but I just loved baseball. So I would be out in the yard, and I would invent my own games against the side of a barn we had, and I would keep score, and it would always be the Yankees against the Cleveland Indians because my team was the Cleveland Indians. The reason for that is that when I was growing up playing Cowboys and Indians, I always rooted for the Indians. And that never changed, and I wound up keeping a scrapbook of the Cleveland Indians of the 1954 season when they won 111 games out of a 154-game schedule.

I just thought the Indians were the underdogs when they fought against the Cowboys. In my make-believe games out in the backwoods, I would always be an Indian. It got ridiculous to the point that the first car I ever bought was a Pontiac because there was a Chief Pontiac (laughing).

And that was not easy getting those daily write-ups and things. I would get them from a New York City newspaper about three days late. I'd listen to games all of the time, and I even had a little game where somebody left a big pile of small stone outside of our driveway, and I used to have an old cracked wooden bat, and I would stand out there for hours just swinging and hitting those stones out into the field. So, I'd get very creative with my love of baseball. I grew up keeping the scorecards of all of the Yankee games, listening to Mel Allan and Jim Woods. I had a yellow legal tablet, a ruler, and a pencil, and I would create my own scorecard every night.

WHITEY HERZOG

Well, I'd have to say that I used to go over and see the St. Louis Browns when the Yankees came to town because I liked DiMaggio, the Yankee Clipper. I was kind of a front-runner. As I got older, being a left-hander, a center fielder, and a first baseman, I followed Musial playing in St. Louis. I'd seen the Cardinals play a lot; I used to skip school and hitchhike over to Bellville and take the bus from Bellville to St. Louis for a dime and another dime to take the streetcar up to Sportsman Park, I guess during the 1940s, even till the time I graduated in 1949 and signed my first contract, Stan the Man was my favorite player.

(Were you a Cardinals fan?) No. I really wasn't; my brother was a Brooklyn fan. And his idol was Billy Herman, the second baseman. And I kind of went through a Browns, Yankee phase in 1942, '43, '44 and of course, I like George McQuinn, the first baseman, and also one of the Yankees, Nick Etten during the war and I, just being a kid, I was playing first base a lot, but I think when I went to see the Yankees after DiMaggio

came back at 1946 or '47, I really idolized him a lot, the way he could play center field and what a player he was.

DOUG FLYNN

Reds. Frank Robinson, Vida Pinson, Johnny Edwards, that bunch . . . Back in those days, now we say we're close to Cincinnati; back in those days, you had two-lane roads; you had to go from here through Cynthia and Falmouth, and it took you two hours to get to Cincinnati where now it takes an hour.

They had a few. I think Waite Hoyt might have been back in those days, but I didn't listen to them as much as I listened to basketball games. Because basketball, I thought, was something that was attainable for me at some point, and I don't know why. Baseball, I didn't know any big-league players. I had met Lew Johnson. Lew was a friend of my dad's, and he played with the Dodgers some; he was from here, but gosh, nobody from Lexington was going to play pro ball, nobody from the state hardly, Pee Wee did, but there weren't that many.

FERGIE JENKINS

Well, my dad used to take me to Tigers Stadium from time to time. Larry Doby was with the Cleveland Indians at the time. I watched him play as an outfielder; pretty good hitter. Al Kaline, he's a couple years older than me; I've seen him play.

Game of the Week; that was the only game you could watch on television. I always told my dad, "Hey, if I ever got good enough, do you think I could play against Willie Mays"? Which I did, seven years I pitched against him and the same thing with Mickey Mantle. I watched, and then I pitched against him in the all-star competition. That was a dream. Every kid has a dream. When I look back, 17/18-years-old, when I signed with the Phillies, we used to watch games . . . most of the games I played in that Miami, Chattanooga, Little Rock area, they were night games. So I got the chance to watch NBC Game of the Week and before I got the chance to get to the big league I'd seen a lot of these pitchers, Camilo Pascual, Whitey Ford, Frank Lary, you watch the guys that pitch in the big leagues and I said, "Man, I can do that (laughing)." You convince yourself; you can do it. Maybe you're having a decent season, but I thought I could do it, and then the Phillies brought me up in 1965, won some ball games, and then they traded me to the Cubs (laughing).

WILLIE BLAIR

Favorite team is probably Cincinnati, they were closer, and during the mid-1970s I knew just about every player on the team and "The Big Red Machine" and then a little bit later I started following the Cubs and the Braves because we were starting to get the Super Station and WGN on our cable at that time and so I got to watch them just about every day. Those are probably the three teams that I followed more, and at that time, the Reds were really good; Braves were really bad, and the Cubs were not real good either; they were okay.

The Big Red Machine; when we were playing Wiffle ball, I could do just about every one of their hitter's stances and swings. I did that all the time and then I used to always try to do my pitching motion like Nolan Ryan and obviously he was, at that time, was just about everybody's idol for anybody that wanted to pitch because he was so fun to watch but yeah, just about the whole Reds team is my favorite, that would be the answer to that one (laughing).

WILLIE HORTON

The player to me was Rocky Colavito.

Yeah, he got me involved in baseball at a young age. Me and my two buddies I mentioned, James Slate, we called him JP . . . and Johnny Mac Barnes. My parents and their parents let us skip school, and we went and seen Jake Wood, and we used to play strike out on old Briggs Stadium when the Tigers were in town. What we did is slip in the ballpark. When the concession trucks come we used to slip in the ballpark and go hide in them dumpsters, and when they open up the gate we'd go up in the bleachers where we sat, and one day we got caught, and Rocky Colavito, he was with Cleveland at the time, and Don Mossi, if you recall, he had some big Mickey Mouse ears, scared the death out of us and so we thought they would detain us or whatever and Colavito said: "Let us have these kids," and Rocky took over, and I think Ray Collins, he used to run the visitor's clubhouse, so we started working down there part-time, and I'd tell people "I'm about the only guy in a Tiger uniform that never paid going in the ballpark, I used to slip in, and hide, and watch the game, and then one day we got called to start working down there, and then I signed with them" (laughing).

But Rocky Colavito, he actually passed left field down to me, later in years he got traded to Detroit before I signed, and I'll never forget Rocky. One winter going into Winter ball, he sat down to talk to me at the end of the year, and he said: "They're going to make room for you." I said, "No, you the Rock, I mean, I'm just enjoying the game," and he said, "No," he said, but he's not through playing. He said, "Let me tell you what you're going to have to remember. When you go out there next year they're going to boo you at first, but if you learn to handle that, that don't mean they don't love you, or they don't like you, they just been used to that old shoe out there, and once they get used to that, them boos will turn into cheers", and I tried to do the same thing to Steve Kemp when I left the Tigers. When he came along, I tried to pass the same words down to him, and he looked up to me like a mentor, but that's what the game of baseball is. You keep up with the game, and you love the game, and when I went and finished my career, I took what I learned from the Tigers.

CHARLIE LOYD

The Cardinals because we could pick them up on radio.

Oh, back then, I kept up with Stan Musial and Enos Slaughter, guys like that. Couple of pitchers, Burkhart and Howie Pollet that pitched for the Cardinals back then in the 1950s, and I kept up with those guys, but I never was much of a fan as I was a player. Most athletes are not much fans, they keep up with it, but they're not much fans. And I remember when I signed with the Yankees . . . I was playing pro ball at the time my first year, and they were talking about Elston Howard, and I said who's Elston Howard and, of course, he was catching for the Yankees behind Berra (laughing) I didn't know who he was (laughing).

13.

BASEBALL CARDS

BOOG POWELL
No, never cared much about it. The only thing we did was just, like a lot of other kids, just put them in your bicycle spokes.

PHIL ROOF
No, it cost money, and we didn't have money back then, and I never collected them whenever I played the game; I just never thought of having an interest in that. My daughter kept those up there, 15 from my career, and I just never did. And we have guys in baseball; Tom Kelly is a good one, he managed in major leagues for 16 years. He's got a great collection of signed autographed baseball cards.

HAWK TAYLOR
No, somehow or the other, that kinda fell through the cracks with me, I was never interested in baseball cards. The bubble gum in them was awful (laughing).

JIM HICKMAN
No. We didn't know what baseball cards were.

KATIE HORSTMAN
Yeah, after I was in the league. After the league dissolved, then I really became interested in baseball cards. I have gobs of them. I used to go to

the sporting goods store here, and they would have big sports memorabilia. I would go there, and I got quite a few good autographs in my collection here.

JIM KAAT

Oh, I sure did. I wish I had my 1952-1953 Mickey Mantle Bowman cards (laughing). They were, as with all of the kids, I'm sure they were in the spokes of my bicycle.

Yeah, eventually, they threw them away. Of course, we would use them to make up a lineup, and then one of our popular games on a rainy day was we played Dice Baseball. So, we had a dice game. Like 4&4 was a home run; 6&6 was a double; things like that. So, we had a little group of kids that had a baseball league, and we would use our trading cards to play; pick out a catcher and pitcher and all of the positions. You would stack them, and then that was your lineup for the day. They might be players from several different teams.

LOU PINIELLA

Yeah, I bought baseball cards all the time; in fact, we lived right across the street from a playground park where they'd play softball at night. The men had softball leagues, and they'd play like three days a week, and I'd always get up early after the game the next morning because I'd go look for some change around second base, or third base, and I'd find . . . a quarter was really hitting it big, but I'd find a lot of nickels and dimes, and what I did with them, I'd go right down to the store (laughing) and buy the bubble gum cards, they were penny-a- piece.

A piece of bubble gum and a card, and then we'd flip them too, we kept the ones that we wanted but the other ones, we'd flip. Did you ever see them flipping cards? Heads or tails. You throw a card down. Alright, and it's face up. So, I had to throw a card face up; if I threw one face down, it was your card.

We'd flip cards all the time, then we'd flip them against the wall, see which one got closer, and I was pretty good at that. I pulled up quite a collection of cards, and I remember I had a really nice collection. I went to play ball, play pro ball and still had them, and when I got back, I forgot about them, and I don't know what happened to them, but I had some nice cards; I had some Mickey Mantle cards. Yeah, I had a Ted Williams card; I wish I still had them today.

LOU WHITAKER

Well, the only time we got baseball cards, and back then, you got them when you bought the Bazooka Bubble Gum. And really you was going after the bubble gum, but you would always look at the baseball card.

I never really was one who kept the cards or looked to get autographs because I was nowhere close to a stadium or a team but seeing what the kids do today, they send all that stuff through the mail. I used to give the autographs all the time at the ballpark and sit down and sign them. Quite a few—I pretty much did a ball every time we went to the stadium. But I never collected any baseball cards in the day.

STEVE BLASS

Oh, yeah. I had a huge collection. I had the shoebox with the rubber bands around each team, and like every other kid in America, my mom did something with them, who knows where they wound up. But I had a great collection. I had a Jackie Robinson rookie card, and it was all kind of stuff. But yeah, I did all of that, absolutely did all of that.

WHITEY HERZOG

Oh, yeah, I remember the baseball cards. From Boston Braves and some of the cards I'd get, and the big piece of bubblegum you'd get and I'd chew that bubblegum and . . . my God, I'd have a wad on my window sill, I'd keep puttin' them together and, God, it looked like I'd have a big wad of tobacco in my mouth when I was 10-years-old, for crying out loud, but the baseball cards, in those days, you know, you could get them for a penny (laughing) but nobody had a penny for crying out loud.

DOUG FLYNN

I did. I grew up and had them and did what everybody else did, put some
in my spokes, probably threw away a pretty comfortable living (laughing). Didn't we all back in those days in the 1950s?

Yeah, mom threw them away (laughing). But we'd play games on the
floor. I'd play little games, invent games with dice and you'd write out
base hits, singles, whatever and then roll the dice and play and I'd have
everybody in their positions on the floor. Yeah, I did all that.

FERGIE JENKINS

Hockey was the big thing. Donruss was the big card company for hockey
players. Gordie Howe, Rocket Richard, ah geez, who else? Doug Harvey,
Boom Boom Geoffrion, there was so many good hockey players back
then, Terry Sawchuk. I followed hockey a lot, but then baseball entered
the picture, I really didn't collect baseball cards, but as a kid, it was hockey
cards.

WILLIE BLAIR

Never had any interest for some reason; I never got autographs or anything from players that were playing from the pro team that I watched.
In our hometown, I never hounded them for autographs. I didn't want to
feel like "Hey, you're better than me," you know what I mean?

WILLIE HORTON

Well, I used to collect them all the time; I wish I would've kept them
(laughing). We used to put them in our bicycle spokes; I had Mantle,
Mays, all the others . . . I had all the great ones. But at the time you
weren't into saving, all we were thinking about was making a motor for
your bike. I had all types of baseball cards, but we made a baseball motor, and I had a buddy . . . we thought, in our mind, we thought certain
players make you sound more like a motor than the other players. That's
that little boy you have in you and that little dream you are talking about.
You might have Mantle, your card sound better than Willie Horton card,
it's funny how you do that. That's the little kid inside of you.

14.

CHATTER, CHATTER, CHATTER

BOOG POWELL

You know, I don't remember anything derogatory towards anybody else; we used to holler for our own guys. You know, holler for our own players and stuff like that, but I don't remember any negative comments about any of the other teams or any of the other ballplayers or anything.

HAWK TAYLOR

Yeah, yeah, chatter was part of it. We didn't call it chatter, I forget what we called it, make some noise or something like that. Yeah, it was part of it, I'm not sure what a big part of it was, but it was done.

More on the chatter, from what I remember, it was more keeping the pitcher in the game, keep him focused, and keeping that focus more than what chatter was.

KATIE HORSTMAN

It was few and far between. I doubt it very much. We were just so anxious to play that we did anything the coach told us. And besides, the priest was there all of the time, so we didn't needle too many times; he'd probably tell me to go to Confession (laughing). I can't ever remember, and if someone swore, they swore in German, because everybody knew German. In fact, when I went to school, I didn't know any English, it was German. We talked German. The biggest thing was, you *dummkopf*, which means 'you dumbhead' (laughing); that was probably the worst word we used because, like I said, It was very religious, and I never even heard my brothers swear . . . my mother would be "Whoa" . . . You just didn't do that, and if you did, somebody in the town would call your mom.

JIM KAAT

Well, I think the way I grew up with chatter, it was always in an encouraging nature for your teammates. I grew up in a very, very conservative, strict, Dutch reform church community. You never did anything to show up your opponents or show off or anything like that. I don't think we ever had anything that you would call bench jockeying like what I got into with professional baseball (laughing).

LOU WHITAKER

Well back then it was, "Come, baby, baby, baby, baby, come, baby, baby" you know, something like that.

And basically, it was chattering for the pitcher, and that was pretty much what we used with all the little kids out on the field doing that; you never forget that either, but as you got a little bit older, you didn't do all the chatter. I grew up playing third base, so being closest to the pitcher, I did a lot of communicating with the pitcher. Telling him, "Let's go, get it over the plate, throw strikes," you know, keeping the pitcher going, keeping the pitcher in a rhythm.

STEVE BLASS

Oh, yeah. Oh yeah. We always hollered at each other, "Come on, batter, batter, batter." You got to understand that was back in the 1950s. There was a whole different world where you didn't have to have a game face on and all that stuff. It was full throttle; you were just having the time of your life.

FERGIE JENKINS

Yeah, as a first baseman, I use to always just try to reassure the pitcher, whoever it was. Dennis Rovey, "Come on, Rovey, let's go, come on." Or Eddie Meyers, "Come on Meyers, let's go. Or Jack Howell. His father was a barber, so they called him "The Barber": "Hey Barber, let's go!" (laughing). He ended up being a barber, he followed in his dad's footsteps, and he kept his dad's business going. But that was just something that, as a kid growing up, there wasn't that much chatter. When I played first base, I just tried to reassure the pitcher, "Come on, let's go, let's go, throw strikes." Everybody had a nickname.

WILLIE BLAIR
Yeah, I think we did; I mean, I think our coach tried to get us to all the time, "Hey batter-batter," stuff like that, but I never did that a lot; I didn't like doing it, but they encourage us to do some.

WILLIE HORTON
Yeah, yeah. Cheerleader. You're not only a ballplayer, but you're a cheerleader. Well, that's how we were raised up to do it. We're there to support, and I remember the first time I saw Pete Rose, he took it to another level. He'd run, everything he did, he was running to go get water when he was a kid, and I take my hat off to him right now. And me and him back in the winter, I think in January, we went into the Ted Williams Hall of Fame together in St. Petersburg, and we were talking about . . . whoever would've thought, we as childhood kids, we'd been going to the big leagues. I think Pete was one of the greatest ballplayers and is the greatest in my time. Other great players, they ask me, should he be in the Hall of Fame? Hall of Fame is not the Hall of Fame until you get him there. He took everything he had and became the best; I mean, this guy probably got 2,000 hits more than Mays and all them greats. And I had a great career, but I'm saying he took what he got, the God-given ability and made himself the best. He told me a joke at the ceremony in St. Pete. Pete and his son were playing ball, and his son came up and said, "Dad, I need some help," and he said, "Help on what?" He said, "I'm batting .240." He said, "Wait a minute, two what?" He said, "Well, I think you better go talk to your God Daddy, Concepcion, I don't know nothing about hittin' no .240 (laughing).

CHARLIE LOYD

Oh yeah, and you know you don't find that much, even in pro sports, even in Legion. They don't even let the dugout bench ride the players anymore, but that was most of it back then.

I don't think it hurts anything; in fact, if nothing else, it keeps people active and keeps people attentive. A lot of time, especially playing in pro ball, you bring a reliever in, he has no idea what the situation is, who's ahead or anything because he's been down, playing Password or some game down in the bullpen (laughing). He couldn't care less unless he's playing.

15.

THE SEASON, THE SPORT

HAWK TAYLOR

In high school, I won the 100-yard dash. I could run pretty good and in high school when I wanted to steal a base, I did. There was no getting thrown out.

Yeah, well see that all factored in, but I also considered myself an athlete, so I played all the different sports. When baseball was over, it was football time, football over it was basketball time, and then in the spring, you had track meets along with the baseball games, so I participated in track, and that's where I developed my running speed.

Well, it's not their picking the sport; I think it's their dad's picking the sports for them, and I think it's very unfortunate. I think a kid ought to be exposed to all the different sports and enjoy them for what they are. And there's a time to come when you specialize in a sport but starting out and that's all you do at the expense of getting to experience football or basketball, I think is the wrong way to do it.

JIM HICKMAN

I remember in high school there was a lot of things my coach wouldn't let me do, and I remember, for some reason, I could throw a shot put pretty good and boy, coach . . . he'd raise cane if he'd catch me throwing that shot put. And I knew how far I could throw it and heck . . . we had a big track meet up there one time, and they were throwing the shot put, and they were four or five feet shorter than what I normally would throw it, and I was sitting there wanting to throw that thing. "No, you're not gonna throw that thing. I don't care if you can throw it 50 feet farther than they can; you're not gonna throw it." He made me watch what I did to protect my arm.

BILL GREASON

(*Did you have a high school baseball team?*) No. just football, we didn't have any fields.

After I finished high school, a fellow there wanted to get a professional football team started; before the Atlanta Falcons came, we had a team called the Atlanta All-Stars. I played two years of football with those guys; I was the quarterback and running back. Didn't weigh but 160 pounds, but we ran from the T, we had another one ran from the single wing, another from the double wing, big ones, we were the small ones. We ran that T, that quick opening stuff. We were always; whenever we played any game, I was always on the small side; I wanted to go against the big guys. I never had any fear of them; I just believed I could outmaneuver them and was fast enough to get away from them.

KATIE HORSTMAN

Oh, I really liked football. Football and basketball were my favorites (laughing), because basketball, I could play by myself in the barn. We had a net and a nice floor, and everything. Basketball was really great! And football . . . I loved to kick the ball. I could out kick my brothers (laughing). That's true. And Minster didn't have a football team then until I came to high school, then we started a football team. The older ones, I don't know if they played. I don't think they played football. They had just basketball and baseball.

I was the best kicker that they had, but the coach was totally against girls playing because he was from Ohio State University, big Buckeye. He was very good, he was taught under Woody Hayes, and so he wanted me off the field, so he made me a cheerleader so I would get off the field (laughing).

JIM KAAT

The seasons then were much more separate where you had a football season in the fall and basketball in the winter and baseball in the spring. So, in the fall in the backyard, we threw a football around because we were fans of the University of Michigan. We didn't have access to the local gymnasium until I got into high school. Obviously, the basketball season was longer than baseball, the baseball season, in Michigan, we probably played ten games in high school. And two of those might have been in snow flurries (laughing).

JIM ZAPP

Basketball in High School. Yeah, Basketball, that's all that school had, a private Catholic school on Lafayette. I laid outta school for two years; when I went back, they had got a guy to volunteer to coach basketball; that's how I started playing basketball.

Each time we played basketball, I said: "Mr. Goodman, I ain't playing that ole' sissy game." We called it an ole' sissy game, basketball; it turned out to be a rough game!

Well, after I started, I loved basketball; they didn't have baseball teams but had high school basketball. I was a big boy during those days, 6'2", the little guys come in under the basket; we'd tease them, "You better not come under that basket (laughing)." Mr. Goodman, he died not too long ago, he'd say, "You better not let them get any easy crip-shots (laughing)," Gosh, those kids would come to the basket; we'd play what you'd call standard guards on defense, playing a zone. And a boy named Butch Mize and Butch Mize would kill them when they'd go to the basket (laughing). They were scared to come under the basket. In those days, he was 6'2", big kid, weighed about 190 lbs.

LOU WHITAKER

Well, I think I was about 12 years old; I played football. Like I said, I was a small guy, so I had to play with kids a year younger than me. I was a running back and ended up being the scoring champ in the Little League football, something like that. I played basketball with my friends in the city park; they were the high school stars. They won the state championship in 1975. I never played football after about 12. I used to see guys older than me messing up their shoulders and messing up their fingers and hurting their legs and stuff like that, so I said, "No football for me," because my main interest was baseball and baseball lasts a lot longer in a career than football. So, I sort of knew what I wanted to do, and I pretty much stayed with just baseball. That's the only sport I started playing after I realized the injuries in football.

Basketball, I really never had an interest, but like I said, I played in the city park with my friends, and one year they told me to go out for basketball, and that was my senior year. I was probably the last man—it was between me and another guy. We were the last two; either one of us could have not been on that team, but they kept both of us because I was a baseball guy, and the other guy was a golf guy, so we both pretty much made the team, but I never played any on the team. I pretty much just sat on the bench, so I quit after about three or four games. Basketball just wasn't what I wanted to do. They talked me into going out, I did and made the team, but I left it to them, and that year they won the state championship.

STEVE BLASS

I played Little League, and I was good. I was good in Little League, and I just made the regular progression up, but I was hooked early. I wasn't hooked on baseball more than the other sports. Before Little League, I invented football games where I would throw it; I would be the passer and the receiver (laughing). I just did all of that stuff. It all turned to baseball primarily because baseball had Little League, and there was no organized football or basketball. All during grade school, I was a good basketball player, and I wanted to play football, but I wasn't big enough. I played my freshman year and then stopped and decided to run cross country instead of playing football. I was a high scoring basketball player. We had an interesting high school team in that when the other team scored, nobody on our team would take the ball out because you would never see it again (laughing). Everybody would want to shoot the minute they got the ball (laughing). That was primarily it: basketball and baseball in high school.

I just always liked to run, so that was just an extension. The reason I chose cross country was that we lived about a mile up the road from the high school, and I could always stop and have lunch. My mother would cook, which is better than the school food, so it was okay. But later on, when I was playing professionally, I loved to run. Some of the guys thought that was work, but I loved to run.

(Sounds like you were always thinking ahead!) Yeah, that prepped me for always wanting to get the edge when I was pitching, always looking for the edge (laughing).

WHITEY HERZOG

Our basketball team at New Athens was with the same group of guys. We wouldn't get the high school gym; we didn't have a grade school gym, so we'd play outside, and on Saturday morning, while the ground was frozen, we'd be playing basketball on an outdoor court. Later on, in the eighth grade or the grade school team, we got to use the high school gymnasium a couple of nights a week after the high school team was done practicing and we ended up, my senior year in high school, we had 49 boys in high school, and we won the district, which the small schools had to do, and we beat Bellville in the regional and then we went to the sectional, a game away from going to the Sweet 16 in Illinois and we got beat by one point, so we finished the season with a 37 and 2 record and lost two games by one point each.

DOUG FLYNN

I played basketball, and then I played Little League football, which I only played for a year when I was nine, and then I quit playing that and just played basketball and baseball. It was just; however, many guys you could get that would determine what game you were going to play.

Basketball was my favorite. I always like basketball better. I played it every single year. Baseball, I played every single year. Football, I didn't play after I was nine until I was a junior in high school.

Actually, the University of Kentucky had signed a guard to play, and from the time that he agreed to come, he ended up being signed by the Cleveland Indians. Now they're left with everything but a point guard, so Coach Hall called and wanted me to come over and be the point guard for the basketball team as a freshman in 1969. That was the year Dan Issel and Mike Pratt were seniors, so I went and played basketball, and then I went to the baseball team and basically was told I wasn't good enough to play. I only had nine at-bats as a freshman; I really wasn't that good, my hands were good, and I can field, but I still hadn't had that little growth spurt . . .

But I remember playing football with them, and they'd hit you, and you'd go "Was that necessary?" and they'd say, "Is the game a little too rough for you?" They were just, they'd test you, but I loved it. The kids today don't play all of the sports because they try to specialize; it's the only time when you're in high school and juniors that you can play all the sports. I didn't want to play football, but Coach Roy Walton got me into football. At 5'6" and 130 pounds, I played as a junior and getting hit and knocked down; when it came time to basketball, to take a charge, wasn't any big deal. Then, playing basketball got my legs in really good shape for baseball, even turning a double play. I tried to turn every double play, and I got knocked down a lot, but if you learn how to get knocked down, you also learn how to fall. If you get your feet off the ground, I knew how to fall. You could come down on somebody and act like you don't know it, but you learn how to do that. Everybody that plays the game learns that. So, every sport helped me. If you look at the NFL draft, 28 out of the first 32 guys drafted were multi-sports guys.

It just tells you that all sports can help each other. Unfortunately, coaches today are trying to make you specialize; why? Because if you'd made me admit it, I'm glad we didn't have all the statistics when I played they do today. I'd never got a chance to play. He's too slow, he's too short, and he's too weak. He's too this and all, but all these statistics can't measure your heart and your head.

FERGIE JENKINS

Definitely, I think that was a good factor too because we had three other pitchers on the ball club, and we all were about the same age; all 16, 17, 18-years-old and we played all the way through Bantam, Midget, Juvenile baseball all the way up. We also played hockey with each other. It was a small town, and we all played certain sports.

WILLIE BLAIR

I played all sports up until I got into high school, and then I just played baseball and basketball. I played football up until high school as well. But honestly, basketball is my favorite sport. That was my favorite sport to play. Now, baseball was my favorite sport when I was pitching because that made things a little different, I felt more comfortable when I was on the mound, but as far as just going out and playing, basketball was my favorite by far.

I think it probably was like my favorite to play, but I guess I was kind of like whatever season is in, that was my favorite sport, but if you just ask me let's go out and throw a baseball or let's go shoot basketball, I'd want to go shoot basketball.

When you're that age and growing up in Eastern Kentucky, everybody wants to play basketball at the University of Kentucky, and obviously, I wasn't that good, but that was the goal from when I was young, is to play at UK. But I actually had a few offers from small NAIA schools to play basketball, but I knew I was much better in baseball.

WILLIE HORTON

I played football for one year, and at Northwestern High School, I played on the basketball team. They kept us busy. You did all types of different sports, and I think today that's what we're cheating our young people out of; we program them to do one thing and keep them from other sports. I think you should have all options because what you learn from different sports, it helps in other parts of your life and helps you out with your decision skills, and I was very fortunate I had the opportunity to do them other things. In my mind, with season change, I changed.

You had other people guide me towards my best sports, but I went out and enjoyed everything I did. Whether basketball, football, whatever. I boxed when I was a kid. I won a Gold Glove back in Detroit. Back there, I put my age up three years, and I won that one year, and then my dad made me quit doing that. But I enjoyed it. Actually, my boxing coach, Martin Gilday, he's still living.

16.

I KNEW I WAS READY WHEN . . .

BOOG POWELL

I guess I got really serious about it when I was; I guess I was 14, and I got to thinking about it, and what am I going to do? I'd done a paper in school that year about . . . I had to pick an occupation, you had to go do a studies about an occupation and being an engineer had always intrigued me, and I did a little research on it, and I decided that was way more than I wanted to do (laughing), because I wasn't very good with math, I was OK, I was just middle of the road student, maybe just a little bit better, I wasn't a real good student, but I just got to the point to where I got to do something here, and I don't know what. Then my senior year, after we get through football season . . . I wasn't going to play football first of all, and then I said, "Ahh man, all my buddies are out there," and there is was no way I wasn't gonna play . . . I mean, I had to go. So then come basketball season. Me and my dad, we talked about it, and he said, "You know, why don't you start working out early and everything and be ready for baseball season and skip basketball and so I went over and talked to the basketball coach, and I told him I wasn't going to play basketball and he said, "OK, I understand, but you come back anytime." The next day I came back. I was sitting there; I said, "If it's OK, I'd like to come back," and he said, "I thought so, so get out there," and that was it. So we played basketball, and we had a good team for Key West, little ole town like Key West, and then we had five guys that played football, five guys that moved from there and was starting five on the basketball team and five out of nine on the baseball team, good athletes. One of them was George Mira. George made All American quarterback at University of Miami, and he was probably a better pitcher

So anyhow that was it, and then after that, one thing kinda lead to another but I was never obsessed with it, you know it was never like, "I gotta do it, I gotta do it, I gotta do it," it was never like that. It was almost like, "I can hit, and I can do it anytime I want."

PHIL ROOF

Probably my sophomore year. Because I was doing things there that were head and shoulders above other youngsters in this area and knew at some point in time, if I keep improving, I'd wind up being a major league player.

You know, once you size up the competition that you're playing against, I knew at that time when I was a sophomore that I could catch, I was a better catcher than Hawk and a better thrower than Hawk, had a stronger arm. He was a much better hitter, and I knew if he got drafted and signed that I was gonna sign too, which I did. Wasn't no draft back then, the highest bidder took you.

HAWK TAYLOR

That was obvious from the get-go that I was going to be a pro ballplayer. I saw my uncles, "Hey, I'm gonna do that," so I made up my mind that's what it was gonna be. Now when did I think the clincher was gonna be when I might have the ability? Like I said, I was pretty cocky (laughing). I guess I'd thought pretty early. I was 13 or 14-years-old, and I'm playing against adults and doing very well, so that helped things out considerably.

Oh, I'm sure of it. You know, I had many opportunities to play. I figured out one summer I was playing on five different baseball teams, and that runs from playing on two different adult teams down to teams my age, so in this framework here that you know, "Yeah, I'm gonna be a professional baseball player," there was no doubt in my mind, I know that . . . there's no doubt in my mind I was going to be a Big League ballplayer because I had all this support system going for me. For one reason, nobody said, "Well, why not? You can't be" nobody ever told me I couldn't be (laughing), so I can be, and it worked. And I think Phil would probably say the same thing to you, "Nobody ever told him he couldn't be," and I betcha he hadn't thought it in that way; in fact, I just now thought it that way. There was nobody told us we couldn't be whatever we wanted to be (laughing).

JIM HICKMAN

Well, I guess I felt that way a little bit in high school, just listening to people talk. The first year or two in high school, when I played, I had a few people tell me some things that made me feel like I could play.

BILL GREASON

No, I didn't know it, but I just believed from watching; I said: "If I get a chance, I believe I can make it." I'd watch other fellows, and we'd go down and watch the sandlot players, and I said, "Shoot, I can do that."

KATIE HORSTMAN

Well, I dreamt about it every night; I just prayed to God; that was my first prayer; I would say every night before I'd go to bed, "Dear Jesus, please find a girl's baseball team (laughing)" I did that every night. I was bound to find something.

JIM KAAT

Well, I didn't really know for sure until I signed in 1957. My dad had a stroke in 1969. He lived until 1983, but he was partially paralyzed and not easy to communicate with. I never really took the time to ask him, so one day, I asked my mother. I said "Did my dad ever say anything about when I was in high school or something that he thought I had a chance to be a player?" and she said "Well, I don't know the exact time, whether it was when I was pitching in high school or wherever, but anyway I guess my dad had said to her one day, "You know Jim has some special talent to play this game." Now he didn't say I was going to the big leagues or anything like that, but I knew after Dick Weincek scouted me, I knew I was going to get a chance, but I had no idea that first year when I went to Superior, Nebraska, whether I would be in over my head playing against the boys from the big city, so I went into it kind of blind. After that first year, I didn't do very well, I was 5 and 6, and my dad had come out to see me for about a week out in Nebraska, but when the season was over I went home, and he said: "Well what did you think, what was the experience like." I said, "You know I didn't do real well. I had a few really dominate games, but then I had some games where I got knocked around," but I said "I didn't feel overmatched, I felt like I wasn't intimidated, but I felt very comfortable with the level of competition" and I kind of felt that way every year I moved up through the minors.

LOU WHITAKER

Well, you know I think the first time I ever thought about Major League Baseball as far as playing, of one day being a major league ballplayer, I think I was about 13-years-old, and it was a guy out there just looking at kids play. Like I just mentioned, I was at third base, and someone walked by me and said something that stuck with me. And I think that was the beginning of thinking about major leagues, one day being a major league ballplayer.

(What was said to you?) I can't remember exactly what he said, but it was pretty much like you keep playing the game the way you're playing–just keep that interest, and someday you could probably get a chance to see what you could do at a higher level.

STEVE BLASS

Well, I didn't know. I had confidence that that's absolutely what I wanted to do since I was eight years old. I didn't really know; I just felt I could. I didn't look at the percentages or anything or how tough it was going to be. I didn't know why I didn't want to be a major leaguer right away, I wanted to be a professional baseball player, and then it just went on from there. Even when I speak now, I tell kids that goals change. Don't make your goals unattainable; make then attainable because you are going to adjust them upwards.

WHITEY HERZOG

Well, you know, it was just ironic that when I got out of high school, I was a pretty good basketball player, and I had seven scholarship offers to go to college. And one of the offers was from Illinois University, combined baseball and basketball scholarship, but in those days, a high school education was all you needed. Everybody looked to get that high school diploma. It didn't seem like that was that important to go to college, and I wasn't what you'd call a guy that hit the books. I used to make teachers cry because I wouldn't study. All I cared about was being eligible to play and getting by. And I wanted to play baseball, kinda knew that I was going to get an opportunity because the scouts started talking to me in my junior year, seeing if I was interested in playing and so forth. And the other difference then was when you signed a professional baseball contract, and you came home, you were kind of looked up to in the community as being a professional baseball player, they just thought you were something special for being able to play in the minor leagues, to play professional baseball.

DOUG FLYNN

When they told me that I did have the talent.

I was going to junior college down in Somerset, and I was playing softball, and guys were watching me play; I'm starting to mature a little bit. I was going in the hole and throwing guys out from left field and swinging the bat pretty good, and then I was playing baseball on Sundays and played softball during the week two or three times, and I played baseball in the Blue Grass League on Sundays, and I was the youngest player because it was mostly men . . . Allen Feldhaus and Scotty Baesler . . . it was all men playing. So, I started playing, then all of a sudden, I started getting a few hits off of some of these men, and I'm thinking . . . "Okay, I'm starting to come around a little bit." I start realizing because now all of a sudden in basketball, when we'd play intramurals and stuff, now I'm able to go out and shoot legitimate jump shots and I can jump pretty good and get up close to the rim, and we did a layup drill one night, we were just screwing around, I went up and dunked one, and the guys went (expression of amazement) and I went "I don't know." It's just, "Something is going on here, and I ain't figured it out yet (laughing)." You could tell everything was just starting to mature, and some friends dared me to go to a tryout camp; that's how it got started. Some friends down in Somerset, they woke me up and said, "Come on, we're going to try out for the Reds," that's how I went. They dared me because I would never have thought of playing pro ball. I was looking to go play three years of basketball in college. I had a scholarship offer to go with a guy named Doug Hines down in Tennessee, and I was going to be a point guard for them.

(University of Tennessee?) No. I wish. It was going to be a little school called Bethel College in Tennessee. Doug Hines was the coach.

I actually went down, and he had me scrimmage with the guys one day. Here I am, I scrimmage against two of their senior guards that were really quick and really good. Held my own pretty good and they had a pretty good team, they were like 6'8", 6'9". They were a big team for a small school. So, I had committed verbally, and then I went to the tryout camp, and I remember calling Coach Hines, "I got good news and bad news." "Well, what's the bad news?" "Coach, I'm not coming." "Really, what's going on?" "Well, we just signed a big contract for $2500 with the Reds." And I told him I'd been to the tryout; he knew I was going to the tryout camps, and there was nobody that could've been happier. And he used to come while I was playing in the big leagues and watch me play.

FERGIE JENKINS

Bantam and Midget baseball, and the next year I turned 17; I was playing senior ball with guys who were 24-25 years old and getting them out! So, I knew I had something (laughing), and a lot of scouts started showing up at my house, and at 17 years old, Cleveland, Pittsburgh, Philly, just a bunch of scouts were showing up; Detroit. Lou Dinunzio was his name because Joe Entevito was the Globetrotter marketing guy. But this guy showed up at my house, wanted to know, "Did I really think that I could become a professional athlete," he wanted to sign me as a First Baseman.

I said, "Well, I'm only 17". I said, "I can't sign until I graduate at 18". I went to an all-boys tech school. I was a tech student. So, to make a long story short, the Phillies worked with me the most; I signed with them right out of high school when I graduated.

Yeah, they basically helped me learn the art of pitching. I knew nothing about pitching (laughing), pick the ball up, and throw it hard. Gene Dziadura, who was a shortstop at the time, taught me a windup, and as I said, the ball just seemed to jump out of my hand. So, I was fortunate that some good things were happening. I signed with them in July and went to Miami for six weeks and won some ball games, and I just kind of proved to the organization that I was capable of pitching.

WILLIE BLAIR

That's a tough question because even when I was young, that was my dream. I wanted to play professional baseball, and I told my parents when I was younger that I wanted to get a college scholarship, and then I'm going to play pro ball, and fortunately, it happened. It don't always happen, and I know that. When I was a junior in high school, and I was out there, and I was watching the Paintsville Yankees, and I'm like, "I can throw that hard," I can throw as hard as that guy when I was only 16-years-old. That's when I realized that I wasn't too far behind those guys, and I felt like my breaking ball was just as good as theirs, and I wasn't cocky; it was just in my mind like I think I could pitch with those guys.

CHARLIE LOYD

Well, I always thought I could; even when I was in high school, I knew I could. But when I saw guys playing pro ball that I wasn't too impressed with and then when I was at Kentucky I had super years up there in the SEC and that SEC is the best league in the country, so I knew if I could do well there, I could play anywhere.

17.

SCOUTING & RECRUITMENT

BOOG POWELL

I was 17 when I signed, I started seeing some scouts when I was about in the 10th grade, and I was still in Lakeland, Florida.

Then our family moved to Key West my next year, and I finished my junior and senior years in Key West Florida, and I had a couple of pretty good years in high school, and every major league franchise was beating on my door constantly, I mean all of them were there.

We went to the state tournament in 1959 in Fort Pierce, and I think I had come off a year I hit .460 that year and had a slugging percentage of 1.200%, something like that, the numbers were just ridiculous, and everybody was there, I mean every club was represented, and they were all just waiting on me to do something really good . . . and I was a bust. I went 1 for 13 in the state tournament, we won in our division, we won the state tournament, we got knocked out oddly enough by Lakeland in the last game, but they were 3A, and we were a 1A school down in Key West, we only graduated like 80 guys out of the senior class.

After the dust cleared, there were three teams left, St Louis and Baltimore, and the Yankees, all the other teams were there, and none of them even wanted to look at me; none even wanted to talk. The Dodgers were really hot after me, the Milwaukee Braves were, I thought for sure that I was going to go with the Braves and in the end, it was . . . the Orioles had a scout named, Freddy "Boot Nose" Hofmann and Freddy "Bootnose" caught Babe Ruth, and he was with him in Boston, and then he went to the Yankees with him, and he was quite a character, and he was there, and St Louis was there, and St. Louis came in and offered me $20,000, and the Orioles came in shortly after that and offered me $25,000 then I was waiting for somebody to come back and let's get on with this bidding you know (laughing), the Yankees came in, oh the Yankees were there too, the Yankees said "Casey Stengel wants to see you in Yankee Stadium," I said "Well, I'm signing tonight! If Mr. Stengel wants to see me, he'll have to sign me."

That was it, so . . . you know a lot of times I wish I wouldn't have rushed right into it, but I was so . . . after we lost the state tournament, I was a little depressed and down, and I was ready to go; I mean, I thought I was ready to go. I signed with Baltimore, and two days later, I was on a plane to Bluefield, West Virginia; that's their Rookie League. That's below D, and that's like the end of the world. We had quite the team down there; we had all the kids they'd just signed, the Orioles signed that year, Dean Chance, a kid named Arne Thorsland, and Bobby Saverine. In the end, I think there was seven of us out of that signing that made it to the big leagues. Of course, Dean Chance won a Cy Young.

I walked into Bluefield that first day and took batting practice against, I think, Thorsland that first day and I said, "What have I gotten myself into." I made a terrible mistake; I can never play here. I can't do this. I mean, it was just because . . . everybody was the best you ever saw, you know in high school you might see one kid the whole year that looked even anything like these guys, and everyone were like the best I ever saw, and I said, "Damn, what did I do?"

PHIL ROOF

Well, there was a lot of pressure because there was always four or five or six scouts there every game, especially my junior and senior year. There was sometimes eight or nine or ten there, and some big-name scouts were there and of course Mother and Daddy, they had chains on me to keep me in line and not let me go out because you don't want to get injured, don't want to get hurt because it was obvious that I was gonna get signed by somebody and there was a relief once it happened, it was a relief for

Mom and Dad and myself. We probably could have got more money had we held our ground and took a trip to Detroit because the Detroit scout, he said: "I'd give you $35 now, been authorized to give you $35 if you will go up and work out with the big club I can probably get you $50,000." Well, once we got all our bids in and offers in we met with Wid Mathews and Dick Keely and he offered $35,000, well Dad said: "Son, we got to take that," so we did, and I don't regret it, don't regret it at all.

Wid Mathews was a special assignment scout for John McCall, who at that time was the general manager, and Wid was the special assignment scout, and if they had difficulty signing people, he would go in and negotiate that deal. He's kinda a pressure guy. Come in and close the deal.

When Hawk came on, Hawk was a great hitter in high school and Legion, and that's why he got that $120,000 or whatever. He got a lot of money, and of course, when I came on two years later, I never hit what Hawk hit; I hit good but not what he hit. They had backed off giving big bonuses at that time because they had to keep you in the big leagues, and you see Hawk stayed up there for a year or two.

HAWK TAYLOR

Well, a good friend of ours, who also knew Phil and his family, played big league baseball and is from my hometown of Metropolis, Illinois. He kinda made it a point where baseball received a little recognition here. We always had some scouts in the area, and they would hold scouting camps and tryout camps, so we were exposed to some pretty good baseball back then.

That was before they had the; what they now call the draft, they didn't have the draft back then. Probably my senior year in 1957, I had 14 of the 16 teams had scouts in the stands; I mean, the stands were full of scouts.

Well, when it came down to deciding because there was so much activity going on, the Cardinals had a rule that if you're going to be considered for a bonus contract, you had to go up to St. Louis for a tryout. I said, "Well, you know, you're just as able as anybody else to see me play while I'm down here playing for all these other teams here," so they weren't in the last go around. There was probably eight or nine that were around bout the time I graduated, and then that dwindled down to three or four as the money kept going higher, less and less teams stayed involved. It came down to who was going to spend the most money. Cubs, Braves, and Philadelphia were the ones.

Yeah, it was a bidding process. In fact, somehow or the other, I don't know, it doesn't sound like my dad but, we'd promised the Dodgers, who were the Brooklyn Dodgers at that time, the last shot but it was 4:30 in the morning when we'd been talking all night with Milwaukee and a few other clubs, "Hey, can't do this anymore, gonna have to shut it off, this is it," but then I found out many years later that dad had made this promise to the Dodgers. They were waiting over at a motel in Paducah Kentucky with a hunk more money than what the Braves were offering (laughing).

Yeah, they had that bonus rule. In fact, that was the only year they had it, no may have been a couple of years, but they did away with it as soon as it was over; it was a stupid rule. If you received a bonus over $4,000, you had to become a member of the 25-man roster, and so that was supposedly to cut down on big-league clubs signing these young guys; all it did was hurt guys like me. I should have been playing in the minor leagues.

Well, now you'd have to go back here and put it in perspective. Now I had an uncle that played big-league baseball, had another uncle who played so I'd been too big league ballparks, I'd been in the dressing rooms, I'd been exposed to all that, and remember before I signed the contract I was in Wrigley Field wearing the uniform and all that so when it came time to sign with them that wasn't that big a deal (laughing). I mean as strange as it may seem, but it wasn't that big a deal.

I just wish the circumstances were different . . . were that I didn't become a hostage rather than being able to do what most other players do, just go out, sign your contract, start playing baseball. Politics were just too big in the issue then, and I got hurt by it.

(Would it have been more beneficial for you, as a baseball player, to have not been a bonus baby, to be able to go into the minor leagues?)

That's kind of a double-edged sword right there. Let me put it this way. Had things been the same and I'd signed a contract with the Chicago Cubs, I'd been very happy. I had a feeling I would have played a bunch with the Chicago Cubs. It was just the Milwaukee Braves had three established catchers and my friend, Wid Mathews, although well-intentioned, was wanting to take care of the home town boy and all that, did not see things all way, he actually ended up hurting probably more than he helped me on that because I never did get squared away in the Milwaukee Brave organization.

JIM HICKMAN

Never, never saw one scout that came to any of our games. I just went to a couple of tryout camps, but as far as seeing scouts at our games, none. We didn't play many games either, we'd play eight or ten games a year, and that was about it. That was high school, and we had an American Legion team.

(Did you play a lot in the summer?) That didn't go over to well because a lot of the kids get to summer vacation, and they didn't want to spend it playing ball, so we didn't really play a lot of baseball.

Well, the guy that signed me had relatives that lived in Ripley, where I went to high school, and he was told about me, and honestly, I can't remember him coming to any of our games. I'm sure he was there a time or two that maybe I didn't know anything about, but no, it wasn't a lot of scouts there.

I wasn't contacted by a Milwaukee Brave scout until I went to college. I went down to Ole Miss, and he was connected with them in some way; he knew the coach down there, and in fact, he got me a job that summer before I went to Ole Miss down in South Carolina. I went down there and played baseball in a semi-pro league down there, Mullens, South Carolina. It was just a semi-pro league, and I worked down there in the tobacco warehouse.

(So, the scout, Sam Allen got you a job at the tobacco warehouse?) Well, he just got me a job playing ball, and when we got down there, we found out we had to work, it wasn't too much fun (laughing). We had to get up at 6:00 in the morning and go to work, and we unloaded the trucks that would come in. Then in the afternoon, we'd . . . I was the guy that took the papers from the auctioneer and run them back to the office. The afternoon wasn't so bad, but the morning was when it was bad, then we'd play that night.

That was one of the toughest jobs I ever had, that tobacco warehouse. They'd bring that tobacco on those old long sticks. You know they'd hang it over them sticks. Our job was that the sticks were long enough so one guy would get the stick and turn it and then like I'd be standing there to unload it, I'd have to run my arm up in there between the leaves, where the tobacco was and then pick it up off that stick and lay it on the trays or whatever it was, and then once I get that half off the stick he'd turn the stick around, and I'd run my arm back up in there and get the other half and put it on there, and all this was in about a 100-degree heat. Those old warehouses in South Carolina in August, man that was awful, and the worst part about it, you'd have to wear a long sleeve shirt or that stuff would just wear your arms out. We unloaded trucks all morning, and then we'd go play that night.

(And after playing semi-pro in South Carolina, you went back to Ole Miss to play basketball?) No, a football scholarship. When I went down there, back then, I guess it's the same way now, the scholarships are limited, and I signed a football scholarship before I went to play baseball that summer and when I came back the scouts that I knew, even Sam Allen said, "Well, you know, playing football you could get hurt." Didn't take much to talk me out of it. So I went down there; I told them, "Well, I just don't want to play football," and they said, "Well, we can't give you a full baseball scholarship; is there anything else you could do?" I said, "Well, I played a little basketball in high school." They said, "Well, if you play basketball and baseball, we'll give you a scholarship or just let this one go ahead" because see they had lost that scholarship for football. They couldn't sign anybody else for that scholarship. So that's the way that came about.

Well, yeah, and St. Louis was really the team that I had more or less made my mind up that I was going to sign with. And the guy, Sam Allen, he tried to get me to sign with Milwaukee. I was just a Cardinal fan and Buddy Lewis, the Cardinal scout; he lived in Memphis, and he had relatives that lived here.

BILL GREASON

They were following me, and when I came out of service, a big-league scout saw me, and I signed with the Oklahoma City Indians. Second black in that league to break the color ban and Dave Hoskins was with Dallas, and Oklahoma City signed me.

Oklahoma City got me; I don't know whether they bought me from the Negro League team I was playing on or what, but I started with them in the middle of 1952. I won 9 and lost 1, had a 2.43 ERA. The Yankees and the Boston Red Sox offered $100,000 cash and players for me, and the owner said: "Next year I can get more than that." He got greedy!!!

The next spring training we were down in Galveston, Texas, we were right by the seashore, didn't have showers or nothing, we had to drive about 10 or 12 miles to a park where we were training and sweating. We'd come back, and then you cool off, and I caught a little cold in my arm, didn't get out of there until about middle of May, and finally, he sold me for $25,000 and players to the Cardinals. I didn't mind; I didn't worry about it. We lived in separate places, we couldn't even eat in the same places, couldn't stay in the same place, same thing when I went to St Louis, it was strange up there, but I didn't mind, I just wanted to represent, first of all, the Lord, then my family and then whoever I was playing for. I never took that stuff to heart; whether you liked me or not, it didn't matter. I knew who I was and what my purpose was. I just stayed with it.

LOIS YOUNGEN

During the summer before my senior year in high school, I went to visit a cousin, a married cousin that lived in Fort Wayne, Indiana, which was home of the Fort Wayne Daisies. The whole family went out for this visit, no particular reason other than we probably were invited to come. So they asked me what I'd like to—we stayed a couple of days, I think, and they asked me if I'd like to go see the Fort Wayne Daisies play because they knew that I played ball. And so, I said, "Well, yes." And so, the whole family, kit & caboodle went. They had four kids; they only had two at that time; they had two more later, but anyway, we all went to the Daisie's game and about the seventh inning, when we had the seventh-inning stretch, I turned to my cousin and said, "You know, I can do that (laughing). And this is a 16-year old talking here like I could play like that. Not too much chutzpah or hubris there (laughing). Anyway, the next morning, I had the tryout with the Fort Wayne Daisies.

Well, my cousin called; obviously, I don't know how he managed to do it all so fast, but the next morning, I had this tryout at the same field where I saw the game. And Max Carey was the manager of the Daisies that year, and he is a Hall of Famer, a great base stealer himself and very instrumental in getting the league and keeping the league going and being involved with the All-American Girls Professional Baseball League. But anyway, he was the manager that year of the Daisies, and so he was there, and there were at least four Daisies. I had an hour and a half or two-hour tryout, and at the end of the tryout, Mr. Carey said to me, "Lois, we will be in touch. We'll let you know." So, we went back to Ohio, and I started my senior year in high school, and in January, I got a letter inviting me to spring training with the Fort Wayne Daisies.

So then came the process of getting myself out of three weeks of school in my senior year, which was no easy task in 1950/51. You just didn't get out of school for anything, no doctor's appointment, no dentist's appointment. I supposed if they called 911, it'd be okay (laughing). But kids just didn't get out of school. It just wasn't something that was done. Well, I finally got permission from everybody except this one teacher that I had for a business course. It was typing and shorthand, and she said only if I would send in my homework every three days to her. So I promised I'd do that and probably had to sign something, I don't remember, but she's not the type to take somebody's word for it, so I'm sure I had to sign something. So, I finally got permission to go.

And the spring training was in Alexandria, Virginia. So, I tooted off to Alexandria, Virginia, and we had spring training with—I don't know if it was the Racine Belles, but we had another team with us. There were two teams that trained together; that way, we had exhibition games against each other, and we traveled a bit down into North Carolina, and we played in Virginia, then we played in West Virginia and in Baltimore. We played there, and then we played in Griffith Stadium in Washington, D.C., where the Senators played, and I had my favorite photograph . . . one of my favorite baseball photographs of all time taken there. Max Carey took another rookie and myself to Griffith Stadium, and we had our picture taken with Clark Griffith, one of the grand old men of baseball, and the stadium was named after him. He and Connie Mack were two of the grand old men, and he must have been in his 80s then, and he wasn't very tall. I'm sure he shrunk because I have (laughing). Anyway, he's in the picture and then next to him, I'm standing next to Clark Griffith, and then there's this girl who was a rookie. She never made the team. So, I have no idea who she is and no one else that I know that I showed the picture to has any idea who she is.

But anyway, the next person is Max Carey. And there's the four of us, and we're all holding this baseball bat long ways . . . horizontally, so we've all got a hold of the bat. And I'm looking into Clark Griffith's eyes, and everybody else was looking down the bat at him. So, it is absolutely my most favorite photo of all time.

And I remember being in Griffith Stadium. I'm not sure if we played one or two games or if one got rained out, but we were there because I remember going up to home plate, and I stood on the right side because I'm a righty, and I said, "Gee, Joe DiMaggio stood here." And then I looked around on the other side of the plate, and I said, "Ted Williams stood here (laughing)." So, I just had a good time. As I said, I had no idea what the score was, we had rainy weather, and I'm not sure whether we really played in Griffith Stadium or not to be honest with you. I'd have to do my homework and go back and look and see if I have any notes or a clipping or something that said we actually played there. But I know we at least got through our infield practice. We might've gotten rained out, but we got through our infield practice anyway. So, then we came back by train, the teams and I got back home to Leroy, Ohio, which is now Westfield Center in time to go to the senior prom and my graduation ceremony. And then I became a Fort Wayne Daisy, and I did it all in three weeks. I got all that in three weeks. I got a contract, and I got to go be a Daisy, and I got to graduate, and I got to go to my senior prom.

So anyway, that's how I became a Fort Wayne Daisy. And I got to Fort Wayne and I—that first year, my roommate was a fellow rookie by the name of Pat Scott, and she was a pitcher, and I was a catcher. And I spent most of that first year sitting on the bench because we had plenty of catchers and plenty of players and I got to catch maybe the last inning or the last two innings depending on what the score was.

KATIE HORSTMAN

Mary Froning, who also played in the AAGPBL, she went the same year that I did. She went to Kenosha, Wisconsin, and I didn't even know it because she already graduated, and I just got through with my sophomore year. A scout came to St. Henry, Ohio, where we played, and he talked to the manager. The scout was in the insurance business, and so, that's why he was down there talking to him. He asked who I was; he says, "I think that girl from Minster could play professional baseball." And so, no one knew what he was talking about (laughing). Fort Wayne was only 65 miles away, and we had no idea because we only got one paper; that was the Minster paper.

Well, they talked to me right after, and he said he was interested in taking me to Fort Wayne, and so I talked to him, and he says, "Do you think you would want to go" and I said, "Of course." And he says, "Well, I would have to have your parent's permission." Well, my dad died when I was 14, and my dad and I were very, very close, and I say, "Oh, nobody's going to stop me from playing, not even those cows! I don't care; they'll have to sell them (laughing)."

Anyways, Mr. Bernard took me to Fort Wayne that next week because it was the first of May, and they just came back from spring training, so they were still a whole week from the season, and they would just have warm-ups in their hometown. He took me, and that's when I tried out, and Max Carey was the manager then, he's also in the Hall of Fame, and so he says "Yes," but don't you have to finish your schooling and I said, "Yeah, I'd better go back and find out." So school was out like May 20th, and so I said: "Yeah, I'll be out in 2 weeks." So anyway, I came back, and the superintendent was super at the time, and so he let me go a week early because he loved baseball himself, and he thought it was a good deal. So I went the week after, and they signed me right away and boy, here I was milking cows for free and babysitting for $2 a night and then when they started me out with $50 a week, well, I thought I was the richest person on earth!

JIM KAAT

The big school then for baseball was Western Michigan College; now it's Western Michigan University. They had a coach named Charlie Maher, and he was known as a kind of legendary coach, so that was sort of the place unless you went to the University of Michigan or Michigan State. Michigan State was just a college then. I thought maybe going to Western Michigan would be good, and then Hope College, they didn't give out scholarships, but they would get you a summer job to help pay your tuition. None of my siblings went to college, so the deal was if I wanted to go to school, I was going to have to earn the money to pay for it myself. I think my tuition for college my first year was about $700. So, these two Hope College Alumni owned the laundry in Holland, Michigan; Modern Laundry, and they gave me a job. I was lifting these big bags of sheets and linens from the local resorts. Zeeland and Holland is right off of Lake Michigan, so it is a pretty popular spot in the summer. So, they kind of talked me into, along with my dad . . . at Hope College, you know you're going to pitch, goin' to Western Michigan, who knows? So, I kind of bought into that and took the summer job and went to Hope College.

Well, the way it worked, I did spend a little . . . Well, I have a Twitter account, and I just did a tweet a couple of weeks ago, they were recognizing some scouts, and I did a tweet on my scout Dick Weincek, who is in the Scout's Hall of Fame. But Dick lived in Kalamazoo, Michigan, and I think he signed over 72 players that went to the big leagues, which is still, I think, an all-time high. I think he signed . . . Canseco was one of them. He had a partial influence in signing them. Often times several scouts might look at you play, but he was at . . . I was pitching against Kalamazoo College, and they had a left-hand pitcher that had promise; I don't even know his name, but Dick went there to see that pitcher, and I had a good game, which I did in all my games. I think I pitched six games; we played 12 games, six doubleheaders; my roommate pitched six, and I pitched six. I was 6 and 0. I think I gave up one run in all six games. I was pitching against Kalamazoo College that day and had a good game, and he said: "Wow, I better go see that kid again." So the next week, I was pitching against Alma College, and on our way home, we traveled in station wagons; I happened to be in the wagon that the coach was driving, and he said, "Oh, I understand that there was a scout at the game today. I don't know who he was looking at." I didn't know if he was pulling my leg (laughing) or what he was doing. But I thought to myself, "Boy, I hope he was looking at me." And then that next week my dad got a call from Dick Weincek and invited me; I think it might have been our last game of the season or one of the last games of the season, he said: "Chicago, where the Washington Senators are playing, go down there for a tryout."

(You signed for less than $4,000, so you wouldn't be classified as a Bonus Baby?) Yeah, that was totally my dad. I had really no kind of concept of what kind of money they were paying players. I just knew I wanted to play professional baseball. So, my dad really followed the history of the game and prior to . . . I believe they changed the rule the next year, but prior to 1958 for about a 10-year period there, teams were signing players; they called them Bonus Babies. They were giving them anywhere from $30,000 or $60,000, or there might have been one or two that got as much as $100,000, but part of the deal was that you were placed on the major league roster for two years; you took up a roster spot. And they did that to discourage the wealthier teams from signing all of the players because for everyone you signed for more than $4,000 . . . I think you were only allowed two and they had to be on the major league roster, and my dad followed these players, and there are very few; it took Sandy Koufax several years; it took my friend Harmon Killebrew several years after their

two year time in the big leagues, they went back to the minors, and it really took them a while to get their career started, to get it on track and in a lot of cases they never made it. And the rule was if you got more than four thousand, you had to do that, but you could get a $4,000 bonus package and go to the minor leagues. I think mine was a $3,200 bonus; I got $300 a month for the two-month season, and I believe I got $200 for incidental expenses. So when Washington offered me that, a scout from Grand Rapids named Pete Milito was scouting for the White Sox, he called my dad and said "I understand your son is going to sign," and he said, "Yeah I think we're going to sign with Washington, $4,000 go to Superior, Nebraska". Pete said, "I think I can get him twenty-five thousand from the White Sox because I think he'll be in the big leagues in a couple of years." And I don't know that this is going on. My dad told me that later and I actually confirmed it when I went into the Grand Rapids Hall of Fame years ago. I talked to Pete Milito and confirmed the story, but my dad said, "No, we're going to take the four and go to the minor leagues," and Washington only had three left-hand pitchers in their organization. Left-handers were pretty rare back then, and so it was a combination of being in an organization where I had a chance to move up rapidly if I did well, and he said: "We'll go to the minor leagues and learn how to play the game the right way." So that was very wise advice. It sure wouldn't happen today (laughing). But it was very helpful to me. Because, you know, I went down there and I got my brains beaten in a few times (laughing) which is kind of new when you come out of a small town, and you're winning about every game you pitch and them all of a sudden you're getting knocked around and you gotta say, "Well am I in over my head or what?" But you know it helped me kind of grow from Class D ball right up through the system, and I actually did get called up to the big leagues in two years, I went back to the minors briefly in 1960, but that was a very wise decision because who knows if I would have ever made it if I took the money upfront.

Yeah, he was the perfect dad, and he followed that (MLB's Bonus Baby Rule) so closely, to know that there were a lot of them like Hawk Taylor. I remember when we had a league called the Instructional League that you went to for about six weeks in the Fall down in Florida and all the Braves guys like Hawk Taylor, they had a pitcher named Brubaker; they had Walter Hriniak; who became an outstanding hitting instructor, and they were all driving around in these sharp Camaros and red sports cars (laughing), and we're driving our old beat up 1954 Mustang.

LOU PINIELLA

Probably when I started playing American Legion ball, and that was our first exposure to scouts, quite a few scouts that came to the game. I was, well, let's see; I was born in 1943. I was probably 15 to 16-years-old.

In high school, scouts would come before the ball games, talk to you and find out your interest, "Do you want to play baseball? Do you want to go to college? Do you want to play pro ball?" They sort of read you a little bit, and it'd give them an idea if you want to play professional baseball, "We could sign you to a contract, but how much money would you be interested signing for?" So, they had sort of read you a little bit. Out of high school, I could have signed for a lot more money than I originally signed for, and the reason being is they wanted to keep you from going to college.

Stay close! Yeah, I really did. I had opportunities to go to different colleges for both basketball and baseball, and I decided . . . first of all, I knew that I was going to try to play pro baseball; I knew that before I decided on a college. Everything was pretty well arranged to go to Auburn University, but the University of Tampa, my hometown, made me an offer. I could play baseball, I could play basketball as a freshman, and the same scouts could watch me play, and there was a kind of newness in the whole thing of college life. I wanted to sign a pro contract outta high school, and my parents wouldn't let me; they wanted me to go to college. So I went to school for a year, and when I took my freshmen exams, I came home, and there are a few scouts sitting in the driveway, and they asked, "Do you want to play pro ball?" I said, "If you can convince my parents (laughing), you know." And finally, I signed with Cleveland, Spud Chandler, a scout from Cleveland was living in St. Petersburg signed me, and I went on to Selma, Alabama, the old Florida/Alabama league. That was the last year of existence in the league.

They figured once you go to college, you go there for four years, and they'd rather have you in their organization, but it worked out fine. I had a long career and really, in pro ball I had to learn how to hit. I was a strict pull hitter that hit a fastball really, really well, had trouble with the breaking ball and I had to learn a lot of things, to stay inside the ball and basically when I really learned to hit I became more of the right/center field, left/center field hitter.

LOU WHITAKER

I had scouts probably follow me from at least 15, just looking and following. You didn't get that many; one here, one there, but by my senior year, I used to have maybe five or six scouts from different teams. I would have some; what I learned later, they were called bird dogs, something like scouts. They scouted, but they passed the information through different organizations. So it wasn't like it was one team, but one particular scout, he would gather information and just put it out on the wire, and I think that was where I was pretty much being seen, just not here. My senior year though I had the Baltimore Orioles and Cincinnati Reds, they were the two teams—wow unbelievable. And they were the two teams that was interested in me. But Cincinnati Reds they wanted to draft me.

I was trying to get more money in the signing bonus. All the people in my neighborhood that had a little influence and in their conversations was telling me what to expect and this and that and getting released and all of that type of stuff. But they were telling me, "What you need to do is ask for about $45,000," or something like that. The man who come to sign me; when I asked him for $45K . . . he had a cigar in his mouth, and he almost choked on it when I asked for that amount of money (laughing).

But I said, "Well, I'm not going to sign; I'll go to college or whatever." And I really did want to go to college, but I played a few more games in Connie Mack, and Mr. Lajoie called me . . . he wanted me to sign, so we talked about a few things, and I eventually signed. They ended up giving me about $11,000. I told 'em, "I'll sign for $10,000 but give my mother $1,000, and I'll sign."

Now my baseball team coaches; they were trying to get me to stay and play with the city team. But again, that's on me to make a decision. Do you stay and play with your friends, or do you take an opportunity and try to go further? You know what I mean?

So, I knew what I wanted to do, and it's a decision . . . you get an opportunity once, and you've got to make the best out of it. If I went to school, who knows, you got a junior who's played third base that's already on the team, and he's doing good or has done good for years and now I sign, where you going to put me? On the bench, because I'm a freshman.

STEVE BLASS

The guy that signed me was a guy by the name of Bob Whalen. We were all free agents because the draft hadn't come into effect yet. I graduated in 1960, and the draft started in 1965; I think with Rick Monday. The scouts were always around because of the reputation of our high school having all these pitchers. Bob Whalen came to watch me, and I pitched in a game that . . . we were in Class B in Connecticut and we constantly played against teams in Class A because we were good and I pitched a game against Torrington High School, and there were 15 scouts there including Bob Whalen and I walked a batter for every scout there (laughing), and I also struck out a batter for every scout, but at the end of the game the only scout left sitting there was Bob Whalen and that had always impressed me. He would come down and work with me at our high school field and what he tried to do was give me a better follow-through, and he said . . . he was a heavy smoker and he'd put a pack of cigarettes out in the front part of the mound, and he said: "every ball you throw I want you to bring your arm down and pick up that pack of cigarettes." So that was a technique he used. I felt like he cared about me a lot, and here is the kicker; I was scouted by the Cleveland Indians.

And I wanted to sign so badly with them, and they offered me $2,500, and I could go to spring training the next year, but the Pirates came in and offered four grand, and I could go play right away. So, I signed with them.

WHITEY HERZOG

I remember when I got out of high school, I had three clubs come talk to me the day after I graduated. The first one that came to see me was the Cubs scout. And he said, "Don't sign with anybody, we'll better anybody's offer," that's what he said; I don't know what he was talking about, but he was probably talking about a thousand or fifteen hundred, and they wanted to sign me as an outfielder. Then the next day, or that same afternoon, the Yankee scout Lou MaGuola came and talked to me, my mother and dad. He told me that DiMaggio was getting old, and he's a center fielder . . . you know, he was a pretty good salesman (laughing) and of course I didn't know Mickey Mantle or Bill Virdon and all those great outfielders the Yankees had. And then the St. Louis Browns called me; Bill Dewitt was the owner, and the General Manager of the club and Jacque Fournier was their farm director and asked if me and my mother will come over on Monday after the Friday when I graduated. So, Monday morning, my mom and I went over to Sportsman Park and talked to them. And I think Jacque Fournier was in East St. Louis when I pitched a no-hitter against Lincoln High School, a seven-inning no-hitter and struck-out all 21.

And they wanted to sign me as a pitcher. And here I am, a 17-year old kid, I wasn't 18 when I graduated from high school, wouldn't be 18 till November. And I said to Mr. Dewitt and Mr. Jacque Fournier, I said, "Now I know why you're in last place if you want to sign me as a pitcher (laughing)." I had an off day that day, I threw strikes, but I was just wild enough to be good (laughing), you understand what I mean, but I just didn't think I could; in those days I was just another wild young lefthander, and that was the favorite expression.

DOUG FLYNN

My dad knew a lot of scouts. He had played a year with Brooklyn Dodgers in the minor leagues. He knew the scouts, and he'd introduced me, so even as I started moving up the ladder, none of them never said anything, so I figured . . . well, I must not be any good. Quite frankly, I wasn't. I was real small. I actually went to college at 5'8" and 147 pounds, played basketball, and on the baseball team (at University of Kentucky). All during my freshman year, I didn't grow until after my freshman year, where I grew three inches and started maturing a little bit, so I was kind of a late bloomer in that respect.

After the first tryout camp, a scout came up to me and said: "We're kinda interested in you a little bit; can we see you again?" I went in a pair of shorts and a tank top, and he said, "Could you put a ball uniform on and come back?" and I went, "Yeah." He said, "You're not real serious about this, are you?" (Shrugged shoulders while laughing). So, I go to the next one in Frankfort, and I thought I looked really good. All you do is take a round of infield, and you get five swings.

(So, you thought . . . "I really look good in this uniform; I'm as good as in!")

Both and nobody said a word after it was over with, "Okay, thanks for coming." So then, I'm sitting at home, and I get another call about two weeks later. They say, "I want you to come to Riverfront. We're gonna have 90 guys from four states come up, and at the tryout camp, you get five swings, take a round of infield, and run the 60-yard dash." So, I did that, and when it was over, the scout came; his name was Chet Montgomery. He said, "I want to see you one more time." So, I'm thinking, "All right, I'm either so bad and funny they're videotaping me and showing it to people, laughing their butt off or something's there that's intriguing (laughing). So, then we came back to Lexington, he brought a couple of other guys with him. We tried out over at Southland Park, and he said: "What would it take for you to be a pro ballplayer?" And I said, "Coke and a hotdog, I don't know," and then I signed for $2500 (laughing).

And then that got me to spring training, that was 1971, got me to spring training in 1972, then I made it to the big leagues in 1975.

FERGIE JENKINS

Yeah, it made me work harder. I got invited to some other camps, I did one in Ann Arbor, one outside of Buffalo, and my hometown Chatham held a couple. The Phillies held a couple of camps, and the Tigers came up and had some instruction; there was like 25-30 young men from around the area, and they were evaluating how we ran, how we threw, that type of thing, what position we played. I always said, "I'm gonna pitch." I tried to open up some eyes, and I think I did in some respect. The Phillies were the only team that really had that big interest, and I ended up signing with them.

My bonus was $6,000 and a plane ticket! Yeah, back then, when scouts see talent, they would go overboard, and sometimes they wouldn't. My first salary, I made $400 a month playing Class D ball. Back then, it was quite the experience, and I got better as I played, and the money increased. It was kind of weird back then; they would be like you only got a $6,000 bonus? And I would say yeah, that is all they gave me.

WILLIE BLAIR

I mean, there was a couple of scouts that came to some games and talked to our coach, but at that time, I was probably 150 pounds soaking wet, and I think that they probably thought I needed to mature; I was really young and only 17 when I graduated. I was 17 for the whole first semester of college. I think everybody kinda' thought I should go to college. They told our coach, "Yeah, we like him, but he needs some time."

WILLIE HORTON

Well, I worked out with Boston. I worked out with the Yankees, and I'd worked out with Baltimore, but the Yankees kind of had me flying in and out of town. I met Yogi Berra when I was very young. Worked out with Cincinnati Reds, I met Frank Robinson and Vada Pinson, and that group in Cincinnati were young, but the chief scout of the Yankees, Mr. Patterson, he sent me a catcher's glove the week before I signed, that's the reason I thought I was going to sign with the Yankees.

I had been working out with the Yankees, and Boston, and all these other teams, and actually, I thought I was gonna sign with the Yankees because the head scout at the time, Mr. Patterson, just sent me a catcher's glove. I'd met Yogi Berra when I was about 14 years old. It was 1961 that Jake Wood, our first African American ballplayer came to the Tiger organization 12 years after Jackie Robinson. My dad let me skip school, and my buddies JP, Johnny Mac, and their parents. We saw Jake Wood play the eighth and the ninth. I asked Papa; I said, "Will I be going out of Detroit?" and he said, "Well, you know, I've decided . . . I talked to Judge Keith and your mom. The young man, Jake Wood, that we let you skip school to see play, maybe you should sign with the Tigers.

So, I remember my dad told me the day I signed, he grabbed my wrist, and he said, "Boozy, you got to make a commitment if you can't do that now, that your life belongs to the fans, and the responsibility of your job, do not sign." And I think I lived that, I made that commitment that day, and I lived my career through that, and things I did beyond the field, I lived that same kind of commitment.

CHARLIE LOYD

I played baseball at Paducah Junior College and then went to the University of Kentucky. I had some big baseball schools I could have gone to, but basically, I went to the University of Kentucky, so I could watch them play basketball (laughing). You know when I was at Kentucky I knew a lot of basketball players, I talked to Kevin Grevey and Kyle Macy and guys like that and they'd tell you they liked baseball better than they did basketball but they just wasn't as good at it.

In the summertime, when I was going to school at Kentucky, I'd spend a lot of summers throwin' batting practice for big league teams for a couple of days. I'd go to St Louis, I'd go up there, and then I'd come home, and I'd go to Chicago with the White Sox and throw batting practice a couple of days, and then I'd go to Cubs, and I'd throw batting practice over there a couple of days. That's the way I spent my summers . . . in fact, when the Yankees scouted me, I was throwing for the White Sox. At the time, the Yankees were in town, and I'd never talked to anybody from the Yankees. I'd talked to the Cardinals and the White Sox, and the Cubs and different players and back then they didn't draft you, wasn't a draft, you just signed with whoever gave you the most money and back then there wasn't but 16 teams. That's why they've diluted; I see guys pitching the big leagues now that couldn't pitch in the SEC (laughing). I mean, they've diluted that talent so much. You just played with whoever gave you the most money. I would just listen to them. Listen to them and decide who I wanted to play with. Now I signed with the Yankees. I figured I got a better chance of getting a World Series share with them than I would with the White Sox but didn't do either (laughing).

(How did you end up pitching batting practice in the summer?) The scouts would call me up and wanted to know if I would come to Chicago in the summertime and throw up there and let the general manager and people see me. That's when I was throwing for the White Sox, and the Yankees saw me up there, well, I got home and couldn't get together with the White Sox, and the guy that signed me had never seen me play, but the guy in Chicago that saw me was a guy named Lou MaGuola, and he called the scout in Lexington who then called me and offered me some money and wanted to know if I could come to Lexington and sign, so I drove to Lexington and signed with them.

You know it was something that I always wanted to do. And they sent me to Greensboro, the first year I played in the Carolina League, which was a super league to play in and I remember going down to Greensboro, flying in there and staying at the old Henry Hotel, I think the team was on the road, and I had to wait a couple of days for them to get back so I was reading the paper to see how these guys were doing and I was wondering if I was gonna be able to fit in or play at that level because I'd just gotten out of the University of Kentucky and hadn't really pitched any in two or three months so I was just kinda apprehensive about meeting all those new guys I didn't know and if I was going to fit in talent-wise but I didn't have any problems.

18.

WISDOM FROM THE DIAMOND

BOOG POWELL

And a lot of just fabulous memories and as a kid growing up we didn't have TV, I don't' think we had TV until about 1955 so when I was growing up on the way home from junior high and stuff we'd stop in front of an appliance store, they had a big overhang out there, and we'd sit there and watch TV, wasn't a big deal. So, I'd just sit out there and watch the games for a little while, but I wasn't obsessed with it; I wanted to do it.

PHIL ROOF

Daddy never pushed much; he never said much; he was just in the crowd and pleased that his sons were able to complete, but as far as knowing anything about the game, he didn't. He just tried to tell us to keep our cool and not lose your cool at a bad call or a strikeout, and we were all pretty good about that. And he got a lot of compliments from fans, "enjoyed watching your son play," he liked those comments.

HAWK TAYLOR

You know, it has all blended in together. The only fair way to answer is I enjoyed it all. All one big part of me and I can't take out any one part of it; it was all one nice time. Now some of the caliber of baseball was a little more advanced than another, but it all was part of growing up, so I enjoyed it all. Man, I'd go through that again in a minute.

JIM HICKMAN

Yeah, that's all you can do is be yourself, and my mom always said that, and every time I'd go out to play baseball, "You just gotta be yourself because you can't be somebody else, just gotta do what you do."

BILL GREASON

My mom taught me, "Son, know who you are. Don't be judged by the color of your skin. But try to develop a character that's worth something, and no matter what people call you, know who you are. First of all, you're God's child, and then you're my son, and you're somebody. You're the only person that God put his hand on when he made man, he took his hand and formed him and everything else he said let there be".

LOIS YOUNGEN

And they got bullied into asking me to quit—but eventually, somebody must have explained to them that it was more important to win with a girl than to lose without one (laughing).

KATIE HORSTMAN

That was always my dream. Every night I would go to bed, I'd pray that there was someplace where they either had girl's baseball or basketball or football. I didn't care; any of the three, I loved them all. I was still grieving for my dad, dying overnight, and a year later, here I am playing baseball. And he knew I loved baseball and I swear it was a miracle.

JIM KAAT

I wish that I had asked my dad more questions about life in general; I so wish that I would have fought to have just sat down with my dad and just say, what was it like during WWI.

LOU PINIELLA

People kept playing into their late 30's, early 40's . . . They kept playing baseball. And I remember going to the skating park, Sundays were special, and they had the doubleheader, four teams played, and I still remember those days. I remember loving to buy snow cones down underneath the stands

I remember those days; it was fun. We played a lot. I mean, we get up in the morning, go to the playground, and played until it got nightfall.

JIM ZAPP

We would put a little bat together, and you'll tape a ball together, stuff like that, and we would play in the open field at St. Cecilia. I had to go all the way around to the Southside to play on an organized team and the ballplayers in my neighborhood; they went all the way to South Nashville.

LOU WHITAKER

Well, I just loved to be outdoors playing and guys at the ballpark; they kept the fields in very good condition, and when they cut that grass, it just smelled soooo good!!! (laughing).

STEVE BLASS

Every morning of school vacation, of summer, the first thing I would do when I got out of bed, I would run over to the window to see if the weather was gonna be good enough for me to play ball. That was the first thing that I did and found out if I could play ball.

When I speak now, I tell kids that goals change. Don't make your goals unattainable; make then attainable because you are going to adjust them upwards. I just would hope that all boys would have that Joy I had with the game of baseball, that simple word. Whenever I sign an autograph, I write Joy. And I hope that as many kids could have that joy.

WHITEY HERZOG

Come summertime; it was baseball every day. We played baseball every day from 8:00 in the morning till our mothers came up to the schoolyard and said it's time to go home and eat.

DOUG FLYNN

I loved youth baseball. I mean, it's some of the best memories of my life.

I was always taught a great lesson about humility from my mom and dad, both of them. I mean, dad was a little cockier than mom, but he used to tell me, he said, "If you're any good people will know about it, you don't have to say anything about it.

FERGIE JENKINS

Yeah, for sure. There is always someone smarter than you and a little bit of knowledge; you just have to have an open ear. My dad used to tell me that all of the time: "Listen, son, listen (laughing)." But to make a long story short, it came easy, but I had to work at it. Nothing ever comes easy, but I had the talent; it was all God-given.

WILLIE BLAIR

As I started playing and making friends and all that kind of stuff, it became not only a thrill to compete but the camaraderie that you build with being part of a team, and that was pretty special.

WILLIE HORTON

When you're a kid, you just play the game, and you just enjoy what you're doing. I never put the game before fans and the people, and I learned that at a young age. You never put the game before fans because its people who make the game, to be able to smile, cheer, or boo you, whatever. That's what makes the game, and I learned that at a young age.

CHARLIE LOYD

I wouldn't trade my childhood for anybody. We had the biggest time. I've talked to some guys I've played with, and they said, "You know we grew up in the best of times. We could leave home in the morning, and our parents didn't have to worry about you; there wasn't any drugs or anything. If your parents were gone, your neighbors watched after you. It was really a good time to grow up.

19.

EXTRA INNINGS WITH THE PROS

BOOG POWELL

And it turned out that I won an MVP, but the Orioles, they gave up on Dean Chance in 1961, two years later when they had the expansion draft, and the California Angels were coming in we had another kid named Arne Thorsland, one of the best pitchers I ever saw. He was head and shoulders above Dean Chance, and the Angels ended up getting Chance in the draft; I hated to see it because Chance was a good pitcher, but anyway, that was pretty much the start of it. *(And that was the end of your youth career.)* Yeah . . . after that, there was no more giving away.

You know, sometimes I wish that I had a little bit better stats so that I could be considered for the Hall of Fame and that kind of stuff, but overall I was pretty happy with what I got. I've got about as much as I could get out of this body. And you had to play hurt. If you didn't play hurt back in those days, somebody else is going to have your job. Yeah, I had a broken finger when I was playing, and one time I had a broken wrist; those were just things that happened, and you learned to live with them, and that's the way it was back then.

Speaking of Jim Kaat, I got my first big league home run off of Jim Kaat, and then he hit me right in the neck the next time up. Right in the neck, and I didn't even move. I don't think I got another hit off him for two more years. The pitch that I hit for a home run . . . I kinda understood as to what he was saying. He said, "If I threw you something inside, you can hit it, but if I make a perfect pitch, you better leave it alone," that was what he was saying in effect. Hank Bauer came up to me one day, and he said, "You know you don't have a hit off him in over a year now, and you faced him like four games. You haven't had a hit in four games against him; do you want to play?" He said, "I will sit you out." I said, "You asking me?" he said, "Yeah," I said, "I do not want out of the lineup!" I said, "If you want to take me out of the lineup, you take me out; I won't be mad or anything, but if you ask me . . . I want in there." He said, "I was hoping you'd say that." So anyway, that was my thinking, and that was the way I felt towards baseball my whole career. There were probably some times that I probably would have hit 50 points higher if I'd paid some attention to him (laughing), but that just wasn't my makeup. I wanted to be out on the field, and even though I wasn't hitting, I was a pretty good fielder. I could field my position, and I helped the team defensively even if I wasn't hitting that day.

PHIL ROOF

Well, because a lot of guys just scribbled their names . . . I've got autographed balls, but not so many over there because the ones you can't read I've got them in a box, but Harmon Killebrew would always fuss at players who didn't sign their name legibly and I use to fuss because I was the caretaker of balls in Seattle for five years. Players would put a gospel verse on the balls; Psalms or whatever and you couldn't half read their name, and you couldn't half read their Psalm so I'd go to each one and I told them "If you're gonna put that message on there, let's make it legible so we can read it, so if your gonna send a message, it's gotta be clear enough so people can read it." So, they got better at it.

I spent four years in the minor leagues; I caught every day. I knew I was going to catch every day, and that was the biggest and best confidence builder you can have knowing that when you walk into the clubhouse, you don't have to look at that lineup card, you know your name is going to be on it. And then the manager would tell me, I had Jack Tighe for two years, and he said: "Your gonna spend ten years in the big leagues." Well, that seems like so far off that I was gonna get ten years in the big leagues and I went up there in 1960 for a month at the end of the season and 1962 I was up there for six weeks before they sent me down as a 20-year-old. And then I came back to stay in 1964, and there was some anxieties in 1962 and '63 before I went back in '64; played winter ball in Puerto Rico, and we had a good year. Won everything down there and then got beat in the final game of the playoff and was asked to come to the Dominican and played for Vern Benson. Vern Benson was the third base coach for the Cardinals, and I said, "No, I want to get home." Because I had been playing in the Instructional League then went to the Winter League in Puerto Rico and played there until about the 10th of January, and by the 15th of February, spring training opens so I come on home. I said, "I want to go home." I first agreed, then I called them back and told them no. Because once we got beat, that let down, I just told him I want to go home, and he understood.

On every team, there was always three or four or five Americans. In fact, on our team, we had Ted Savage, Tommie Aaron, Camilo Estevis, myself, Frank Krusters, Taylor Phillips. That's six. We probably had at least six to seven Americans, and the team would be 18 or 19. Jose Pagen was on my team. The day I made my major league appearance . . . that's Willie Mays up there hitting, and I'm catching. The day I made my major league appearance, he hit two home runs that day.

I got traded in 1964, I got traded to the American League, which was a benefit, and I spent the next 13 years in the American League.

Well, it was an honor. By the time I got there Del had been traded to the Giants and Ed Bailey had come to the Braves and then it was Joe Torre, Bailey and myself, and by that time Hawk had been traded to the New York Mets, and then they traded me to the Angels that fall, and I was a half year with the Angels and then with Cleveland, a half year and I ran into Alvin Dark. Alvin Dark was with the Braves in 1960, and I saw him on the elevator in Kansas City. And I said, "Alvin, what are you doing?" "He said, "Oh, I'm here scouting," I said, "Who for"? He said, "For the A's," and I said, "Oh," he said, "Can't talk about it." Two weeks after the season ended, he traded for me, and he's the one that gave me a chance to play. He's in Greenville, South Carolina. He'll probably be 88 years old, good man.

I know this, when Alvin Dark was the San Diego Padres manager, he hired me as a coach in 1978, he got fired because he wanted Ozzie Smith to be his opening day shortstop and he told me that winter in January, he said, "Phil, I got a kid that's going to be opening day shortstop." And I said, "What has he done?" "Well, he came out of college and only played four to five games, but Phil, he can catch every ball that comes his way." "What's he gonna hit?" "If he hits his weight, he will be lucky." I said, "What about Billy Almon?" Billy was runner up to the Rookie of the Year the year before, and he said, "Phil, Billy can't hold a light to this guy." So, we go into spring training, and he said: "I want you to hit him ground balls every day" and, of course, Ozzie's young and all.

We get about 15, 16 games into the spring training, and we're like 8 and 8, something like that, and Ozzie's doing a good job at shortstop. And Alvin comes to me after the game, and he said, "Phil," he said, "Keep your fingers crossed, there's a chance I may get fired tonight." I said, "Over Ozzie?" and he said, "Yeah." I said, "What's the deal," he said, "Gaylord Perry, Randy Jones, Bob Owchinko, Rollie Fingers." All those guys loved Billy Almond because he come and done a good job as a rookie the year before, and he said: "I think I got Ballard Smith on my side, but they want me to send Ozzie down and then put Billy Almon back at shortstop." I told Roger Craig and Don Williams, our two coaches, about it, and we came into the ballpark the next morning at 7:30, and Alvin is packing his bag. I walked in, and he's got tears in his eyes, and I said "Alvin," and he said "I thought Ballard Smith was on my side," and I said, "Who's gonna get it" and he said, "I think Roger Craig will get it." So, I go in, and I tell Roger, I said, "Roger, Alvin just got fired," and he said, "You're kidding," I said, "No." "Over what?" I said, "Over Ozzie Smith." I said, "You're probably gonna be the manager." So once Alvin got out of the clubhouse, Bob Fontaine came in, and he called Roger and told him he's gonna be the manager. So, he came back in the coaches' office, and he said: "What should I do." I said, "You just tell them you're glad to be the manager, glad to be the leader here." In about three days you'll have your policies all lined out about what to do, and I said "When you end your meeting you tell them, Ozzie Smith is my opening day shortstop" because if you don't put your foot down right now they will disrespect you from every day on, and you hold to it, and he did. There was never another word about that. When Ozzie Smith was elected to the Hall of Fame, he paid for Alvin Dark to fly into Cooperstown and be his guest.

HAWK TAYLOR

I've got to tell you about this one right here; you'll get a kick out of this. I got traded to the New York Mets. Man, I'm looking forward to it; I'm gonna get a chance to play for Casey Stengel. I hadn't been playing any with the Milwaukee Braves, man this is just great, and Jim's (Hickman) locker was right next to mine, and I'm sitting here, and I say; telling Jim and I'm kinda prouder than words, "Jim you know I'm really looking forward to playing for Casey, just can't wait to get started." He gave me a funny look over there; he said, "Now, just you wait," (laughing) I thought that was kinda a strange thing to say. "He said, "Just you wait; he'll make a bad ballplayer out of you (laughing)." It didn't take long; I knew what he was talking about.

JIM HICKMAN

(You had the game-winning hit in the 12th inning of the 1970 All-Star Game that scored Pete Rose in a collision with Ray Fosse at the plate, what are your memories of that game?) Well, we didn't know that he got hurt that bad. We're just glad to win the game, and I know the clubhouse was full of sportswriters, and we were in a hurry to get to the airport and get back to Chicago.

I was in a rush the whole time I was there. I was late getting to Cincinnati, and then when the game was over, we were in a rush to get back to catch a plane to Chicago, so it was just a run . . . run . . . run . . . the whole time I was there.

I didn't go down for all of the pre-game stuff; I didn't go down until game time. I was gonna leave Chicago at like 3:00 because it wasn't a very long flight; 3:00 in the afternoon and get there in time to go to the ballpark. Well, we got to the airport in Chicago, and we sit on the plane for about an hour, and they finally told us, the airline said: "Well the plane, something's wrong with it, you'll have to change planes." So we got off that plane and walked all the way to the other end of O'Hare airport, and you know, that Chicago airport is pretty good size and we got down there and got on that plane, and they said "No, we got the other one fixed," so we had to turn around and go all the way back to the other plane and we didn't get out of Chicago until, I don't know, heck it was 5:00 or later. We got to Cincinnati, and when I went out and finally got dressed and got out on the field, it was game time. Yeah, we didn't take batting practice or anything, no infield; I just barely got there. I came in the game pretty early. I played quite a bit of the game; I think I went in about the second or third inning, I went in, and I played left field for several innings, and then I moved to 1st base. That's where I ended up.

Well, when I went to this tryout camp over here, I worked out as a third baseman. Then when I came back from South Carolina, I went to St Louis for that try-out. That's when the guy told me he said: "Well, I think you'd be a better outfielder." I saw you out there shagging balls in batting practice, and I saw you go catch a fly ball one time; I think you'd probably work out as an outfielder better."

You know, you talk about Hawk Taylor. Hawk came to the Mets when I was still there, and he had a bat, a model bat that I started using, and I used that bat the rest of my career; made just for him because the number of the bat was a T115. Next time you see him, you can ask him about that, and the T was for Taylor, I guess. Any time they made a special bat model for somebody, that's what they did, just like Musial's bats. He always had an M110 or M159 or different bats like that, and I started using that bat, and I liked it.

Oh, I used a Babe Ruth bat for a while, an R43 that I used. Of course, we'd change bats in the minor leagues. Back then, we didn't have many bats, and if you happened to break one of your bats, you had to use something else, and of course, being in the St Louis organization, we had a lot of old Musial bats. We had the old M110 and M159's; had quite a few of those. I changed model bats, and everyone thought the bat had something to do with it. If we changed bats, we'd get better, but that didn't work that way. We used quite a few different bats when I got to the big leagues; I don't remember what year Hawk came over there; it was after we moved to Shea stadium.

(laughing) Well, I don't remember saying that, of course, I could have said it but . . . Ole' Casey (Stengel) was all right, he was hard to understand, but he was alright.

(You were a hitting coach in the minors, did you ever want to be a manager?) No, not managing in the big leagues but managing in the minor leagues, of course. But that's the way to go if you're gonna try to progress is be a manager. As far as a pitching coach or hitting coach, that's a little bit tougher to get to the big leagues that way. But they asked me, "Would I be interested in managing," I said, "Man, no, I have enough trouble taking care of myself; I don't want to take care of 25 players." I never did have a desire to do that because you know how young kids are . . . boy, every day we'd go to the ballpark, it'd be something different. Somebody was either in jail or some problem with something, and I didn't want to do that, and I said Man, no. I've raised four kids; I don't want to raise any more.

BILL GREASON

So I stayed here until a part of 1951 when I was called back into the Marines because when I came out in 1946, I re-upped for four years, not believing or thinking there would be another war, but the Korean War broke out. I had six months to go before my time was up, but the Marines called me back. I just pitched in Houston, Texas, against the Memphis Red Sox and beat them 1 to 0. I was pretty good (laughing); yeah, pretty good, and I called my mom, and I said, "Mom, do you have any correspondence for me?" And she said, "Yeah, I have a brown letter here, has US War Dept or something on it." That was on a Sunday night, and I said, "Well, open it and tell me what's in it," she said, "You are to report to Camp Lejeune, Tuesday morning at 8:00 am". I said, "Ohhhhhhhhh!" I cried and cussed; I wasn't a Christian then (still laughing); no, I wasn't a Christian then. I cried, but I told the fellas to take care of my stuff, and Tuesday morning, I reported in and served. In the

Marines Corp., they have such strange ways of disciplining you. As soon as I get in, they said, "I'm gonna put you in the mess hall for 30 days", and so I didn't fuss, and I went on. They assigned me a certain part I had to take care of and make sure the utensils was clean.

I took it, and after that, it was about time for spring training to start back up the next year, and we went down to . . . where did we train? I don't know exactly where we was, but I do remember when we began to play, our manager somehow got us a trip to Orlando to see Washington Senators play during spring training. At that time there was no integration, but I had on my Marine uniform, I'm sitting in there with the other Marines, I'm the only black in the whole park, then all of a sudden I feel somebody hitting on the heal of my shoe, and I look down, it's the sheriff knocking, I just ignored it. He comes around to the front, and he points, then he called out to me, "You, come from up there." I couldn't go, so I said to Skip, "What're we gonna do?" he said, "He wants you to leave." I got on my Marine uniform; that's one of the most hurting feelings I ever had in my life, and he said, "Let's go." The whole team got up and left. I felt pretty good that they left with me, but it hurt me for me to be in a uniform; we just sitting there watching the game and be called out, but I moved on, and I soon forgot it because I learned that you don't be troubled by being mistreated.

That Texas League was something; there was only two of us in the league, Dave Hoskins, with Dallas, and I was with Oklahoma City. It was a strange thing that they didn't want us to play, but when Dave and I confronted each other in a game, we were both starting pitchers; you couldn't even get in the ballpark. The largest crowd they ever had. I've got a little article at home, over 11,000 folks were there, and I beat Dave that night, and sometimes you wonder about it; how can you try to stop people from enjoying what you enjoy. It's not costing you anything. That's a strange thing to me, you know. We're not trying to reside or stay, we just want to share and enjoy the same things that don't belong to any of us, all of it belongs to the Lord, we just using it for a little while, but those are some things that I did, but I think God that he was with me.

I remember when I was in Houston, fella not far from here, Harry Walker. We were in Shreveport one night, and they were calling me all kinds of . . . "nigga this" and "nigga that," "ya hit it, nigga." So, Harry told me . . . I was doing real well; I had a shutout going in the seventh inning. And they started from the dugout, the players, so when I came back in, he said, "Bill, you watch me. Whenever you see me touch my cap, I want you to touch his cap, and every time you don't do it, it's going to cost you twenty-five dollars." So, I brushed the guy back, and boy, they sounded off. The guy stepped out and told the umpire, "He's throwing at me" because they were watching Harry and saw what he was doing, so the umpire said, "The next time you do it, you're out of here." I didn't care what he said; I was watching Harry because $25 was coming out of my salary. Other team's player did it again, so Harry took me out; he wouldn't let them put me out; he just said, "That's enough. You're not going to pitch anymore here." You know it didn't bother me, you know it just made me push harder, and this is the way it's always been with me; I always felt that I had to push harder if I was going to excel in whatever I attempted to do, ministry or whatever.

I played from 1948 to 1958 except those years in the Marines; I played in the Latin Leagues, Mexican League, and Puerto Rican League. I played in Santa Domingo, played in Cuba . . . in Cuba with Sentan Ferger and Mexican League with Los Mochis (Caneros de Los Mochis), and Guadalajara and I played in Puerto Rican League with Santurce (Cangrejeros). In 1954, boy, we had a team, out of sight. That's when the Giants won the World Series, and Willie Mays was allowed to come to Puerto Rico, and that was down there in the same hometown Roberto Clemente grew up right in, so he was down there. He was my best friend, Roberto Clemente. Oh, yeah. He'd call me. It really hurt me when I heard that he'd died in that plane crash.

I remember when he first started down in Puerto Rico, and in 1954, we had a team; we won the Caribbean series. We had Bob Thurman in left field, Willie Mays in center field, and Roberto Clemente in right field. Boy, what a team. And we had a fellow named Buzz Clarkson played third base, Don Zimmer at shortstop, Ron Samford at second, George Crowe at first and Harry Chiti was our catcher. We had Rubin Gomez, Giant Sam Jones with the Cubs, and couldn't nobody take nothing from us (laughing). That was great, and the owner Pedrin Zorrilla. Great man in Puerto Rico. He was a businessman; Pete was. He was a fine brother. I played for him for about six years. I had some good years down there; last year, I played, I think was 1958.

My wife went with me one year down there, and she did the cooking for us and taking care of us. The other guy brought his wife down. I played with some great ballplayers, Ray Dandridge. I played against some of the top major leaguers. I did pretty good over in a town called Caguas. They had Victor Payos played first base and Hank Aaron. Of course, you had the choice to play and one thing about it, if you went to those places and if you didn't produce in three or four outings, they'd send you back home (laughing).

When I was with the Barons in 1948, we'd play Kansas City Monarchs, and whoever would win would go to the Negro League World Series against the Homestead Grays. We had a couple of rainouts in Kansas City, and so we were tied three games and Piper Davis; the manager asked Powell and Alonzo Perry, who was supposed to be the aces if they was ready to pitch and both said: "My arms stiff." I said, "Skip, give me the ball," I said, "Give it to me!" He said, "You got it." And I pitched us into the Negro World Series against Homestead Grays. I just always believed that anything I got in; I was gonna succeed. Just like the ministry, I never wanted to be no preacher, but that one night on Iwo Jima, two of my best friends were killed, and I prayed that night, I said, "Lord if you get me off this island, anything you want me to do, I'll do it." So, I dodged it for a long time; I could feel a different attitude had come into my life about things and about people.

I just thank God for the fellows I played with, and of course, all this baseball now is behind me, and I'm just concentrating on the ministry.

LOIS YOUNGEN

One of the things that I wanted to tell you was that in 1954 they changed the size of the ball, which happened from time to time. I'm sure that this was a plan to pull more fans in because it seems like every time they made a change in the size of the ball, it increased attendance. We started throwing underhand as softball; we ended up throwing the ball overhand. We went from underhand pitching to throwing overhand with a 10-inch ball for the three and a half years while I played 1951, '52, '53, and part of '54.

Right after the 4th of July, we changed, without any fanfare whatsoever, from this 10-inch ball to a regulation 9-inch ball. They moved the pitching mound back. Every time the ball got smaller, they had to adjust all the distances, so the pitcher's mound got pushed back, and the baselines were lengthened, and then they had to adjust, maybe the outfield fences.

Throwing the ball overhand, it did dip, and it curved, and it dropped too. It did all the right things that baseballs do. The only adjustment that they didn't make was they didn't shorten the baseline, I think instead of 90 feet, I think we stayed at 85 because we were much—you know, we're not six-foot-two or three.

So, I think they left the baselines right around. I could double-check that, but right around 85 feet. But everything else—everything else went major league except the fences weren't back as far as the major league's fences would be. But what's so funny is, and I've talked to some of my teammates about this, no one remembers doing much practicing with this 9-inch ball, we came out one evening, we head into practice with it, everything had been changed, and we played (laughing), "what's this?"— When I look back on it, it seems very strange that we didn't have a couple of morning practices with this new 9-inch ball. I guess because it was so close to the 10-inch ball, but it sure made a difference to me because I've got short fingers and boy when we had that 9-inch ball could I handle that. It never slipped out of my hand like the 10-inch ball would every once in a while; if it were wet at all in the outfield occasionally, it'd slip out of my hand. But that 9-inch ball was absolute perfection. And so, from about July 4th until the end of August of that last season, we played with the 9-inch ball.

A hundred and eighteen games, yes. Anyway, we played with the 9-inch ball, and we ended the season playing with the 9-inch ball, and then we got letters in the mail telling us that the League was shutting down . . . we all knew that there was a question mark whether or not we would be around the next year.

So, I'm not sure that the 9-inch ball brought in any more people. I don't remember what kind of impact it had—I didn't pay any attention to how many people we had in the stands, whether we had a hundred more after we added the 9-inch ball or not. That wasn't something that I paid any attention to, but I don't know if our attendance went up or not after we changed ball size.

You know, there's no question about that. The 10-inch ball was made for us by a company here in New England because we've gotten some replicas made that are 10-inch balls that were made in China that we were trying to sell; we're a non-profit players association trying to keep our head above water by selling certain merchandise. As I tell people, we raised most of our money selling t-shirts to each other (laughing). So, we got these baseballs that are made in China, and we've been taking them to various softball tournaments in the south, and they would go on in the winter down in Southern California and Arizona. I'm up here in Oregon, so I don't get to them. But anyways, the balls are stamped China, and there's no way that we should get confused with the balls, our vintage balls; however, one of my theories a long time ago was we didn't have any money. The teams, individual city teams, didn't have any money, and those 10-inch balls had to be handmade because you couldn't go into Wilson Sporting Goods store and buy 10-inch women's baseball.

So, by switching to the regulation 9-inch, they saved a batch of money I'm thinking. But it's gotta be more than that, so you were on the right track because that was one of my original theories with cost related to the balls. But it's got to be more than that. They didn't have to buy these expensive balls, but I think it was also for fan appeal. We see that change. We bring in a few more fans.

KATIE HORSTMAN

We were the first ones to have a League, and it wouldn't have been if not for Phil Wrigley from the Cubs and President Roosevelt; because the whole thing was that the guys were going to the war, all of the baseball players. I don't think you would see that today.

Oh, yeah, I kept everything from my time with the All Americans. I got all my balls. You could keep a ball only if you pitched and if you won. So, I got quite a few balls in my trophy case. My whole living room is full of trophies.

JIM KAAT

Oh, yeah, I have the baseball guides going back to 1900. I don't have as many of the current ones because it's kind of changed in its size, but yeah, my dad had them all re-bound. So if somebody says, "Oh my son or somebody played in the minor leagues and didn't make it to the big leagues, but he played in the minor leagues," and I'd say "Oh well what year did he play?" You can go back in those guidebooks and see. Years ago, they had 20-some minor leagues back in the 1940s. So yeah, I still have all those record books and history books as well as . . . it's more like a booklet than a book. It's called Who's Who in Baseball. I have those going back to 1937. And I have the baseball guides going back to 1900.

I did a CD for my grandkids that I gave to each one of them sort of talking about what life was like in the 1940s and how I got my interest in baseball, among other things. I so wish that I would have fought to have just sat down with my dad and just say, "What was it like during WWI?" or "When do you remember?"- they didn't go to any games. The first game that he took me to was in June of 1946 in Detroit. He didn't go to big league games, but he would listen to them on the radio. So, it would have been interesting to see exactly where he did get his interest.

(How did you feel your first day as a Pro Ballplayer?) Well, I was eager; we all flew into Superior, Nebraska. One of our teammates was two days late; he thought the team was in Superior, Wisconsin, so he went to the wrong state (laughing). I was just really apprehensive. I wondered what my teammates were going to be like. Were they bigger, stronger, faster?

So that was the biggest thing . . . that along with going to the ballpark every day instead of once a week. All of a sudden, you are doing this like school. You are getting paid for it, but you are going every day, and I think that is still true today, although kids play so many games in college now. That was a big thing to get over and to adjust to.

LOU PINIELLA

I drove up from Tampa with my uncle and the manager; he was a very nice man, Pinky May; lived in St. Petersburg. And I played, I played with his son and coached against his son.

And I can't think of his name but anyway, I remember my first at-bat, I blooped a double to right field, and I was always concerned a little bit about hitting the breaking ball. I knew I could hit the fastball really well. It's amazing, I hit with a pretty square stance my whole life, but when I went into pro ball, I switched it immediately to a little more closed stance so I could hit the breaking ball better. And I found out that they were jamming me a little bit, so I went back to what I started with and it worked out pretty well.

I played in the minor leagues half a year in 1962, a full year of 1963 in the Carolina League; then I had a year in the service, then I had a full year in Double A in Elmira, New York. I played for Earl Weaver. And then I played three years in the Pacific Coast League with the Portland Beavers. So, I had basically five and a half seasons of minor league ball, which, at that time it wasn't all that unusual. Now, they get to the big leagues much quicker, but there are a lot more players and less teams.

JIM ZAPP

But you know I never did take it too seriously, like I said, in Aiea, we had two teams and Edgar Jones, he integrated a team and took me and another boy from Michigan, put us on the white team, so I never paid too much attention to it.

Butch McCord, he introduced me to integrated baseball. He would play with Paris Illinois in the Mississippi Ohio Valley League. He recommended me for Paris. That was in 1953, and we only had four blacks; Me, Butch, Quincy Smith, and Bebop Gordon, four of us.

In the stands, man, you never seen anything like it. When I first saw him (Josh Gibson), I'd gone out and played for the Nashville Elite Giants team on the weekend; we'd go to Washington and play on a Sunday. You see, I'm the only military guy on the team, and we're playing the Homestead Grays in Washington. That's when I saw Buck Leonard, Josh, and Cool Papa Bell; that Homestead Gray's team. Josh Gibson hit one down the left-field line, about 410 down the left-field line in old Griffith Stadium. Josh hit one right in those stands that day; he was powerful.

Well, Nashville Vols had a trainer by the name of Willy White. He was there for years, and he'd say, and I'd listen to him; he said, "If Joe DiMaggio had Zapp's legs, he'd still be playing now." I never had no leg problems.

I was in the Navy for three years, two months, and 11 days (laughing). You know where I was when the war was over? Shore duty in Harlem; Yeah. I have SP on my arm . . . boy you talk about some celebration, I took my gun all in the bars and celebrated with them. It was a happy day.

LOU WHITAKER

When I signed with the Tigers, I went to the minor leagues, and they had already started their season. So, I'd sit on the bench for a little bit, and I rooted for my teammates. Got a chance to play in my first game, the coach told me that I was going to be playing third base in the second game of a doubleheader, and I think from that day, I may not have started the next game, but I was playing every day after that. I didn't do well, the season was over, I go home, and my uncle said "Come pick me up," they were telling me, "Well you didn't do too good," and all this stuff but I tell you what, next year I go on, and I learned a few things there, just listening to other players. First time ever being away from home that long.

Went home and got ready for the next spring. Go to spring training in Florida. Actually, when I was first back in Florida, they had me back on the Rookie team to just work out and whatever. And Jim Leyland got me from the Rookie team, put me on third base on the Florida State team, which is Class A, and had the third baseman, made him the designated hitter. I was the most valuable player in the Florida State League; I hit about .379; that's what my friends tell me; I thought I hit much lower. Stole quite a few bases, 42 to 44 bases.

We won the Florida State League. I had other teams interested in trying to buy me from the Tigers. I had the Yankees and the St. Louis Cardinals come down to watch me play, and they were trying to make a trade through the minor leagues to get me. The Tigers said, "Uh, huh, no, no, no" (laughing).

And the next year or that winter after Florida State League, they get all their prospects and have like a little instructional league where you work out, and then you play games later in the afternoon, and that's when the Tigers made me a second baseman, and that's when Trammel and I first met. And we played together in AA the full season the next year in '77 and got called up at the end of the season to the major leagues.

STEVE BLASS

Well, I had never . . . I had only flown one other time in my life, so I flew from Hartford to Tri-Cities, Kingsport, Tennessee. I got off the plane, and a guy met me and took me to a boarding house, and there were like eight other kids that had just signed. Every morning you woke up, four of them would be gone, and four more would come in. I had never been on my own, so my first day, I went out and bought a six-pack of beer and a watermelon . . . I didn't leave the bathroom for a day and a half (laughing), but I was on my own, man; I was living the life (laughing). I went to a laundry mat, I had some underwear and socks, and I had never been to a laundry mat so, I went down there, and I threw them in the thing, and I saw this vending machine up on the wall, had these little soapboxes, so I figured, "Well, I got 11 items here so I should have a box for each one." And that didn't work out well, and the suds started coming out of the top, and for the rest of the summer, I mailed my laundry back to my mother in Connecticut, and she would clean it and mail it back to me. That worked until one time, she had a batch, and she decided to put some chocolate chips cookies in with the laundry, and it was the middle of August, and when that arrived, I decided I better learn how the laundry mat works (laughing).

(I bet it was fun hanging out with you) Well, I wasn't dull; let's put it that way (laughing).

WHITEY HERZOG

I was a pretty good player, and I had the big leagues looking at me; to have scouts come look at you knowing you only had 16 major league clubs, but there was 50-some minor leagues, when you did sign a contract, if you didn't do well at one level or one team, they'd send you to another team. You didn't get released and sent home. I think you had a little bit better chance to succeed if you matured a little bit later. I was only 5'9" and 155 pounds when I got out of high school. When I took my assignment with the New York Yankees, I grew to be like everybody else who seemed like they were 5'10" to 6'1", 180 pounds.

When I talk about the great ballplayers of my era and the big leaguers, they all seem to be . . . every once in a while, you'd get a Steeple Schultz or Dave Kingman, but most of them were . . . the Musial's, the Mays', Aaron's all the great kids, all the ballplayers they got in the National League. Maris, when I played with him in Kansas City, he was about 6'0", 185 pounds before he went to the Yankees, but we were all about the same size. I remember one time, I went in the weight room at Busch Stadium with Stan Musial, and I guess they had about $2 million worth of equipment in there. And I said, "Stan," I said, "Now, you're one of the great ballplayers that ever lived, you got a .337 lifetime batting average, 3000 and something hits, does it take all this to play baseball?" And you know what his answer was? He said, "No." He said, "I just used a rubber ball." Which meant he had a rubber ball in his pocket at all times, squeezing that ball to make his wrist strong.

That's all they ever did. Nowadays, people keep asking about the injuries and everything else that happens and how many people on the disabled list, well, the ballplayers make enough money, they don't have to work, they're in the weight room year-round. They're like, what I call, like violins. They're so well-tuned, in such good shape that when they make a false move or slip on a wet turf, they pull muscles. In those days, I don't remember anybody having Charley horses, and we all eat meat and potatoes, vegetables out of the garden and even when I got to the big leagues, and we traveled by train, we'd have two roomettes and a dining car in between the two, and we'd finish a series, and we're moving somewhere else . . . you'd have a few cases of beer on there and everybody get a baked potato and a big steak and salad. That's all we ate. Now, they're vegetarians, and they train, and sometimes I think that's part of the injuries now.

Well, today I saw somebody tie Joe DiMaggio's home run record with 362. You know, when you think about Ted Williams and DiMaggio, Musial only missed one year in the service, Bob Feller, they missed four prime years during World War II. How many games would Feller have won if he's pitched in 1942, '43, '44, '45? He comes back from service after being gone for four years, and on Opening Day, he pitched a no-hitter. Set the strike-out record and broke Rube Waddell's record and how many home runs would Ted Williams had hit. The fact that he missed in 1941; he missed 1942, '43, '44, and '45. He came back, lead the league in hitting in '46 when the Red Sox won the pennant. You look at the numbers they put up, and Williams hitting five hundred and seventy home runs and missed four years during World War II, missed half a year when he broke his collarbone in the All-Star Game. Went to the Korean War as a Marine flyer because he had such great eyesight, and they didn't have radar. Williams and the other pilot that broke the sound barrier, all the pilots wanted to fly in their squadrons because of their eyesight. When you talk about Ted Williams, and you talk about all the hitters . . . I only saw Babe Ruth on film, but I don't think there's ever been a hitter that I've ever seen who was—in all my years, even in professional baseball, that was as good as Ted Williams with a bat in his hands.

Well, when you talk about the great players in our game and the history of our game, when I was a kid, and I'm sure up from the time he died of throat cancer even after he quit playing, everybody knew who

Babe Ruth was. Not only was he the great home run hitter, he's a guy that did for baseball what Arnold Palmer did for golf. I think that Babe Ruth may not only have been the best hitter of all time, but he was also a great left-hand pitcher. You know, he held the World Series record for innings pitched without allowing a run in World Series play. So I would say that, number one, even to this day, with all the great players we have, things that they're doing now, that Babe Ruth will still be the number one player if you took a poll, of who was the greatest player in the history of baseball.

DOUG FLYNN

Just having a ball and playing. It's too bad you can't keep that same attitude when you're getting into professional baseball. It's hard to do. The fun part is hard to do because there's always the pressure of something on you all the time to perform or do this. In Cincinnati, I had a ball; I was lucky there too, with good teams. Then, when I went to New York, it changes . . . they did so many things to me when I was there. I even got them calling now about the 40 year anniversary of the Tom Seaver trade (Seaver to the Reds for Doug Flynn, Steve Henderson, Dan Norman, and Pat Zachry to the Mets). and had them call me the other day, and I say, "I really don't want to talk about it; I think everything has been said." "Well, I'm trying to get a different perspective." and I said, "That's another reason why I don't think we need to talk about this (laughing)." There's only one perspective.

We had a guy named Pete Flynn, was a groundskeeper in New York. And I say, "Pete, when you water the field, can you put a little extra out on second base?" I said, "I'm not going to make any money with my bat, but I might make some with the glove, so I like it little damper, I don't want dry or anything, just getting it, so the wind's not going to mess it up." He says, "What, you want extra water on that?" I said, "Yeah." He says, "You know, if you had good hands, you wouldn't have to worry about that (laughing)." When I won the Gold Glove in 1980, I bought all the grounds crew, watches, and it said on the back, "Doug Flynn's Gold Glove Grounds Crew."

I went back up there three years ago, and one of the grounds crew guys still had the watch on. He said, "What do you think of that?" "I think I bought a better watch than I thought I did; that's what I think (laughing)."

I remember winning the Gold Glove in 1980, and we go to spring training in 1981, first spring training game; we're playing 30 games, so you got time to get yourself in shape, so it's the first game. It's the first or second inning, a left-hander for the Phillies hits a rocket. Hits about two or three feet in front of me; comes up, bangs off my shoulder . . . error! I wasn't smart enough to get out of the way. We were always taught to "center everything up." Today's guys don't do that. So, I get an error; it's all right. Then, the ball gets hit in the gap. I go out for the relay, get it. The runner is going to third; I throw it. It hits off his arm and kind of squirts away. The guy that hit it goes from first to second, so I get two errors . . . Didn't cost us any runs, nothing happens, so no big deal but the New York paper the next day, it says "Golden Boy not so Golden" (laughing) . . . The guy that did it was a guy named Jack Lange. I said, "Jack, it's the first spring training game." and I said, "When you read your article, it didn't say that the errors cost us anything but down at the end you have to write and Doug Flynn, last year's Gold Glove winner had two errors." I said, "I guess I just don't understand." And so, from then on, I only gave him yes and no answers.

FERGIE JENKINS

Leo Durocher, he was the kind of a guy that knew talent. We had Robin Roberts; he was the pitching coach and Joe Becker. The pitching coach that helped me the most, Cal McLish. Maybe that name is not familiar, pitched with Cleveland, and was in the Philly organization. I went to Winter ball a couple of seasons in Puerto Rico; he taught me the slider, taught me mound awareness. You don't ever leave the mound . . . that is where your job is. You don't run around the infield like Mark "The Bird" Fidrych (laughing). I never did that. I stayed right on the hill; that's where your job is. He gave me that opportunity to learn that when

I went to winter ball in Puerto Rico, won some ball games, did really well. After the season, the Phillies decided to bring me up in 1965. They were grooming me as a bullpen pitcher out of Little Rock when I was there because they had Chris Short, Bunning, Roebuck, Ray Culp . . . they had a bunch of guys that were ahead of me, and they wanted me to pitch in the bullpen, which I did. I thought I was successful, but then I was involved in a trade.

I didn't fall into that trap, which is something that happens to a lot of players. Nobody is going to replace Ernie Banks at first base, Ron Santo at third, Kessinger when he really became an All-Star at shortstop, so the pitching aspect and I've tried to reiterate it to people, there was only nine pitchers made the staff back then; nine pitchers, 16 position players, so when it comes to making the ball club, you better show the organization that you can play. Gene Mauch was that type of guy. When I made the ball club at the beginning of the 1966 season . . . my uniform was number 70, the first big league camp, then it went to 46 and then 30. When I got to 30, the number 30, I said: "I've got this ball club made (laughing)." I had a low number; I had a pitching number. Now guys want 99, 57, 72; it's crazy now. But back then, all pitching numbers, the highest number was Drysdale, like 52, I think or 53. None of the numbers were higher than that as a pitcher, so if you got 30, you were right in the mix to make a ball club. I knew I had it, not had it made, but I knew I was going to make this ball club so long as I kept doing all of the positive things.

My roommate, when I got to the big leagues, was Alex Johnson, and we signed together with the Phillies, and then when I got traded to the Cubs, Ernie Banks was my roommate. I roomed with Ernie Banks the last three years he played. He would tell me all the time, "Focus in on what you are trying to accomplish. Your talent is as good as the next guy's." He never talked about himself, always about the team. He always talked baseball, always talked baseball. He loved the game.

Oh yeah, with Ernie, incredible. As you said, passing on knowledge from one youngster to another youngster. When I came back to the Cubs,

I tried to tutor Lee Smith some. We weren't roommates, but we would hang out together, went out to eat. He knew nothing about pitching and the release (laughing), not a thing. I didn't for almost two seasons; part of 1965 and almost the whole season of 1966. I said, "You gotta get yourself prepared within 15 pitches (starting the game); 15! Then you got another eight when you get to the mound. So that's 25 pitches to get your act together. He couldn't realize that. He said, "What do you mean 25"? I said, "You've got to concentrate on what you are trying to do. You got men in scoring position", which now they pitch with nobody on base. And Lee Smith; he was a hell of a relief pitcher. He took that to heart; he had a hell of a career. I'm not saying that it was me that helped him; I just tried to give him a little advice.

(Do you watch ball games on TV?) Oh yeah, I watch and criticize (laughing). I used to tell myself. Where is the scouting report on this guy? He should know better; this guy is a first-ball hitter, this guy hits deep in the count, this guy cannot hit a breaking ball, don't throw him fastballs, gees (laughing)!!! You can see the talent that some of these young men have, and then you look at the scouting report; I say, "Who's scouting this guy?" The game is remarkable. Every game is different. I criticize by speaking out sometimes; I've done that a few times. Don Zimmer didn't like it. When Don Zimmer coached Boston, he didn't like me to speak up (laughing). Bill Lee and I, at team meetings, we always had something to say. Don Zimmer didn't like it. To this day, if he was around, he would say, "Jenkins, shut up (laughing)." That was me. I just thought that to have an input, you gotta speak up. It was just something that . . . I didn't try to criticize, but I thought it was a helpful idea. Some cases it worked and some it didn't (laughing).

Three hundred innings was big in my era: Juan Marichal, Bob Gibson, Don Drysdale, Sandy Koufax, myself, so many guys, Gaylord Perry, Don Sutton. I could name 100 guys, Steve Carlton. Three hundred innings, that's what the game was, had a four-man rotation. And if you were in control of the game, you stayed in the game. That was it. And if you look at these guys, all of them were decent hitters too, being able to bunt and hit.

WILLIE BLAIR

I tease my kids all the time about "Get out and play some Wiffle ball, you're in there playing video games" and now as a coach in professional baseball I kind of put the video games and piece that in with a theory that I have because a lot of guys . . . when I was coming up through the minor leagues, just about every pitcher had the good fastball and at least one really good breaking ball, whether it'd be a slider or a curveball. Well now you got guys that have a good fastball and a good change-up, but there's very few, I wouldn't say very few, there's not as many kids nowadays that have that really nasty breaking ball, and I think it's because they're playing video games growing up. They're not outside throwing, playing Wiffle ball and spinning a plastic ball and that kind of thing. That's just my theory, but I really believe that. I've coached now for two years in pro ball, and on both teams, we've had a few players that had absolutely no feel for a breaking ball. But they have a great change-up and a great fastball. Now, they'll flash a good breaking ball every now and then, but they're just not consistent, and it's kind of strange to me because; like I said when I was growing up everybody had a good fastball and a breaking ball and they learned their change-up after they got to Double A and Triple A.

The first game that I ever was a part of in the big leagues, I didn't pitch in, I was a reliever at the time, and I didn't pitch in the game, but it's my first time being on the field for Opening Day, and that was pretty neat. Nolan Ryan, who was an idol growing up, was pitching against us, and he had a no-hitter for five innings. I was 24-years-old, and I think that was his 23rd or 24th season in the big leagues, so that was pretty neat. I didn't pitch for another couple days, maybe the third game of the season where I remember getting out there and feeling my knees shaking. It was unbelievable; I wasn't scared . . . it was just; I was so excited, maybe a little nervous, but I wasn't scared of it. I was just anxious.

I think I had a little bit better experience in Colorado than I did in Arizona. In Colorado, we were all a bunch of young guys . . . kinda cast-offs from other teams that we came together, and we knew we were coming to a new city that was baseball crazy, but we also knew that we're playing at "Mile High" altitude, and we knew it's going to be tough. That group kind of bonded together better than some other teams I've been on. As far as the way the team handled everything, it was great. I think we were sold out most of that year, and it was just a great experience. I think we broke the single-game attendance record, and they did that by adding a bunch of temporary bleachers and seats, which they were still working on during batting practice (laughing), and they were up there too. I don't know if I would have sat on them.

Arizona, it was a great stadium, great people. I had a little bit of a bad experience there just based on performance. I just didn't perform as well as I should have, but our team wasn't very good either. We had a bunch of injuries, and we had people playing out of position. That was my first year as a free agent, and I was supposed to be relied upon for giving innings and getting wins, being a veteran on the staff, and things just didn't work out. I ended up getting traded with about two months to go on the season. I was like 4 and 15 or something. That wasn't a great one, but when you look at it, the year before I was 16 and 8 and that year, I ended up 5 and 16, and when you look at my numbers, they were very similar. But the year before I was playing on a better defensive team, the team scored some runs and the second year when I was 5 and 16 I think I was shut out seven times that year on the games I pitched, and I think I led all of baseball in least run support that year. It wore on me, and it got frustrating. I had nothing to do with it; I wasn't mad at anybody; it was just circumstances. I was just struggling, and I felt like I was letting the team down, and it was just not as good an experience as the other one.

Playing for the Detroit Tigers, there was a difference because you look around in Tiger Stadium and you see all of these Hall of Famers around, the jerseys hanging up and the numbers hanging up, so you understand that there's a ton of history there and you go to Arizona, and it's all new. Fans are great; they loved us, and we had sharp uniforms, and all this stuff and the stadium was unbelievable, second to none, so it was neat. It was a neat experience, but as far as the difference, there wasn't any history there. The part of history that we were is that we were the first team that franchise had. That was pretty neat.

(Is there anything you would change about youth baseball today?) I'd have to think about that one a little bit. I think there's a couple of things that I would do with the leagues that I played in and the leagues that my sons have come up playing in. The nine through 12-year-olds play in the same league, and it's really . . . there's arguments from both sides; the nine-year-olds get better because they're around older players, and they're around coaches that are teaching the fundamentals and all that. But for every one of those, I think there's a nine-year-old that will get turned off because he is so intimated by a 12-year-old. I think the nines and tens should play together. Eleven's and 12's should play together. That's one thing. The bats nowadays, which they're getting better about it but up until this past year or two, the bats were so unbelievable strong or "hot" that it was dangerous. I remember when my kids were playing in Cal Ripken League and some of those bats, man, the kids would hit a ball, and a big 12-year-old kid would hit a ball, and another 11 or 12-year-old kid or even a nine-year-old kid, they couldn't defend themselves, it would be hit so hard. I think the equipment needs to be moderated a little bit to make it a little bit safer. That's about it really. Baseball is just baseball, and I just think that they got carried away with the bats there for a while, and I think keeping kids in their age group is a factor.

WILLIE HORTON

Jake Wood, he's still living, and I got him back involved with the Tiger organization; he helped me with a lot of things in Detroit and down in Lakeland, Florida. It was a great opportunity when I signed, and then I left home, and then after that going to Florida. I didn't know anything about racial problems or stuff like that, but I had to walk six miles to spring training from the bus stop; I think the little baseball kept me all together where I was trying to do things. It might be hard, but you take it in and get through it and help other people. It's a game that you enjoy, meet a lot of people in life, and I think that walking in the beginning and what I do right now in life has taught me beyond the field, it was just the way life was at the time, and Papa always told me "That change would come with people, don't rush it, it would take change," and I got involved through that belief.

The great sports announcers for the Tigers for many years, Ernie Harwell and George Kell, they tried to tell me about things up North going to happen, and I didn't quite understand, I didn't know all about that, I just wanted to play baseball, and then Gates Brown telling me that "You're a franchise player." and I said, "I'm a ballplayer (laughing), I don't know nothing about franchise." I didn't know what that was, but they got me ready, and Ernie introduced me to Hank Greenberg when I came to the Tigers, and he kind of sit me down, and talked to me and got me involved with Jackie Robinson, and learned me about Larry Doby, and that's when I really started learning about what this game does and what that baseball can do. The only way you can learn, you got to keep the little boy in you to keep learning. That little round ball, yeah, you might go through pain, but with your learning curve, you can still expend that; decision skills and good foundation come from people that you meet, and that's the reason I'm doing what I do today. I'm just very fortunate, but all that took some hard time. I remember Hank Greenberg telling me what I'm gonna have to go through with the Tigers, and you know, I said, "Hey, I'm a ballplayer," and you know, I went through some Jackie Robinson time my first four, five years here.

I look at a baseball game, and it brings people together; it brings people together, and I think when you bring people together, it makes it worthwhile in life. I always say right now I wish I was a politician and could go to all the open games in Detroit, and around the country, and see black, white, and all nationality of people smile. They go "Oh" and then they go back to the office and make the right decision for the people. The people that put you in that position. I think if everybody would do that, we wouldn't have all the problems that we have in the world.

CHARLIE LOYD

Paducah Junior College. That's when it was downtown on seventh and Broadway. It was right there at Broadway Methodist Church, and right next door, that was the college. We had a super ball club down there too.

We went to the national tournament; was never beaten by a junior college team. Yeah, we had a super baseball team.

Yeah, baseball is a hard sport to play because there is no place to hide you; you can be a third baseman, you got to catch balls hit at you at over 100 mph, and then you gotta throw them out, then after you learn how to do that you got a go up there and hit one (laughing), which is the hardest part.

Baseball is a great game; I go to the College World Series every year out in Omaha. It's more fun than the American League and National League World Series, I mean it is, everybody that's a baseball fan should go at least once in their lives

In order to play pro ball, you got to live it, eat it, and sleep it. It is just constantly on your mind, and you're always thinking, always thinking, how can I get just a little bit better? Where do I need to go to hone these talents? You watch other guys, and you watch film.

When I was playing pro ball, I just kinda got bored with it. I could see that I was never gonna make it. That's the most desolate place there is, waiting to hear from somebody in the big leagues. You never hear from them, good, bad, or indifferent. You play, and you come home, you have no idea of what they think about you then next spring, they'd invite me to spring training with the major league club, and they would tell me, "Well, you need to go down and work on this." I talk to some of those guys that had been up there for years, and they weren't making any money either. I thought, to hell with this, I didn't go to college to bang around like this, and I had two daughters, and I wasn't there when either one of them was born. We had a first baseman, Mike Hegan, and his dad was a bullpen coach. He had caught for Cleveland, they had Bob Feller, Garcia, Wynn, and that bunch, super catcher, and his boy was with the Yankees in spring training . . . he'd never seen him play.

Never seen him play because he was always with Cleveland, and his son was back home in Milwaukee, going to school and playing. The only time his Dad got to see him was when he went to spring training. You got to give up a lot. It just wasn't worth it to me. I just got to where I thought, "Man, this is not what I want to do."

(How many players do you think got held up in the minors during the 1950s because there was fewer teams?) A bunch of them. How'd you like to have been playing . . . See, there weren't any free agents, so you couldn't leave. We had two center fielders playing behind Mantle; led the league in home runs every year; they weren't going anywhere. In fact, one of them at the end of his career, Philadelphia signed him, bought him, took him to Philadelphia, and he hit ten home runs just right away. Then the other one was Roger Repoz. The Angels bought him. He played for a couple of years for the Angels, and he's at the end of his career, and the guy should have been in the big leagues long before this.

Yankees had a great scouting system. If I'm not mistaken, I think we only had 90 players in our entire organization. That's minor leagues and major leagues. They had 90 premium players. Just about all of them at the end of their career played for somebody else . . . where they could have, if the Yankees had traded them, they could've gone somewhere else. The first year that I played at Greensboro, I had a super year and went to spring training with the Yankees the next year and had a good spring and during the offseason, they had bought Tex Clevenger and Bud Daley from Kansas City, and they had Bobby Shantz, trying to make the team; had Robin Roberts trying to make the team and they already had Bob Turley, had Ralph Terry who had won 22 games, had Whitey Ford who'd won 27 games, Rollie Sheldon, Billy Stafford. Yankees said, "Well, Chuck, we're gonna send you to Texas League. "Okay, see you later (laughing)."

(Looking back, would you have preferred signing with a team other than the Yankees?) I don't know. You know, just the opportunity might have been better, but I had a good life regardless; I never looked back. I enjoyed playing when I did, and I've enjoyed working, and I enjoyed being home with my family. You'll find out those kids don't stick around long. They grow up and are gone in a hurry.

The best stories about baseball are usually minor leagues because guys are down there, and they're bored to death, and they're going nowhere. We were playing in the Southern League one year, it was a Double A League, and we're playing in Columbus, Georgia. Across the street from the ballpark was a restaurant, so we'd get these guys to go over there and buy sandwiches and stuff like that. One day this place was closed, so we sent them down to the market to buy some hotdogs and buns (laughing). We're sitting out in the bullpen, and the bullpen came down behind the dugout, and the coaches couldn't see us from the dugout, so we built us a fire in the bullpen (laughing). This is a Double A league; I mean, this is a big-time league. We're cooking these hotdogs (laughing); Rube Walker, who used to catch for the Dodgers, was our manager. He walked down to see where the smoke was coming from, and after the game, he called us all together and had a clubhouse meeting. He said, "Guys, when you guys went across the street and bought hotdogs and cokes, stuff like that, drank them in the bullpen, that's all right, I didn't mind, but when you come to the ballpark and start cooking your damned meals, that's a little bit too much (laughing)." If there's a minor league team around, that's where you go. That's where the baseball is played. In the big leagues, there's 22 cameras on them; they can't do much; they'd get fined.

We're down in Columbus one year; Fort Benning's down there, and they're big on community work. The 4th of July . . . they had a big fireworks display in our ballpark; well, we had a couple of pitchers that stole a bunch of rockets and Roman candles. Well, every place we'd go, whenever the other team would hit a home run, they always had a damn cannon right behind our dugout, so they'd fire that damn cannon and it used to piss us off so bad. So, we stole a bunch of Roman Candles and rockets from these guys, and we took them down there every night to the bullpen, and we'd wrap them . . . even the other pitchers didn't know we had them. So we waited about three days; nobody hit a home run, and finally, we had the coke bottles, and everything sitting back there ready to put the rockets in . . . this big ole' center fielder hit a towering home run. We lit those rockets and started firing those rockets off (laughing). We had a guy from Vancouver named Bob Lasko, and his buddy was playing center field, we was playing Macon and Pete Rose was on that team. Lasko's nickname was Rockhead. He said, "Rockhead, what the hell are you doing?" So Lasko lit one of those Roman candles (laughing), shooting them across center field. Oh god, you talk about going nuts, the manager went nuts, the president of the league; they fined us all (still laughing). They went nuts. But I tell you, you got to entertain yourself when you're in the minor leagues.

Let me tell you this story. I wasn't involved in this, but this is the greatest story. You might have heard it; the clubhouse guy is telling me the story. Billy Martin's going deer hunting, and Billy told Mantle they was going to go deer hunting up in New York where Martin lives, and he said, "I've got a guy up there, he's got a big farm, he'll let us deer hunt up here." He pulled up there early one morning and told Mantle, "I'll be right back; I'm gonna go in here and tell him I'm here." So, Billy went in there and told the farmer, "You know, Mickey and I's up here, and thought we'd let you know we're here." He said, "Good, go ahead and help yourself." Then the farmer said, "Will you do something for me?" And Martin said, "What's that?" He said, "I've got an old mule out there that's 17-years-old." He said, "You know, the rendering plant won't pick him up as long as he's alive, and I've had him since he was born; I just can't shoot him; would you shoot him for me?" And Martin said, "Yeah, I'll shoot him for you." So, he went out there and told Mantle, "That no-good son of a bitch is not gonna let us hunt; I'm gonna shoot his f . . . king mule." So, Martin shot . . . Bam!!! and then he heard Bam!!! Bam!!! Mantle said, "Let's go; I got two of his cows too." The trainer said he was in the clubhouse one day, and Mantle gave him a check for something like $800. He asked what it was; Mantle said: "Mail this to so and so, I've got to pay the guy for the cows (laughing)."

I mean, those Mantle years, that Yankee team I was on. The 1961 Yankee team; we went to spring training; they're supposed to be the best team ever put together. The days we'd play, we'd have other ballplayers from major league teams like Baltimore and Cleveland and St. Louis in the clubhouse getting these guys autographs.

I talked to Cotton Nash; he played at Kentucky when I was up there. Cotton's a good friend of mine. He said, when he was with the White Sox, they was gonna take batting practice sometime around 7:00 p.m. Some of the players was going to the ballpark, it was 4:00 p.m. and he said, "Where in the hell you guys going?" They said, "We're going to the ballpark." He said, "We don't hit till 7:00." They said, "No, but Mantle starts at 4:30." They all went to watch Mantle take batting practice. You know that 1961 team the Yankees had, the catchers hit over 60 home runs. They had Johnny Blanchard, Elston Howard, and Yogi Berra; combined hit over 60 home runs. Man, they had some players; had Skowron at first base, Richardson at second, Kubek at short, Clete Boyer, Mantle, and Maris.

They had some players. It's unbelievable. It is a shame what some of those guys made. Just like old Yogi said, the most he had ever made was $55,000 a year. Of course, Mantle made a lot of money, and Maris made a lot of money, especially for back then, but when you see these guys now, signing a $200 million contract . . . the media asked Mantle one time . . . he had been retired and ask him what he'd been making if he was playing today; he said, "I don't know, but I'd knock on George Steinbrenner's door, and when he came to the door, I'd say, "Hello partner (laughing)."

They were making a movie down at Fort Lauderdale called Safe at Home, and we were all extras and stand-ins. It was about Mantle and Maris. It's been on TV a couple of times. We're playing pepper there at the screen at Fort Lauderdale; that's where we trained at the time. Me and a couple of pitchers, Mantle was hitting some pepper to us. They said, "Come on, let's go, guys, we're ready to start, shooting is over." We was getting ready to start batting practice; I guess I'm as close to Mantle as here to that wall (10 feet). He said, "Chuck roll me one," and I'm standing next to the bucket of balls, which meant throw him a little curve ball so he took that bat and BAM, hit that thing straight up over that net, and that net was probably 50 to 60 feet high out in the parking lot, and I'm sitting there, and my knees are shaking. If he tops this ball, I'm dead. But he had no idea; he had no idea that he could top it. He knew he was going to hit it. But my knees were shaking, scared me to death (laughing). Yeah, those guys, they'd throw batting practice, they wouldn't put that screen up, because that screen bothered them. When Mantle came up to hit, they put that screen up; he'd hit that ball through the infield, looked like a ping pong ball. He had the best put together body that I'd ever seen, and he never lifted a weight in his life.

REFERENCES

https://www.aagpbl.org/ – All American Girls Professional Baseball
    League
https://www.amazon.com/ – Amazon
https://www.baseball-almanac.com/ – Baseball Almanac
https://www.baseball-reference.com/ – Baseball-Reference
https://www.google.com/maps – Google Maps
https://www.milb.com/ – Minor League Baseball
https://www.mlb.com/ – Major League Baseball
https://nlbm.com/ – Negro League Baseball Museum
https://sabr.org/bioproject/ – Society for American Baseball Research
    Biography Project
https://en.wikipedia.org/ – Wikipedia-The Free Encyclopedia

ABOUT THE AUTHOR

MR. KELLY G. PARK is a retired sandlot athlete, never having the skills to "take it to the next level," but enjoying every moment of those pick-up games. Since 1988, Kelly has worked as a safety and risk manager. *Just Like Me: When the Pros Played on the Sandlot Volume 1*, is the author's debut book.

Mr. Kelly lives in Benton, Kentucky, with his wife, Mrs. Kelly (yes, that's right, they have the same name) and dogs Griffin and Rufus.

Made in the USA
Monee, IL
24 October 2020